THE CUTTING EDGE

The Story of the Beatles' Hairdresser Who Defined an Era

Leslie Cavendish

with
Eduardo Jáuregui
and
Neil McNaughton

ALMA BOOKS

AND

FOX & CROW BOOKS

ALMA BOOKS LTD
3 Castle Yard
Richmond
Surrey TW10 6TF
United Kingdom
www.almabooks.com

First published by Alma Books Limited in 2017
Copyright © Book on a Tree Ltd, 2017

Art director Fox & Crow Books: Andrea Cavallini

Leslie Cavendish asserts his moral right to be identified as the author of
this work in accordance with the Copyright, Designs and Patents Act 1988

Printed and bound by CPI Group (UK) Ltd, Croydon, CR0 4YY

ISBN: 978-1-84688-431-3
eBook ISBN : 978-1-84688-432-0

CONTENTS

DEDICATED TO THE MEMORY OF ERNIE,

MY ROCK-'N'-ROLL SPANIEL

THE CUTTING EDGE

1

The Cutting Edge

London, 1961. I always did have a knack for being in the right place at the right time. The Swinging Sixties were about to explode right then and there, in sync with a couple of other world hotspots of psychedelia, sexual liberation, mind-expanding drugs and peaceful utopias. And I was about to get swept up in one of its central tangles, which oddly enough turned out to be a tangle of hair.

Let's face it: the Sixties revolution was, among other things, a revolution in hair. Long, shaggy locks. Flowing beards and flower-studded braids. Hair that grew wildly, in the face of established norms that tried to comb, straighten, part and otherwise civilize those millions of potentially wayward strands. Hair that screamed for a "proper haircut", because that was its very message: *I do apologize, old chap, but I really couldn't care less about what is or isn't "proper"*. It's no coincidence that the iconic musical of the age was titled *Hair*, its main track one long manifesto to the glory of the messy stuff that grows from our scalps.

Of course, I didn't have the foggiest idea that any of this was about to happen. Who could? If you'd told me, back then, that I'd be personally involved in such a world-changing counter-culture, I would have advised you to ease off your drink. I was nothing but a mixed-up fourteen-year-old kid living in Burnt Oak, an undistinguished North London suburb. Never heard of it? Can't say I'm surprised.

My grandparents were Jewish refugees who had fled the pogroms in Russia, Poland and Georgia before the First World War, looking for a safer life in England. Originally, they settled in the East End of London, a favourite destination for such immigrants, being one of the cheapest (and poorest) areas in the city.

That's where I was born, in 1947, on Cable Street. As the years passed and members of this community prospered, they typically moved to the northern suburbs of London, to Golders Green, Hendon or Edgware. If you couldn't afford any of these, you ended up in Burnt Oak. That's where I grew up from age two, together with a large, loud Jewish family: my mother's parents, my parents, my aunts Gladys and Marilyn, my cousins Lynn and Russell, and me. Nine people in two contiguous semi-detached houses.

So I can safely say that, in 1961, I felt nowhere near the cutting edge of art or fashion, let alone any kind of social revolution. From my point of view, the eight miles that separated my neighbourhood from Chelsea was a gulf as wide as the distance between my chummy East End slang and the sophisticated elocution of the announcers on the BBC. Years of living in Burnt Oak had assured me that nothing of relevance ever happened there, other than the occasional brawl outside the pubs. Even today, on Wikipedia, its only noteworthy claim to fame is having hosted the first Tesco supermarket in 1929.

If I had any clear ideas about what I wanted to do with my life, it certainly wasn't hairdressing. At the age of six, I would have probably been happy to join the family business, a small shoe shop near Elephant and Castle that had grown from my grandfather's horse-drawn market stall. This little world of leather and cardboard boxes used to fascinate me as a child, when Grandpa would take me along on Sundays to the East Street market. My mother, the son he had never had, always helped him with the stall, and then later the shop, learning every trick in the trade. Known locally as "Betty Boots", she liked to brag that she could sell snow to the Eskimos – and she wasn't exaggerating. My father had also recently joined the business, helping them run the financial side of things. He'd worked previously as a bookkeeper at the Eros Film Company, which produced films that never quite became box-office hits, like *The Man Who Watched Trains Go By* or *Behemoth, the Sea Monster*. But then he lost his job in 1961, when Eros, perhaps unsurprisingly, went bankrupt. While helping out at the shoe shop on 98 East Street, my father also moonlighted as a bookmaker at three greyhound tracks in London, figuring out the odds and paying out the winners.

Mum and Dad hoped I would improve on their own humble careers with a proper job in accounting. Unfortunately for them, I wasn't to be persuaded. My parents' aspirations would have required me to stay in school beyond the compulsory age of fifteen, and go on to study at university. I myself wasn't keen on studying and passing exams, and even less on all the rules and discipline that kept me and my schoolmates in check – with the aid of a stinging cane on our bums when necessary.

Also, my best friend Lawrence Falk and I were two of only three Jewish boys in the entire school. Every morning, we were excluded from the assembly, where Christian prayers and songs were recited. We didn't mind too much, as it gave us some extra time to prepare our homework assignments at the last minute. Still, it didn't make us feel particularly welcome, since we were bundled together in a room chillingly known back then as "Form Nought" – children who were dyslexic or had other learning disabilities. And that wasn't the only way we were made to feel different. The class bullies would regularly hassle us for being

"Jew boys", just as they hassled our only black classmate for being a "nigger". I never quite understood where all this hatred came from. On one occasion, a certain Ollie gripped me in such a vicious headlock that a biro in his shirt pocket pierced my lip. The two stitches I received soon healed, but the sense that I was unwanted in that educational institution never fully went away.

Only when we excelled on the football pitch did Lawrence and I feel like we were fully accepted by our classmates, and maybe that explains how we got to be so good. For a while, I nurtured quite serious fantasies that I might turn my passion for football into a professional career. True, Lawrence was the better of us two, scoring the goals as a striker while I played centre back. But still, in my previous school I'd been named team captain, and so I held on, for as long as possible, to the chance that I might become a professional defender. Was it too much to ask from the universe? It's not like I expected to join Chelsea or Arsenal. My favourite team was the third-division Queens Park Rangers, who played at a small ground in West London, and whose cool shirts and unique style of football were virtually unknown except to me and a few other loyal fanatics. That would have been plenty for me. Tragically, however, as I reached my teens, it became increasingly clear that even this modest dream was beyond my reach. When Lawrence, whom I had always admired as a greatly superior player, gave up his football hopes, I was forced to do so as well.

Another of my passions was music. My father had been a frustrated orchestra conductor, who loved to wave his arms erratically in front of our television set to "direct" the BBC Symphony Orchestra, imagining himself to be Sir John Barbirolli. Though I wasn't that inspired by Mozart or Beethoven, I had an additional musical influence right next door to our house, where my cousin Russell lived with the rest of the extended family. Russell's dad, my uncle Tony, was more generally known as Tony Crombie, a talented jazz drummer and band leader who played with the likes of Duke Ellington and Ella Fitzgerald. He also toured with Annie Ross, whose song 'I Want You to Be My Baby' had been banned on the BBC for the phrase "Come upstairs and have some loving". Uncle Tony followed Ross's lyrics quite literally, and my auntie Gladys was no less infuriated than the BBC. So that's how she and my cousin Russell came to live in our double home.

More crucially for me, Uncle Tony had also created the Rockets, the first British band to record a single in the new and exciting style that took the world by storm in the 1950s: rock 'n' roll. While I never quite understood jazz the way my cousin Russell seemed to, the driving beat of this wild new American sound grabbed me at once. From the first time my ears were assaulted, at age eleven, by the jangly guitar and thumping piano of Eddie Cochran's 'C'mon Everybody', I was ready to answer Eddie's generational call to party.

Unless you were there, it's difficult to imagine just how radical rock 'n' roll sounded at the time. The only music that was played by the British Broadcasting Corporation, which had the monopoly over the airwaves, was as safe and proper as the mellifluous accent spoken by the Queen's equerry. You couldn't "rock around the clock" on the BBC, no more than you could "go upstairs and have some loving". Its programmers favoured family-friendly crooners like Frank Sinatra, Perry Como and Frankie Vaughan. No parent would ever object to the charming strains of 'Moon River' or 'Catch a Falling Star'. Rock 'n' roll, on the other hand, sounded sexy, unpredictable and dangerous. Which is why parents feared it... and we loved it.

Listening to Little Richard or Buddy Holly was almost like sampling drugs – and indeed, getting your fix could be a challenge. Due to trade restrictions, you couldn't buy many of these records in the shops. For most people, the only available option was tuning the radio to a very crackly Radio Luxembourg or, a bit later, to Radio Caroline, a pirate station that broadcast from a ship anchored four miles off the southern English coast. If you had contacts in America, however, you could get your hands on the hottest new records from the Billboard chart directly. Luckily, I did. My cousins on the other side of the Atlantic were able to provide me with a steady supply of this explosive and practically illegal new music.

As soon as my new shipment of James Brown, Jerry Lee Lewis or Chuck Berry would arrive, I'd invite all my friends over and blast out the new rhythms over the loudspeakers of my most prized possession: the Decca Gramophone record player I got for my eleventh birthday. We could easily listen to a single album five times straight, letting the new tunes work themselves into our bones. My mother was much less enthusiastic, and I often quarrelled with her over what the appropriate volume was, but I suppose she preferred my musical parties to the gambling sessions many of my other friends were into. Having a rocking uncle like Tony also helped, of course. In fact, by the time I turned fifteen, Tony was sneaking Lawrence and me into the notorious Flamingo Club, a sweaty and smoky cellar where he and a jazzier version of the Rockets would often play late at night to a mixture of mods, West Indian immigrants and visiting American GIs.

As you can imagine, another of my fantasies became making it as a rock star. Sadly, there were too many obstacles in the way. I didn't live in America, or anywhere else with the right kind of scene. My parents would have considered music lessons an extravagance, and the measly income I made as a bicycle delivery boy for Bernie's, a local Jewish deli, barely paid for my records as it was. I could have tried to teach myself, I suppose, playing by ear with the help of my record collection. I'm sure I didn't lack the motivation. But the few times I tried picking up a guitar, I found myself to be all thumbs.

So, accounting was out, and so were football and music. What was I to do when I finished my studies? I never had a career counsellor. The closest to that kind of advice we had at my school was when companies would visit to offer us "exciting new job opportunities", such as becoming a steelworker or learning to fix fridges – which never attracted me in the least. There was only one other thing that I really had a passion for. In fact, I suppose that if I'd met with a proper career counsellor back then, and was asked if there was anything else I *really* liked, my answer would have been quick and enthusiastic: girls. Yes, indeed. That was my honest-to-goodness vocation in 1961. Biology, if you like, but of a more practical kind. Admittedly, it wasn't the most promising basis for a professional career. And yet it was to be this genuine and ardent yearning for the opposite sex which would finally lead me down the path to fame, fortune and the Fab Four.

*   *   *

One day, after school, I met my mother at the local hairdresser's. As soon as I arrived at the salon, I noticed an American car parked outside. It was a flashy Buick, a rare sight anywhere in London in those days, let alone a backwater like Burnt Oak. It gave off an aura of opulence and sex appeal. I can tell you: I was impressed.

As I walked into the premises, I checked out the owner of the car and the salon. He wasn't a particularly good-looking guy, and yet he was surrounded by a dozen women, three of them his young staff and the rest his customers. My first thought was: "This seems like a pretty good working environment. I need to find out more!"

There weren't many men in the hairdressing industry at that time. It was seen as a mostly "feminine" profession, and I could easily picture what Ollie and the other class bullies would have thought of me as a male stylist: one more reason for sticking a pen through my lip. But from that day onwards, I secretly began to imagine a new future for myself. I had seen the light. Girls! Glamour! Sexy cars! What more could a teenager like myself possibly want?

A few months later, I met up with my mate Lawrence Falk, whom I hadn't seen for some time. Being older than me, he'd already left school the previous year, while I still had another three months to go before I gained my own freedom. I asked him what he was planning to do, and his answer astonished me:

"I'm going to train to become a ladies' hairdresser."

"Right, yeah, bet you are, Falky..." I chuckled, not sure if he was, as we Londoners like to say, *taking the mickey*.

"No, really," he said earnestly. "I've signed up for an apprenticeship at a salon called Eric's of Baker Street, in London. Hairdressing's a smashing job, Leslie. You'd love it!"

"Would I?" I asked in wonder. It appeared my old friend had been attracted to the very same career path I had secretly been considering.

Then he grinned and winked at me conspiratorially.

"You wouldn't believe the sexy birds that go have their hair done at Eric's. It's like a non-stop fashion show in that place..."

Good old Lawrence! It's no wonder we'd always been so close. I burst into laughter and confessed to him my own scheme. Until that moment, it had only been a vague and uncertain idea. But now my mind was made up. If my best friend thought hairdressing was a brilliant career move, then that did it.

The question now was, where should I do my apprenticeship? I could have joined Lawrence at Eric's, of course. Another obvious choice would have been the flamboyant Raymond Bessone. Raymond was the original celebrity stylist, a larger-than-life character whose pencil-thin moustache, faux-French accent and bright, colourful suits made him an instant sensation from his first television appearance, in which he showed off his precision-cutting abilities by snipping off "a teasy-weasy bit here and a teasy-weasy bit there". Mr Teasy-Weasy, as he came to be known, transformed his salon into a baroque stage, chandeliers and champagne fountains included, in which he waved around his extra-long cigarettes with his inimitable camp style.

By the time I finished school, however, Lawrence had already spent several months training at Eric's, and his inside knowledge of the industry provided me with another option. One afternoon, we jumped on a trolley bus towards the West End. These buses, electrically driven from wires suspended above the road, were the best way to move around central London at the time. They were both silent and, thanks to their rubber tyres, also quite comfortable. At one point, we passed Eric's salon.

"There's the place where I'm training," Lawrence pointed out proudly.

"Blimey," I replied, genuinely impressed.

It certainly seemed more glamorous than my mum's place back home, even from the top of a bus.

"Do you think I could get into a place like that?"

"Oh, you shouldn't go there," Lawrence said, to my surprise. "You should try somewhere more fashionable."

"More fashionable?" I took a second look at Eric's. It looked fashionable enough to me.

"Go to Vidal Sassoon."

"*Lidel the Soon*? Where's that?"

Lawrence found this hilarious. Clearly, I wasn't up on the latest fashion trends. It took him a while to control his amusement before he could reply.

"Vi-dal Sas-soon," he said, as if to a complete moron. "It's not a place. It's the name of the hairdresser. You know that Mr Teasy-Weasy bloke on the telly? Vidal trained with him, but he's becoming even more famous himself now. I'm telling you, Eric spends half of his time trying to copy Sassoon's ideas. His salon is right at the centre of things, a real hip place."

I had no idea how true this was, or just how true it would prove to be. Lawrence and I are close friends to this day, and I still occasionally thank him for that advice.

Back home, when I had finally learnt to pronounce "Vidal Sassoon" and told my mum that I was thinking of working for him, things took another favourable turn. Her sister, my auntie Gladys, suddenly became very animated.

"Oh, I know Vidal. We used to go to the same club in the East End, in Whitechapel. I used to see him all the time."

It turned out that Vidal Sassoon also came from a Jewish East End family. The street where I was born, near Tower Bridge, had been the site of the infamous 1936 riots known as the Battle of Cable Street. Oswald Mosley's Black Shirts tried to march through the district, but were stopped by an anti-fascist counter-demonstration. It was a violent episode in the history of London, and also a highly significant one, since it focused public attention on what fascism was really all about. Towards the end of World War II, in the same district, a Jewish anti-fascist group was formed, known as the 43 Group. Among its leading members was a young man named Vidal Sassoon.

Within twenty years of the formation of the 43 Group, Sassoon was to occupy the very centre of a very different social movement, a revolution in fashion and culture that was sweeping through London. I suppose my aunt Gladys had no inkling that this might be in progress. But when she heard I was planning to go to Sassoon's for an interview, she was excited nonetheless.

"When you get there, just mention to Vidal that Gladys Hamer says hello."

Full of confidence, I called Vidal's salon, told them I wanted to become a hairdresser and asked how I should I go about realizing my ambition. I was told the best way was to make an appointment to see Gordon, the general manager, which I did. On the day of the interview, however, I worked myself into a state of panic. How was I going to convince the people at Vidal Sassoon's that I would make a great hairdresser? Mentioning my auntie Gladys wouldn't cut much ice, I feared. And there was an ugly truth I had hardly considered, but which I began to realize with growing dismay probably mattered much more: I was useless at art, and hopeless with my hands.

That morning, as I paced my room trying to figure out my strategy, I noticed something on a high shelf that gave me an idea. It wasn't a great idea, I freely admit. But to my fifteen-year-old mind, in that moment of desperation, it seemed like a stroke of genius – just the kind of thing I needed to tip the situation in my favour. At school, I had made a wooden fruit bowl on a lathe. It was rather lumpy and misshapen, but I had kept it anyway – who knows why? Now, there it was, gathering dust between my books. Before the interview, I cleaned the bowl up a bit, put it into a plastic bag and made my way to Vidal's salon.

Walking down Bond Street was quite a revelation for me. As I looked into the windows of Cartier and Asprey, I was almost blinded by the gold and jewellery that glittered back at me. For the first time in my life, I realized how wealthy London really was. The streets may not have been paved with gold, but these shop windows certainly had plenty of it on display. At last I found number 171, Vidal Sassoon's famous establishment. I took a deep breath and pushed my way through the door.

Straight away, I was fascinated. It was filled with chatter and, of course, women – just as my mother's hairdresser's had been. But there was more to it than that. The place was huge, with a raised mezzanine overlooking the main body of the salon, where elegant ladies relaxed on chaises longues while they received their manicure, their heads crowned with gleaming, rocket-shaped hairdryers. The Bauhaus interior design, black chairs on white tiles, together with the enormous photographs of famous models sporting Sassoon's radical haircuts, gave me the sensation of having stepped into an art gallery. Instead of the chemical smell of lacquer and peroxide, I was greeted by the perfume of fresh lilies arranged in vases around the reception area. As for the stylists themselves, they seemed to work and glide through the place in sync with some kind of imaginary music. Lawrence had told me it was fashionable, but that was a serious understatement. I had never experienced such an atmosphere. Sassoon's was, quite literally, the cutting edge. And now, more than ever, I wanted desperately to be a part of it.

One of the receptionists accompanied me downstairs to Gordon's office. Like the stylists in the salon, the manager was smartly dressed in a black suit, white shirt and black tie. As he greeted me with a limp handshake and invited me to sit down, I was immediately impressed by the effeminate elegance with which he carried himself. In my boyish innocence, I had no idea what it implied when people were so obviously camp. For the moment, it simply added to the oddity of this foreign world. At the start of the interview, Gordon cut straight to the chase:

"So, Mister Cavendish, what makes you think you'd like to be a hairdresser?"

"Well," I said, trying to conceal how very out of place I was feeling, "first of all, please tell Vidal that Gladys Hamer gives her regards."

No reaction. I ploughed on regardless.

"May I also tell you that I am very confident around women, and artistic enough to be a hairdresser. Look, I've brought something with me that will prove it to you." I opened up my bag and fished out the wooden bowl. Then I plonked it on the table with a satisfied air. "In the same way I moulded this bowl," I boasted, "I'm sure I can mould people's hair."

To this day, I still wince at the memory. The naivety of it! What was I thinking?

Sassoon's general manager looked down at my wonky creation in silence. Then he fixed me with a quizzical expression. I imagine he was probably trying to suppress a grin. Gordon ignored the bowl completely and proceeded to ask me a few mundane, predictable questions. I answered as best as I could, still hoping to save the situation or, at the very least, my dignity. Then, before I knew what was happening, he brought the interview to a rapid close.

"OK, we'll let you know."

It was a relief.

When I walked out of the salon, I still held on to a smidgen of hope. Perhaps the meeting hadn't started off too well, but when I ran through the answers I had given Gordon, they seemed reasonable enough. As the days passed, however, I became increasingly pessimistic. I couldn't even bear to look at that awful, misshapen hunk of wood. How could I have been so daft? The true extent of my disaster was becoming as clear as the surface of the spotless mirrors in Sassoon's elegant salon. A glamorous outfit like that would never take in a clumsy kid like me.

To my astonishment, however, I got a call from Gordon a week later.

"Hello, Leslie," he said. "If you're still interested, we'd be happy to take you on as a junior."

I almost dropped the phone. It was as if Queens Park Rangers had selected me to play centre forward. All my dark clouds dissipated at once, and I felt bathed in the bright lights of that heavenly Bond Street atmosphere I could still remember so fondly.

For about two seconds.

"You'll have to pay an apprentice fee, of course," he added.

I gulped.

"Of... of course," I stammered. "And how much would that be?"

The deal was you had to pay Vidal two hundred guineas to be taught by him. It was a vast sum for my family's modest means – over £3,000 in twenty-first-century money. I said I couldn't possibly afford that, but we got talking. He seemed to like me and, in the end, we came to an arrangement. My parents some-how managed to scrape together one hundred guineas, which proved enough for Gordon and, presumably, for the Sassoon management.

What had got me the job? Was it my crooked little bowl? Was it my auntie Gladys's message? Was it my dynamic personality and charm? A week later I had my answer. Gordon, now my new general manager, took me aside after my first day's training.

"Leslie, obviously, I couldn't say anything at the time, but when I told the others that you had brought in a wooden bowl to show us that you could be a hairdresser, well... we just fell about laughing!"

It seems that my bold step, half ingenuity and half chutzpah, had landed me the job that would change my life for ever. It was my first inkling that, perhaps, I did have some kind of mysterious talent to offer the world.

* * *

Almost at the same time, in mid-1962, a group of four young pop musicians from Liverpool also had the lucky break that would kick-start their career. Known variously as the Blackjacks, the Quarrymen, Johnny and the Moondogs, and then – inspired by Buddy Holly and the Crickets – the Silver Beetles, they had finally settled on the simpler and more playful name "The Beatles". Like myself, these youngsters came from working-class neighbourhoods, and they had also been hooked for years on American records, which had reached Liverpool thanks to its famous docks, the largest port in the country. The Beatles played a mixture of American sounds and a jazzy-folk style known as "skiffle" at tiny clubs like the Cavern, a brick basement so stifling that sweat would drip down the walls during concerts, causing the amps to short-circuit. Though there were many similar bands in Liverpool – three or four guitarists singing in harmony over a simple drumbeat – a young aspiring musical manager, Brian Epstein, had seen something special in these particular kids. Epstein polished up their act, convinced them to wear a smart set of matching suits and Chelsea boots, and landed them their first proper recording contract with EMI's Parlophone label.

By 1962, the Beatles were already famous in their own city and also in Hamburg, Germany, where they had spent several months playing in underground joints of the red-light district. But they were still unknown to the rest of the world when they arrived in June of that year at EMI Studios on Abbey Road, just a couple of miles away from Vidal Sassoon's salon. Perhaps they deserved a lucky break. After several record companies had turned them down, Brian Epstein had convinced Decca to invite them for an audition in January, only to see them rejected once again. According to the executives who made the decision, "guitar groups are on their way out" and "the Beatles have no future in show business". Then, in April, Stuart Sutcliffe, one of the five original band members, tragically died from a brain haemorrhage, either the consequence of an earlier attack by thugs after a concert or, as others claim, the result of a bad fall down a flight of stairs.

To the Beatles, therefore, the Parlophone contract must have seemed like their last shot at success. And yet it almost turned into their final and definitive disaster. At EMI Studios, they were due to record a number by a young up-and-coming songwriter called Mitch Murray, entitled 'How Do You Do It?', which they didn't particularly like. The Beatles hadn't written it themselves, and though they tried adapting it to their style, their lack of enthusiasm must have been evident on the recording. Neither Murray, nor the producer, George Martin, were impressed. At the time, it was very rare for unknown artists to record their own music, but the cheeky Liverpudlians must have brought out their own chutzpah, for the band managed to persuade Martin to let them try. A bit like my misshapen bowl, the song had been scribbled in a notebook while Paul McCartney was still at school. It was called 'Love Me Do'.

As in my own case, the gamble could have turned out badly for the Beatles. 'How Do You Do It?' was recorded by another of Brian Epstein's bands, Gerry and the Pacemakers, and became a number-one hit in early 1963 – a much bigger hit, in fact, than the Beatles' slow and simple tune, with Ringo Starr's tambourine clinking over John Lennon's harmonica, which only reached number seventeen. But their third single, 'From Me to You', displaced 'How Do You Do It?' at number one in April 1963, and there was no looking back after that. Almost every single and album they released in the following years would top the British charts.

Like many thousands of others, I became an instant fan of this new musical phenomenon. The first time I listened to their songs on Radio Luxembourg, I could hardly believe what I was hearing. It moved me like that fresh, fun, rocking music I had been importing from the States for so many years. And yet these lads, not much older than myself, didn't speak with the familiar American twang. Nor was it the aristocratic British drawl of the BBC and their safe and charming crooners. It sounded like a working-class Liverpudlian accent. Was that even possible? Did that mean that anyone, even me and my mates, could just pick up a bunch of guitars and churn out a rock-'n'-roll hit? People who weren't around at that time have a difficulty understanding Beatlemania: the screaming fans, the hysteria, the fainting. But what you have to realize is that no one had ever heard such music before. And much less the cheeky, self-assured witticisms that popped out of these four youngsters' mouths in answer to reporters' questions:

PRESS: Where do your hairdos originate from?
GEORGE: Our scalps.

PRESS: What do the Beatles think of topless swimming suits?
PAUL: We've been wearing them for years!

PRESS: How did you enjoy the Royal Variety show?

GEORGE: It was great! Fabulous! Yeah, you know, the audience was much better than we expected.

JOHN: ...much taller.

GEORGE: Yeah.

PRESS: You Beatles have conquered five continents. What would you like to do next?

BEATLES (*in unison*): ...conquer six!

Their rocking music, their stage antics, their all-around impudence and, of course, their overgrown, mushroom-shaped hair... It was as if a crack had broken through the great wall of British propriety, and we were suddenly afforded a tantalizing view into the future: psychedelia, playful rebellion, naked bodies dancing in the mud. Oh yes, there was a lot to scream about.

In fact I think I did scream when I first saw the ad.

It was featured in the most unlikely publication imaginable, the weekly *Jewish Chronicle*, which was delivered to our home on Fridays, just in time for the Sabbath. Among stories about Israeli politics, outbursts of anti-Semitism or the opening of new synagogues, it listed ads for all sorts of social events in our community (also known as "Jew Do's"), including a series of charity dances that were held on Sunday nights at 9 p.m. at a small venue near Piccadilly called the Pigalle Club. I'd been to a few of these with Lawrence, but the groups playing there tended to be established bands past their peak, or anonymous new talent – certainly not the biggest sensation in music since Elvis. And yet, there it was, in black and white:

Sunday, April 21st, 8.00–11.30 p.m.
The most sensational group in England
The fabulous
BEATLES
Plus Dave Anthony and the Druids
All at the luxurious Pigalle.
Admission twelve shillings and sixpence.

You can imagine how little time I wasted in applying for those tickets.

How was such a thing possible? I already knew that on the afternoon of 21st April the Beatles would be playing at the *New Musical Express* 1963 Poll-Winners' All-Star Concert. This massive show would be held at the largest venue in the country, the Empire Pool, later to be renamed Wembley Arena. And yet, after performing in front of 10,000 fans, the Fab Four would be rushing off to a tiny Jew Do in the West End, for the benefit of less than one hundred and fifty lucky readers of the *Chronicle*. It didn't make any sense.

On the night of the concert, the mystery was cleared up. It turned out the promoters had booked the Beatles a year in advance, before their hit singles had even been recorded at Abbey Road. Brian Epstein was Jewish, so it was probably one of the first gigs he managed to secure for them. In mid-1962, no one could have imagined how famous this anonymous band would have become just a few months later, when me and my wide-eyed friends walked into the Pigalle, still half-wondering if it wasn't all some kind of belated April Fool's joke.

That night, however, the Beatles did indeed strut onto the little stage, sporting their collarless suits, their Cuban-heeled boots and their famous haircuts, which looked like I could have styled with the help of my wooden bowl. For the first time in my life, I actually felt lucky to be Jewish. The chosen people indeed! All of that hassle from the school bullies almost seemed to have been worth it.

As the three guitarists lined up in front of their microphones, they introduced themselves and the drummer in the back. I suppose their audiences weren't expected to know their names yet.

"Hi, I'm Paul. That's John, George and Ringo."

With those words, they began their set – 'Love Me Do', 'Please Please Me', 'From Me to You', 'Long Tall Sally', 'Twist and Shout'... After the enormous concert at the Empire Pool, which must have been quite a nerve-racking experience for the young lads, they now seemed totally relaxed, even playful, feeding off our boundless enthusiasm, as if it were just another night at the Cavern back in Liverpool.

As for the rest of us at the club, we were spellbound. The way they shook that floppy hair to the beat! Normally, the charity events at the Pigalle were dances, and the music was just a rhythm to which we would move as we mingled and chatted. But this concert was another story. We didn't twist and shout. We didn't shake it all out. We just stood there, trying to take it all in. And then, after each song, we'd all go completely wild, returning to these four budding pop stars all of the energy they'd belted out of their amplified instruments.

It was an evening I would remember – and brag about – for years. In fact, here I am, bragging about it still! Even at the time, though, I was well aware what a privilege it was to watch the Beatles play in such intimate surroundings. As it turned out, that magical night was to be only the first step in a long and highly improbable relationship.

2

No Sex Please, We're Stylists

In the meantime, however, I had a lot to learn. Scissors, brushes, rollers, pins; cutting, washing, perming, drying; types of hair and types of client; when to talk and when to smile. At Vidal Sassoon's Bond Street salon, there was an entire room devoted just to shampoo, with a bewildering assortment of products for every possible level of shine, volume and moisture: cream shampoo, zero-soap shampoo... even egg shampoo! As an apprentice, or "junior", my job was to watch and learn from Stephen, the first stylist to which I was assigned, while I carried out menial jobs like preparing the tools, sweeping up hair or picking up combs that fell to the floor – and immediately dropping them into a jar of disinfectant.

What I saw simply flabbergasted me. I thought I had been stunned enough on my first visit, but the more I learnt, the more I felt like I had been marooned on another planet. This is hardly surprising, as the whole operation had been designed by its owner to impress the most fashionable ladies in London. Vidal Sassoon's, in the 1960s, was to hairdressing salons what Cirque du Soleil would later be to circuses, or elBulli to restaurants. A hairdresser to celebrities, Sassoon had become a celebrity in his own right, and for good reasons. It wasn't simply that his "geometric" haircuts were so radical that they often made the newspaper headlines. The man had completely reinvented the

31

hairdressing experience, transforming every detail, elevating the profession into an art form – for those who could afford it, of course.

Nothing was as you might expect. Hair was cut dry, not wet. Brushes were eschewed whenever possible, in favour of the stylist's own hands, which were run through the "fabric" of hair like upturned claws. Clients were asked to change out of their clothes and into loosely fitting gowns, so that their locks could be cut against their naked skin. The hairstyles themselves, which could take hours to perfect, were often outlandish: a fringe cut at right angles, one side longer than the other, or the famous five-point cut, with its downward spikes at the ears and neck. In a move that would have shocked my grandpa's instincts as a salesman, clients were turned away if they asked for a style the hairdresser was not prepared to offer.

"Back-comb your hair, madam? I'm afraid that wouldn't suit you."

"But that's the way I want it!" the lady would protest.

"Then I'm very sorry, but we cannot complement your hair, madam. May I suggest you visit another establishment…"

"Excuse me?" the woman would then unfailingly balk. "Who do you think you are talking to? I am very wealthy, you know."

"Money doesn't come into it, madam. We simply would not feel comfortable sending you off with such a look."

The hairdressers at Vidal's were artists, and they had standards which could not be transgressed.

Within days, I suspected I had made a terrible mistake. How could I ever develop the dexterity and sophistication required of a qualified stylist? I was having a hard enough time using my clumsy fingers to put together the sponge rollers we juniors prepared by hand, like Belgian chocolates, to prevent the crinkles and waves left by ordinary plastic ones. The idea of actually crafting one of Sassoon's geometric hairdos myself, on a living client, before the watchful eye of the senior stylists, seemed no less fantastical to me than scoring goals for Queens Park Rangers, or playing lead guitar in a chart-topping pop band.

Stephen, the hairdresser I watched and assisted day after day, seemed to me an accomplished artist, but even he would occasionally make mistakes, and when your art requires you to brandish sharp scissors within millimetres of your clients' skin, these can sometimes become quite gory. One morning, Stephen was having an animated chat with an elegant Mayfair client, when he suddenly snipped off a third of her earlobe. Being one of the least sensitive parts of the body, the piece of flesh simply flipped up into the air and then dropped to the floor, without the lady even blinking. The two of us, however, couldn't fail to notice the cataract of blood that gushed out from her sliced lobe. I quickly reached for some wet wipes to stop the bleeding, while looking back at Stephen's pale countenance.

"What are you going to tell her?" I mouthed, trying to get the stricken stylist to react.

"Umm... madam," he finally spoke up, "I'm afraid I've just cut a bit of your lobe off..."

"Oh my God!!" the lady wailed.

Before she could get a good look at the damage, though, I managed to cover it up with the wad of wet wipes and pressed tightly.

"Oh, it's just a scratch, really," I smiled with all of the sweet innocence I could muster.

And off we all went to the back room for some first aid, amidst a flurry of apologies. As we cared for the mutilated ear, all I could think of was this: *If Stephen, who seems so graceful and competent, can make such a gross mistake, how can I ever hope to make it as a stylist?*

*   *   *

Despite these misgivings, I have to admit that, once I started to get a hang of the junior's routine, I did begin to enjoy the buzzing atmosphere that had attracted me on my first visit. I mean, there I was, fifteen years old and surrounded by all those glamorous ladies I had dreamt about. Indeed, things were even more exciting than I'd expected, as some of these ladies were actual celebrities. Vidal Sassoon's stylists cared for many of the coiffures that would grace the newspapers, magazines, films and album covers of the 1960s. Mia Farrow, for example, would soon become a regular at the salon. It was Vidal who created her "pixie" look, which was a shorter, softer version of the bob, and was widely copied at the time. You can see her sporting it in one of her best-known roles, the hapless mother in Roman Polanski's terrifying *Rosemary's Baby*. In fact, she even boasts about the haircut to a shocked character in the film: "It's Vidal Sassoon! It's very in…"

To be honest, half of the time I didn't have a clue who these famous women were. Princess Lee Radziwill? She may have been Jackie Kennedy's sister, but in Burnt Oak you'd be better off asking about Betty Boots. And who'd ever heard of Mary Quant? Or Zandra Rhodes? My football mates had never once mentioned the names of these trendy fashion designers. Even Jean Shrimpton and other *Vogue* cover girls were just anonymous beauties to me.

In my first summer at the salon, I was asked to come in early one morning to prepare for the arrival of two clients who would be testifying in an important trial at the Crown Court. Vidal

Sassoon wouldn't be styling their hair himself, as he had more important business to attend to. He was recreating his famous five-point cut on Grace Coddington, a leading model who later became creative director of *Vogue* USA. So the job fell to Roger Thompson, Sassoon's second-in-command, whom I had just started to work for. One of my tasks as a junior was to get the client into her ribbon-fronted gown and then invite her to sit in preparation for the stylist. After the cut, I would then take her to the basins at the back to wash her hair.

Roger asked me to attend to a certain Mandy, whereas my fellow junior, Alan, looked after her friend Christine. They were both gorgeous and stylish ladies, just the kind I'd been hoping to meet at this incredible job of mine. But I was a million miles from getting anywhere with Mandy, as she seemed in no mood to chat with Roger that morning, let alone his lowly apprentice. So I had no way of teasing out any further clues as to her identity, and just got on with my job.

After their hair had been styled, they were ready to be on their way. I watched them leave from the reception window. A Rolls-Royce waited outside, its leopard-skin seat covers clearly visible, the liveried driver standing by the open rear door ready to take them to the Old Bailey. As I watched them go, I wondered who these two stunning ladies might be, and what kind of trouble they might have got themselves into.

My failure to recognize Mandy and Christine only shows how little I was reading the newspapers, aside from the sports section. It turned out that they were none other than Mandy Rice-Davies and Christine Keeler, the two high-class call girls at the centre of the great political scandal of the age, the Profumo Affair, which brought down a prominent minister and threatened the very survival of the government. The bizarre tale involved a society osteopath, Stephen Ward, who had organized a series of parties attended by many prominent people, at which liaisons were organized with prostitutes. This might have been nothing more than a typical "kiss and tell" story, until it was revealed that one of the participants was a suspected Soviet spy, Yevgeny Ivanov. At the height of the Cold War, only months after the Cuban missile crisis that almost led to a nuclear war, you can imagine the national outrage when Christine Keeler confessed to having slept with both Ivanov and John Profumo, British Minister of War! The consequences of the bombshell were dire. Stephen Ward took an overdose before the verdict was passed and died without receiving his subsequent conviction. Profumo, the implicated minister, was forced to resign. The government survived until the next general election a year later, but then it did lose office, probably in part due to this scandal.

And yet to clueless Leslie, junior at Vidal Sassoon's, all of this was nothing but another wash and blow-dry. When I saw my two clients on the front pages of the next day's papers and read all about the trial, I was a bit embarrassed at my ignorance, to say the least. Later, I discovered that the whole affair had been set off by a knife fight between another two of Christine Keeler's lovers at the very Flamingo Club where I'd spent so many nights with Lawrence, invited by my uncle Tony. One of these men, known as "Psycho" Gordon, had a brother who actually played in the same jazz band as my uncle, Georgie Fame and the Blue Flames. And still, to my shame, I had remained blissfully unaware of the whole drama.

On the other hand, I have to say that the work on Mandy and Christine's hair was impeccable. I don't know if it had any impact on the proceedings, but I still get a kick out of looking at those press pictures and imagining I had a small part to play in Cold War history.

* * *

A celebrity I recognized the moment she walked through the door was Shirley Bassey. That first time, I was understandably excited. The big-voiced singer was already becoming one of the great British divas of the age, especially after she recorded the theme song to the Bond movie, *Goldfinger*. Like many other up-and-coming starlets, she was a regular visitor to the salon, so I actually got to meet her on several occasions. I remember Shirley best, however, as my first lesson in the most valuable of Vidal Sassoon's teachings, which had nothing to do with scissors or shampoo.

The majority of well-known people I came into contact with in my hairdressing days were charming and pleasant with the staff. I must confess that Shirley was a bit different. She certainly knew how famous she was becoming, and seemed keen on making sure everyone else knew it as well. For instance, she had a habit of snapping her fingers whenever she wanted something, as if we were supposed to be at her beck and call. Now, I may have been a mere fifteen-year-old apprentice from Burnt Oak – but even so, I felt that Miss Bassey was taking things a bit too far.

Not once, however, did I ever let her know my displeasure. Like the rest of the staff, and under the guidance of Vidal Sassoon himself, I made every effort to treat all our "problem clients" with the utmost courtesy in their presence, and even after they were gone. There was no question of gossiping with our mates after work about Shirley Bassey's latest display of arrogance. In fact, of all the celebrities I met at the salon, this talented singer happened to be my mother's favourite. So, whenever she called in, I'd have to lie to my own mother afterwards.

"I saw Shirley Bassey today."

"Oh, Les, that's amazing! Isn't she fabulous?"

"She is, Mum, definitely."

When I look back at those early days, I have to admit that it was often the difficult clients who made for the most interesting memories. Two of my favourite characters, in this sense, were the Rahvis sisters, Dora and Raemonde, a pair of costume designers for many successful films in the Forties and Fifties. They were – shall we say – exotic, with their flame-red hair and collection of long-haired Yorkshire terriers, which Vidal allowed into the salon despite the chaos they often caused. If I thought Shirley Bassey was challenging, these two sisters and their dogs were something else altogether. Dora, the more dictatorial of the two, would often shout at me with the air of an Eastern European aristocrat:

"Would you mind getting a move on, Leslie!"

At this early stage of my apprenticeship, such imperious commands would only make me more flustered and confused.

Dora had a large number of hairpieces. One day, she was demanding quick service, as usual. At one point, she turned to the stylist I was working under at the time.

"Ricci," she said with her typical abruptness, "would you tell Leslie to get me my hairpieces?"

In my panic, as I rushed over, I grabbed one of her dogs by mistake. I should say that the dogs had matching red hair, so I suppose it was an accident waiting to happen. The terrier, who had a similar temperament to its owner, went berserk, and chaos ensued. Dogs, hairpieces, brushes and combs were suddenly flying everywhere.

With hindsight, I now realize that these demanding clients provided perhaps the most valuable part of my training. The sophisticated hairdressing techniques of the salon had to be mastered, of course. But that alone would never have got me into Abbey Road Studios, to style the world's four most iconic heads of hair. What Vidal Sassoon taught me, above all else, was the old-fashioned value of discretion, otherwise known as "keeping your mouth shut".

Not that we couldn't chat with the clients. Of course we could. We were encouraged to handle their problems, their hopes and their fears like we handled their hair, according to their style and personality – sometimes with the utmost delicacy, other times with frivolous abandon or even radical violence.

But the crucial thing was that as soon as they left the door, it was all swept away, every last lock and curl, leaving the white tiles as clean as if nothing had taken place there at all. Our clientele had to be able to trust their stylists completely. Only then could they sit comfortably in our adjustable chairs, in front of the bright lights and mirrors, and surrender their heads to our simple art.

*　*　*

As for Mr Sassoon himself (and that was how we *always* referred to him), I joined his salon just as he was about to create the hairstyles that would garner him worldwide fame. Inspired by the Art Deco of the Twenties and Thirties, and the German Bauhaus design movement, the first example of his new style was sported by the glamorous Hong Kong-born American actress Nancy Kwan. This bob, with its sharp, face-framing points, caused a sensation due to its severe geometry, in contrast to the previous softer, wavier styles. Soon afterwards, Sassoon teamed up with fashion designer Mary Quant to popularize the female look of the mid-1960s. This new gamine hair design was associated with ultra-slim figures, short skirts and heavy dark eyeshading that stood out against a background of pale pancake make-up. The motherly, full-bodied ideal, as represented by Marilyn Monroe and Diana Dors, was on its way out, to be replaced by the slender shapes of women like Mia Farrow, Twiggy and Cilla Black. These changes were symbols of the new role of women in society, no longer simply housewives, but increasingly working ladies who couldn't spend hours caring for carefully lacquered beehives.

Watching Vidal Sassoon at work was like admiring a world-class performer. He would take a whole hour to perfect a cut, calculating angles along the skull, analysing the texture and shape of the hair, using combs and scissors like extensions of his own nimble fingers. His body, perfectly toned by daily sessions of swimming and yoga, stepped around the client with the grace of a ballet dancer, while his face reflected the concentration of a tortured artist, twisting into eccentric grimaces that spoke of genius, or madness – or both. At some point Vidal would whip off his jacket and continue in his beautiful white waistcoat, his "VS" cufflinks gleaming in the bright lights as his hands fluttered around the client's head. With the peculiar whisper he always used, he would command the client to sit or stand for different moments of his creation. Then, at the end, he would make a final flourish, like a matador after defeating his beast, and fall back, exhausted from the effort. His haircuts cost ten times the rate of the other stylists, but his clients were never disappointed. The experience was simply mesmerizing.

I was in awe of our master stylist, and in many ways felt a close kinship with him. Like me, he was the son of Jewish refugees, and had harboured hopes of becoming a professional footballer before taking up hairdressing as an apprentice. He too came from a family of East Enders, although he had had a much tougher upbringing than me. Raised by a single parent from the age of three, he had spent eight years of his childhood in an orphanage. He even had to take elocution lessons for three years just to get a job at Raymond Bessone's gaudy salon. I suspect that was also the reason for his peculiar whisper: to disguise his cockney roots.

Mr Sassoon, however, was a demanding boss, and he had rules. Some, like cutting hair dry or avoiding lacquer, were simply stylistic innovations that we quickly adapted to. Others, like the requirement to use only handmade sponge rollers, could certainly make the lives of us juniors a bit tedious at times. A few, like maintaining the utmost discretion about our clients' private revelations, were downright challenging. But there was one particular rule – *the* rule – that made life a living hell for the teenage Leslie Cavendish.

It turned out that those divine women that strutted into the salon day after day, the very source of my professional vocation, the models and starlets whose shapes filled out our flimsy hairdresser's gowns, were strictly out of bounds. Forbidden. Untouchable. Vidal Sassoon was adamant that we should never have any sexual relations with the clients. Not because he was a puritan and disapproved of such things. On the contrary. His "no sex" rule was grounded in solid business reasons. Such entanglements might embarrass clients, to the extent that they stopped coming to the salon.

At first, I couldn't believe he was serious. In fact, I don't think I fully understood what our great master was on about. Surely, such a draconian commandment might allow for a few exceptions? I suspected that not everyone around me could be so pure, including Vidal Sassoon himself, who definitely seemed keen on some of the ladies whose heads he styled. Eventually, I discovered evidence that proved me right.

For a while, I was appointed junior to a stylist named Warren. As I've mentioned, we juniors would carry out basic jobs, such as greeting and sitting down clients, or sweeping away the hair at the end of a cut. But my main occupation was simply watching Warren at work, at close quarters. And in Warren's case, when I say "work", I don't just mean styling hair. Warren had an account at the local Royal Florist's in nearby Brook Street. Sometimes he would send me out to fetch a single rose. He would then place the flower in front of the selected client. After a while, curiosity got the better of me, and I asked him what the rose was for, and why some clients got one and others didn't.

"Watch and learn," was all he said.

I did watch and I did learn. It turned out that the rose was his subtle way of saying, "I'm interested. Are you?" I was amazed to see how often the ploy succeeded. And if it worked for Warren, there was hope for me as well. My new stylist had demonstrated, beyond a shadow of a doubt, that it was possible to circumvent Vidal Sassoon's frightful rule. He had even provided me with a winning strategy.

My delight was short-lived, however. Over time, I observed that Vidal's assessment was correct after all. Within a year, Warren barely had any clients left. Once they tired of him, or he of them, they couldn't return and went elsewhere. Shorn of his clientele, Warren was eventually asked to leave the salon, and I had learnt my lesson. If I wanted to get involved with women, I came to realize with dismay, Vidal Sassoon's was the last place I should try.

As you can imagine, this separation of business and pleasure was a constant challenge. My insides churned as I attended to many of the most beautiful women in the city, some of them clearly susceptible to the charms of a young, innocent and (frankly) not unhandsome styling apprentice. My fingers dug into their wet hair, day after day, massaging the scalps and necks of these half-naked ladies who would abandon their heads on the basins and occasionally smile at me. And yet, maddeningly, I was to remain impassive.

The relationship between a client and a hairdresser can get quite intimate, particularly when she really begins to *talk*. I was often shocked, as a junior, at how much of their private lives these women might reveal as their hair was being pampered. But again, these revelations were generally not an invitation to carry on the relationship outside the salon's walls. They arose precisely because we were strangers, and moreover bound by an implicit vow of secrecy. It was assumed that whatever was spoken in front of our brightly lit mirrors should be received with the detached interest of a lawyer or a psychotherapist. Alas! Little had I realized, when I was hired as an apprentice at Vidal Sassoon's, that the paradise I had dreamt of would actually turn out to be a living nightmare.

Nothing can illustrate this dilemma as clearly, perhaps, as my *professional* relationship with Diana Dors. Diana was Britain's answer to the typical American beauty queen, as represented by the likes of Marilyn Monroe, Jane Russell or Jayne Mansfield. Though conceptions of beauty were to change drastically in the following years, Hollywood stars were still "full figured" – a euphemistic phrase which referred to a large bosom, generous hips and a narrow waist to offset them both. The ideal "vital statistics" of a woman were considered to be 36"–24"–36", and the most desirable bra cup size D or above. Bathing beauty contests were still popular, and the feminist movement had not yet developed enough to challenge them seriously.

Diana Dors, who filled out this profile to the inch, became a regular client at Sassoon's. Her stylist was a wonderful character called Ricci Burns, a kind of hairdressing stand-up comedian who somehow could get away with the cheekiest replies to any of our clients' questions.

"Ricci, what would you do with my hair?" one of the fashionable ladies on his chair would ask.

"Madam," he'd declare with mock seriousness, "this is a comb, not a magic wand."

And if Ricci received a tip that he considered ridiculously small, he'd hand back the coin with an air of concern:

"Excuse me, madam. I think you need it more than I do."

It was Ricci who first told me about the notorious parties held at the Ad Lib Club, a celebrity haunt in Leicester Square from 1965 onwards. According to Ricci, Brian Epstein and the Beatles were frequent visitors, as were many other prominent bands of the day, including the Stones and the Yardbirds. His lurid accounts of nights there mentioned glamorous women, American pop music and, of course, drug-taking. I was desperate to get down to the Ad Lib, but I was still not eighteen, and so, according to Ricci, too young.

Ricci also used to go to parties held at Diana Dors's Weybridge home. It sounded like the Ad Lib Club transported to suburban Surrey, including many of the same guests. At the time, I was starting to become quite chummy with Diana, so I thought my big chance had come. Who knows? Perhaps I might even meet the Beatles…

"Can I come to one of your parties, Diana?" I would ask her whenever she came into the salon.

But she seemed to have joined into some kind of parental-control alliance with Ricci.

"I'll tell you when you're old enough, Leslie..." she would say with a wink.

Frankly, I didn't understand what Diana and Ricci could possibly mean. After several all-nighters at the seedy, multiracial Flamingo Club with my uncle Tony, where knife fights broke out over call girls that caused government ministers to resign, I already thought of myself as a real Jack the Lad. By then I was smoking not just tobacco, but the potent and forbidden cannabis, or "weed", that was becoming fashionable at the time. I'd also seen plenty of people taking "uppers", though I had not wanted to try them myself. So what could go on in those parties that I couldn't experience?

I liked Diana. She wasn't just sexy: she also had a great sense of humour. That lady was certainly aware of the effect she had on men – that they turned to jelly before her astounding figure. And she liked to play around with us goggle-eyed, adoring little creatures. I have to say that, in my case at least, I wasn't complaining.

"I'm bringing in a friend of mine tomorrow," she teasingly announced on one occasion. "She's coming to have her hair done. I think you'll like her. In fact, I'm sure you will."

"Who is it?" I asked, already heating up.

"You'll see," she replied, mysteriously.

I couldn't wait. Was she serious? Could anyone be as sexy as Diana? The next day, I turned up at work in a state of acute anticipation. I tried to concentrate on my job, but my eyes kept flitting to the stairs at the entrance of the salon.

Finally, there they were. Diana came down first, and behind her sauntered in the proof that she had not been joking in the least. I was dumbstruck. It was none other than the sensationally upholstered blonde actress Jayne Mansfield, widely tipped as the natural successor to Marilyn Monroe. Everyone in the salon, both male and female, simply stared at the extraordinary figure that had entered. As for me, I felt like a schoolboy again. Too young indeed...

Jayne and Diana wanted their roots touching up, and for that they had to go upstairs to the colouring room. I was asked to look after them, so after they were changed into their gowns I took them up in the lift. Now, I must stress that this lift was small – very small. So you can imagine how I felt, wedged between two of the most glorious bosoms in the Western hemisphere, their owners wearing only loose-fitting gowns tied with big ribbons right over their D-sized brassieres. I could scarcely breathe, and I didn't know where to put my eyes.

Some of my male colleagues weren't subject to this sort of dilemma. I discovered that Vidal's "no sex" rule posed no problem for them whatsoever. To my surprise, it turned out that these men weren't interested in the female clients at all. Call me naive, but I had received quite a sheltered upbringing from my parents in Burnt Oak. The concept of a homosexual, to me, was something unreal – a schoolboy joke, an insult, not an actual human being. In my neighbourhood, men were men, women were women, and there wasn't much else to be said about gender. But at the salon, things didn't seem so simple.

Of course, this wasn't unique to Sassoon's. Many male hairdressers at that time, and indeed since, have been very camp to say the least. I don't want to imply that it was a profession dominated by gay men. Vidal himself certainly wasn't, as many of his female clients found out for themselves. Lawrence Falk, over at Eric's, and myself were also straight as anything. Even so, we often joined in with the atmosphere and learnt to speak Polari among ourselves. Some of the gay hairdressers in the salon were using it, and it was fun for us to copy them, not to mention useful in a more practical sense.

Polari was a form of slang used within the gay community in the 1960s. Homosexual acts between adults were still a criminal offence in England, and would not be legalized until 1967. In such a repressive social atmosphere, this coded language was one way that gay men could identify each other without risk of discovery. For those of us who weren't homosexual, it was also a way to hide what we were saying from the clients. So, for example, if we said "Varder that polone, such a bona eek", it meant: "Look at that girl, what a nice face". Indeed the term *varder*, to watch or look at, had become a hairdressing term in itself. It was how we were taught; we were *varderers*, watching the master at work and learning his techniques.

So, after a couple of years in the business, I had picked up that there was a certain amount of gender ambivalence in the world of celebrity hairdressing, and had come to feel comfortable and familiar with it. My cheeky colleague Ricci Burns, for instance, was the ultimate example in dubious sexuality. None of us knew whether he was gay or straight, and he was happy to leave us in doubt. It was all part of his ongoing funny-man act, and was a source of continuous comic relief during our busy working days.

However, in 1964 I discovered I still had much to learn. One of the most stunning clients at the salon was a shapely woman named Audrey. She was a regular at Sassoon's, and I began to look forward to her frequent visits.

One day, while I was drying her hair, she unexpectedly blurted out a question that almost caused me to drop my blow-dryer.

"Leslie, what do you think of my boobs?"

To be sure, by then I had heard many things from clients that had surprised me, but this was well outside my comfort zone. I felt myself blush a deep red, completely flummoxed. If I said something like "They're great!" she might think me presumptuous – on the other hand, if I said "They're OK – I hadn't really noticed", I might offend her. I can't remember what I answered. Probably just an incoherent and non-committal mumble over the cover of the loud blow-dryer. The experience did get me thinking, however, that there was something unusual about Audrey. I just couldn't put my finger on it.

It was some time later before I discovered the true cause of my unease. We had become friends after a few visits, and began to take tea together at the Grosvenor House lounge. By then, Vidal had branched out from his original salon in Mayfair and opened a new place in the swanky Park Lane hotel, perfectly situated for his well-heeled clients. The tea lounge was through the back of the reception area of the salon, so was very convenient. Clients often relaxed there after having their hair cut and styled.

Audrey had told me she often entertained her "men friends" there. I wasn't sure exactly what she meant by that particular category, but each time she invited me to the lounge I felt more than happy to be included. One afternoon, while we were having our tea, she didn't seem her usual sprightly self, so I asked her what was wrong.

"Oh, Leslie, I'm due to have the cut-and-tuck soon, and I'm *very* worried about it."

I had no idea what she meant, and didn't understand why she should be so anxious. Most women were delighted at the prospect of a new image.

"Cut-and-tuck?" I said over my teacup. "I've never heard of that hairstyle. What's it like?"

She laughed heartily at my words. I was happy to have cheered her up, though I couldn't quite understand what was so funny.

"Oh Leslie," she said when she'd recovered. "You are so very sweet. It's not a hairstyle, silly. I'm having the operation, you know, to complete my change… from a man to a woman. I thought you knew!"

I barely managed to keep my cup on its saucer. My legs instinctively huddled over my manhood, as I imagined the cut-and-tuck in all its gory, clinical detail. I had no idea such a thing was possible, let alone desirable. In this case, it wasn't just my naivety. At the time, such procedures were very uncommon anywhere, unknown in the UK and hugely expensive. As Audrey explained to me what the operation involved, I listened with growing incredulity. Any romantic thoughts I had entertained about her vanished instantly. Audrey a man! About to change into a woman! No wonder she had asked me about her *boobs*… How had she managed to grow those?! The shock took days to wear off.

In the coming years, I would come to know several other non-binary celebrities at Sassoon's, completing my education on gender-bending matters. The most notable of these was undoubtedly Amanda Lear, one of the most celebrated women of the Swinging Sixties. In truth, nobody has ever conclusively proven whether she was born a boy or a girl, though to see this ravishing blonde in 1965, with her voluptuous hair and figure to match, you would never have guessed such a doubt was possible. Like everyone else in the salon, I was absolutely spellbound by her, from the moment she first set her high heels on Sassoon's tiled floors. With clients like these, gender switches soon began to sound as commonplace as changes in hairstyle.

As for Audrey and me, we remained good friends. She would sometimes ask me to give her a lift in my car to clubs and parties in the local area. Whenever I dropped her off, I'd ask if I could come in with her. Like Ricci and Diana, she always told me I was too young. What was up with these people? And what could possibly go on at these places that an eighteen-year-old couldn't be allowed to experience? With hindsight, perhaps it was for the best. I'm not sure I wanted to grow up *too* quickly.

Speaking of which, I did eventually manage to make a few discreet exceptions to Vidal Sassoon's "no sex" rule. While I was an apprentice, Tuesdays and Wednesdays were "model nights". The deal was this: we juniors got a chance to practise what we had learnt on willing guinea pigs, after hours, from six thirty to ten thirty; these were often young models and out-of-work actresses who couldn't afford the salon's prices; so, if they were willing to be cut and styled by juniors, they could get a haircut for free. Tuesdays would be long-hair nights, whereas on Wednesdays we would cut short hair. One Tuesday, after I finished with my model, she asked me what appeared to be an innocent question:

"Leslie, would you mind walking me to Bond Street Station?"

I agreed at once, of course. A beautiful girl on my arm for a few minutes — not a bad prospect at all. But I was totally unprepared for what was about to happen.

Just as you reach the top of New Bond Street, a little alleyway leads into Dering Street. As we were passing this small opening, the girl suddenly pulled me into it. Without a word, she began to kiss me passionately, and then, before I knew what was happening, undid my trousers and, well… let's just say that Vidal would not have approved!

I was seventeen. She was twenty-three.

On the Northern Line going back to boring old Burnt Oak, my body all a tingle, my mind in a whirl, I wondered… *Blimey, did I just dream that, or did it really happen?*

Just to make sure it had, every subsequent Tuesday night I insisted I cut that particular model's hair. Unfortunately, the supervising stylist, Robert, became suspicious. One day, he took me aside and confronted me.

"You're supposed to be varying your haircuts. Why do you keep on cutting this same girl's hair?"

I couldn't think of an answer. I certainly wasn't going to tell him the truth. My game was up, and I knew it.

So, regretfully, I agreed to change my Tuesday-night model.

3

Almost the Pete Best of the Hairdressing World

Remember Pete Best?

Not many people do. He was the Beatles' original drummer, hired in 1960 when the band travelled to Hamburg for the first time. The young and dashing lad was, by many accounts, the Beatles' most popular member, particularly among female fans. For two years, Pete played hundreds of concerts with Paul, John, George and Stuart, both in Germany and in Liverpool, and was with the Beatles when they signed the Parlophone contract that would launch their career. He also participated in many of their early adventures, including the post-concert fight in which Stuart Sutcliffe was injured, or the incident in which he and Paul McCartney were arrested for arson and deported from Germany after setting fire to a condom in a music venue.

Tragically for Pete, however, he was fired from the band in 1962, just before the Beatles recorded their first hit, 'Love Me Do'. The reasons for his dismissal have never been fully cleared up. The producer, George Martin, suggested to Brian Epstein that he be replaced on the Parlophone recordings, preferring a more technically proficient session drummer. However, Martin has always claimed that he never intended for the band to sack Pete permanently. Perhaps his companions used this as an excuse to get rid of him, whether for musical or other reasons. Some sources have suggested that he never fully got on with the rest of the group. Perhaps he was too conventional, refusing to take drugs or to adopt the famous "mop top" hairstyle they began to sport in Hamburg.

Whatever the reason, it was understandably tough to be Pete Best after 1963. Over the years, he would watch the Beatles become chart-topping stars, then a global sensation and finally the most legendary pop band in history. Depressed, he gave up music and, in the mid-Sixties, tried to commit suicide by gassing himself. Luckily, he was saved by his mother and brother, and went on to rebuild his life, becoming a civil servant and eventually, in 1988, returning to music with the Pete Best Band. Today, in media interviews, Pete is able to reflect on this colossal missed opportunity with grace and wisdom. But it has been a long, winding and painful road.

I've often thought of Pete Best when I recall the Saturday morning, in September 1966, when my own opportunity came to become a part of the Beatles' story. On that fateful day, I was about to audition for the top position any hairdresser could have dreamt of in the Sixties. And I almost blew it, big time.

* * *

By then, I had been working at Vidal Sassoon for four years. Gone was the clumsiness and anxiety of my early days. Slowly, I had gained confidence in the art of high-fashion hairdressing, first by watching my seniors, and then by trial and error on the heads of the models who came in for a free cut after hours. My graduation arrived when I was appointed junior to the maestro himself, the great Vidal Sassoon, who barely spoke a word during his styling sessions, and expected me to understand, from a whispered grunt or a flick of the hand, exactly what he wanted. After this trial by fire, I was now a qualified hairdresser in my own right, with a junior at my service.

The challenge, in those early days, was building up my own clientele. Most visitors to Sassoon's would set up appointments with their favourite stylist. So I would usually be assigned first-timers – or, if the salon was very busy, clients who were unable to book an appointment with their regular hairdresser. I have to say that, in this sense, my name was an unexpected advantage. When a new client came in, she might be told that three stylists were available: Robert, Howard and Leslie. Many women preferred to be tended to by a female hairdresser, so they chose "Leslie".

"Oh," I'd often hear, as they sat down in my chair, "I thought you'd be a woman."

"Not as far as I know," I'd reply, flashing them my best smile.

And that little joke would be my first step towards turning a slightly disappointed newcomer into a highly satisfied repeat customer. Not so much by virtue of my hairdressing ability, which couldn't compete with the skills of the senior stylists, but thanks to a talent I had discovered during my days as a junior: salesmanship.

Though I had never suspected such a thing before, some of Betty Boots's ability to sell snow to the Eskimos seemed to have rubbed off on me. Or perhaps it had been my direct contact with her own guru, my smooth-talking granddad, when I'd visit him at his East Street market stall. To this day, I can recall with crystal clarity the time that a tall gentleman with brush-like whiskers picked up a shoe he liked, a nice black brogue.

"Can I try the other one?" he asked.

"Of course, sir," my granddad said. "Here's the pair."

My eyes almost popped out, and so did the customer's, when Granddad brought out the other brogue, equally shiny and new, but completely white.

"Umm…" the customer said, pressing down on his moustache. "But it's… white."

"Oh, not a problem at all, sir. You'll find some shoe polish in a shop just round the corner. Put some on, and you've got yourself a pair of the finest black brogues, no one's the wiser – and at what a price! Best in London, sir."

I watched in awe as the man paid for the shoes and went off happily in search of his polish. What impressed me wasn't so much the sale, but the customer's evident satisfaction. My granddad had convinced this gentleman that he was making the best purchase of the year. And he wasn't fooling him either. I'm certain Grandpa believed what he was saying, one hundred per cent. I don't think he could have pulled it off otherwise.

At the salon, I discovered a similar talent in myself. What I lacked in manual dexterity I made up for in social abilities: a knack for listening carefully, for asking the right questions, for speaking when chatting was sought and keeping quiet when it wasn't. These are the skills that allow you to build up a solid relationship with clients, making them feel as comfortable in the hairdressing chair as on their own sofa at home. Once you've got that going, you can sell anything to anyone.

My fine customers would come in for a haircut, but they'd often end up undergoing a whole set of treatments over several visits, once I had examined their hair and broken the news, with the stern face of a doctor, regarding their split ends or unseemly dryness. The truth was that they needed these treatments, of course, if they wanted the luscious, shiny hair which, in fact, my lady clients did want, without exception. No one has perfect hair, so there's always a bit of additional care to be lavished on it. And as in the case of my grandfather's "mismatched brogues" customer, my clients were always delighted to go along with the extra treatments, positively thankful for my expert advice. So if I ever felt any qualms about my sales work, it was only when I felt, as with some of the young office workers that occasionally came into Vidal's, that they might not be able to afford it on their limited budgets. In those cases, I was not always as strict about the state of their hair.

I discovered this talent of mine as a junior, in contrast to some of my seniors' complete lack of sales ability. Though stylists received a commission for each extra haircare session they sold, many of them felt uncomfortable flogging additional treatments to their customers. On the other hand, I actually enjoyed this part of my work, and so made quite a bit of money for my seniors. Unsurprisingly, most of them were absolutely delighted to have me as an apprentice, and quite loath to letting me go. In fact Roger Thompson, the senior stylist at the Grosvenor House salon, didn't want me to graduate at all, and tried his best to delay the moment in which I would become a qualified hairdresser. In the end, however, even he wasn't able to block my progress.

Once I did graduate, my sales abilities came in very handy. Within a few months, I had accumulated a respectable clientele and was earning a decent living, between hairdressing fees, commissions and tips. With this hard-earned cash, I made one of the happiest purchases of my entire life: a black Morris Mini, with tinted windows and pretty headlights that reminded me of the big eyes of some of the models whose hair I styled. My Mini was my pride and joy – small but undeniably stylish, and as useful for zipping around London as any flashy sports car.

In addition to my female clients, I had also started to cut men's hair at the salon, after hours. Strange as it may sound nowadays, unisex salons were still a radical idea in 1966. A man at a hairdresser's? Perish the thought! Men were supposed to settle for barber shops, with their spinning poles and simple, no-nonsense haircuts. However, not everyone was satisfied with the conventional "short back and sides" treatment. At the same time that women's haircuts were becoming shorter and more masculine, on the other side of the gender divide, many men were becoming more fashion-conscious, with hairstyles that had begun to grow longer and required more care.

Part of the reason for this change, of course, was the unstoppable media storm surrounding the Beatles, who had not paid a visit to their traditional Penny Lane barber for a very long time now. Their "mop top" style had been gracing the pages of newspapers and magazines for over three years. Like me, the up-and-coming musicians who had kick-started their career back in 1963 had now graduated to a new level: world-spanning tours, innovative sounds and a depth to their lyrics inspired by the poetry and marijuana to which Bob Dylan had introduced them. One consequence was that their mushroom-shaped style had proliferated all over the world – including, of course, my own increasingly furry scalp.

For all of these reasons, at Vidal Sassoon clients began to ask whether the art of "hair geometry" might be applied to their husbands' or boyfriends' growing manes. These reasonable enquiries had to be turned down at first. It was inconceivable that men (other than our own staff) could penetrate the private female world of our hairdressing establishment. The only exception I can remember was when Peter O'Toole came in for some artistic highlights and colouring while he was filming *Lawrence of Arabia*. You can actually notice the effect of these touches in the film, his hair setting off those piercing blue eyes for which he was so renowned. But even in this case, Peter wasn't allowed to sit in one of the black hairdressing chairs on the ground floor, which would have raised a scandal among our lightly clad female customers. Instead, he was whisked upstairs to the private tinting room, away from the main action. That was scandal enough.

Howard, one of my favourite stylists at the salon, began to change all of this. He obtained Vidal Sassoon's permission to invite a few male clients after closing hours. It all started with Chris Stamp, who was co-manager of the Who, and he was quickly joined by the new band's lead guitarist, the future rock star Pete Townshend. The Who had just released their single 'I Can't Explain', which quickly entered the charts thanks to their exposure on pirate station Radio Caroline. Their rowdier style was accompanied by aggressive stage antics like smashing up guitars or destroying the drum kit in front of their gleeful audiences. Their hair was a symbol of that recklessness which, like that of the Beatles, had begun to sprout right over their ears. Amusingly, the band had even considered naming themselves "The Hair" at one point. And though their scruffy heads may have seemed careless and unkempt, they did need careful grooming.

Howard introduced me to this after-hours business he'd established on the side, and even passed on a few clients. Then, one day, Howard announced that he was leaving Vidal Sassoon to pursue other career interests. As I was the only stylist cutting men's hair, I suddenly inherited all of these customers in one go.

One of the most colourful examples was Keith Moon, the Who's drummer, who later gained a reputation for being the wildest man in rock music. Aside from destroying his own drum sets on stage, he would frequently toss TVs and other furniture from hotel windows – and, even more bizarrely, he became fond of making toilets explode by flushing live dynamite down them. I have to say, though, when I met Keith he seemed a nice enough bloke. Bubbly to be sure, but hardly a menace. It turned out he was from Wembley, which was not too far from Burnt Oak. He was only a few months older than me, and of course a huge fan of American music, so we had a lot in common. I suppose he still hadn't started ingesting the large quantities of amphetamines and other drugs that would later exacerbate his destructive tendencies and cause him repeatedly to pass out on stage.

One evening, after styling his hair, Keith invited me to join him, Chris Stamp and the rest of the Who at the Cromwellian Club, one of the hippest venues on the London scene. I'd never been to such an exclusive joint before. As I checked out the three floors of the place – a casino upstairs, a cocktail bar on the ground floor and a disco in the cellar – I recall thinking, *So this is how my clients spend their evenings*. But what I remember most about that night is trying champagne for the first time. In fact, this sweet, bubbly drink flowed so freely that I remember little else about what happened. Maybe I was trying to keep up with Keith. In any case, it was a fitting taster of the intoxicating world of pop music into which I was about to be introduced.

* * *

Unfortunately, on the day the invitation arrived, I was set to miss out on it as catastrophically as Pete Best himself. And all because of a football match.

It was the third of September 1966, exactly two months after the first major anti-Vietnam demonstration wreaked chaos in front of the American Embassy on Grosvenor Square, just around the corner from the salon. Now things were much calmer out on the street, but the salon floor was bustling with the usual Saturday-morning rush. The place was packed, and several women waited upstairs in the reception area, chatting among themselves or reading magazines. The only empty chair was mine, since my 11.30 client had cancelled. I kept looking up at the clock restlessly: 11.40, 11.55, 12.00... As soon as that clock struck one, I'd be jumping into my Morris Mini towards Loftus Road Stadium in Shepherd's Bush. That's where I'd be meeting a group of fellow Queens Park Rangers fans for one of our team's first matches of the season against Swindon Town. After a week of snipping and sculpting and making small talk with high-society ladies, I was bursting for a spot of simple laddish pleasures: drinking beer, cheering and hooting, the thrill of good old-fashioned footie. But I still had over an hour to wait. I sighed, looking ruefully towards the entrance of the salon, where my weekend would finally begin.

Suddenly, a slim young woman walked in through those glass doors into the reception area. I recognized her at once: Jane Asher. Who wouldn't, at that time? Her photographs were all over the press, on billboards and buses. Not only had she co-starred in one of the summer's hit comedies, *Alfie*, with the dashing man of the moment, Michael Caine – but for three years she'd been the girlfriend of the one and only Paul McCartney.

Jane was what we used to call an "English rose", delicately featured, clear-skinned, sensuous but not overtly sexy. She was wearing a fashionably short dress, but it was her hair that caught the eye. It was thick, luxuriant, and a warm strawberry blonde. As an apprentice to Roger, I had occasionally washed and blow-dried that luscious hair. But now that I was a junior stylist myself, she was out of my domain. As she spoke with Joanna, the receptionist, I noticed how her hair fell over her shoulders and then divided, half resting in front, the rest down her back. She wore a heavy fringe, cut just above the eyebrows. I wasn't the only one to notice. As if drawn by her aura, all of the staff looked up from their work.

To my surprise, Joanna began to lead her towards me.

"Roger says he's too busy to take care of her today," the receptionist whispered. "I know you've done her hair before. Can you step in?"

"Sure, no problem," I said, as nonchalantly as I could.

In truth, I was more than a little apprehensive. It was a privilege, of course, to work on that magnificent mane, belonging to such a famous client. But, at the same time, it was no small responsibility.

Before leaving, Joanna only added to my nerves:

"She's a bit frustrated that Roger isn't available, OK?"

I nodded confidently with the tight-lipped smile of that qualified hairdresser I had now become, as if to say, "Leave it in my hands, I'll take care of it."

Before I had time to think out my strategy, Jane was taking a seat in the black leather chair.

"Good morning," she said. "How are you today, Leslie?"

She sounded cordial enough, though her disappointment was obvious. I suppose she remembered me as Roger's apprentice, which I had been only a year earlier.

"I'm doing fine, thanks, Jane. What can I do for you this morning?"

I guess she must have noticed the effort I was putting in to make her feel comfortable. She smiled and even seemed to relax a little into the chair, resigning herself to how things seemed to be going.

"Oh, just give me a blow-dry today, please."

I knew it hadn't been the only time Roger had stood her up or made her wait. As a junior, I had learnt a great deal from

Roger Thompson's faultless hairdressing technique. Even today, he is considered within the profession as one of the greatest hair artists that has ever wielded a pair of scissors. But it had to be said that his eye for detail made him terrifically slow. This meant that, on busy days, he often ended up with a long queue of frustrated clients.

On the other hand, as I began to brush through Jane's hair, checking for knots, I became conscious that I might be hurrying a bit too much. The clock was ticking towards my football match, but the thickness of her hair made the job a delicate one. If I wanted Jane Asher to be satisfied, the thing couldn't be rushed. So I slowed down deliberately, reminding myself of whose girlfriend she was, and that Queens Park Rangers could wait. I asked her about her current projects, and she began to tell me about her latest play, a production of *A Winter's Tale* that had premiered at the Edinburgh Festival. As she spoke about her role as Perdita, a peasant who turns out to be a princess, I got the feeling that her frustration was beginning to recede. She was a charming girl, not much older than myself, and I remember thinking that she did exhibit both the simplicity of a peasant and the elegance of a princess. I had to give it to McCartney. He had great taste in women.

After my junior had washed her hair at the back of the salon, I towelled it dry, sectioned the hair and again checked for knots. Then I began to blow-dry the thick mane, carefully working my way through the back, then the sides and finally the top. I took my time, using my fingers as a brush, because that way I had more control in manoeuvring the rich fabric of golden strands. Finally, I stood behind her and checked in the mirror that both sides looked the same. I noticed a few ends weren't perfectly even, so I trimmed these with my scissors. All in all, the job took about forty-five minutes and, by the end of it, the English rose looked like she had just flowered.

As I held up the mirror for her to see the back of her head, she admired herself and smiled with childlike surprise.

"Leslie, that's just the way I like it," she said.

I was mightily relieved – and proud that I had resisted my temptation to rush the job.

"By the way," she then added, "do you ever make house calls? My boyfriend needs a haircut. Would you be free this afternoon? He would prefer it if you came to our place. It's in St John's Wood."

My boyfriend, she had said. Paul McCartney. The Beatle. The Mop-Top. One of the four most famous heads of hair in the world. The very hair that swishes around before millions of screaming fans. And she wants *me* to cut it, at the Macca's own home, in St John's Wood.

It was the most exciting haircutting gig I could have possibly been offered. Once again, I had found myself at the right place, at the right time.

And yet, I hesitated. There was a problem, and it was burning in my pocket: the ticket to the Queens Park Rangers match against Swindon. My eye flitted up to the clock. It was already time for me to jump into my car, dash through London and meet my mates at the stadium. I know, I know. It sounds insane that I could even consider such a thing. To this day, I continue to wonder in dismay that I could have risked such a once-in-a-lifetime chance because of a third-division football game. But nevertheless, I must admit that it fills me with a certain pride.

You must understand how I felt, and still feel, about Queens Park Rangers. They weren't a team I had been born into, as is the case with many football fans whose loyalty runs in the family. They weren't popular, established or wealthy – no. QPR was a team I had deliberately chosen, at age thirteen, despite the fact that hardly anyone knew or cared about them. Perhaps even for that very reason. In my neighbourhood, most people supported either Arsenal or Spurs, and the rivalry was bitter, aggressive and violent. There was something in that fanaticism that didn't sit with me. It reminded me of the vicious, irrational hatred the school bullies had directed at "Jew boys" and "niggers". So I chose a team that just liked to play football – their own original, attractive brand of football. Their shirts, blue with white hoops, also seemed to me infinitely cooler.

So, in a way, Queens Park Rangers meant as much to me as the Beatles themselves. I was constantly the butt of jokes, of course, for supporting a bunch of third-division nobodies. But that only hardened my loyalty, in the same way as the flames of Beatlemania were fanned by outraged parents' mockery and disdain. To make matters worse (or better, depending on how you look at it), QPR was going through the finest moment in its eighty-year history. Its new manager, Alec Stock, had turned the club around completely, and under his guidance the boys seemed destined for glory. Indeed, the season that was just getting under way would turn out to be QPR's most successful year, the momentous time that my beloved team would not only win the third-division championship, but also become the first team in that division to take the League Cup on 4th March 1967, beating West Bromwich Albion 3-2. I couldn't know any of this, of course. But for some reason, my heart was telling me that I needed to be with the Rangers that afternoon.

I did a quick calculation. The match would end just before five. How long would I take to drive from Shepherd's Bush to

St John's Wood? Less than an hour, I decided. By that time, I had learnt all the short cuts known to the most cunning of London cabbies. So, with a bit of luck, I could both watch the game and meet my music idol, all in a single afternoon.

"How about six p.m.?" I said to Jane.

At the salon, I had learnt that clients could be very fickle. One minute they might share a backstage anecdote with you, giggling carelessly as if you were their dearest friend, and the next they might snap at you for trimming too much off their fringe. So my attempt to delay Jane's appointment until such a late hour might have easily put her off. She might have decided to forget the whole idea. Or to ask Roger if he'd be free at a more reasonable time. If that had happened, then I suppose I would have spent the rest of my life regretting my idiotic question, wondering what it would have been like to have cut and styled the Beatles' hair, perhaps even cursing Queens Park Rangers for getting in the way. I would have become, indeed, the Pete Best of the hairdressing world.

Fortunately, I got lucky.

"Fine," Jane said, fishing inside her handbag. "I'll give you the address."

She pulled a notepad out of her bag and scribbled on one of its pages. When she passed it over and I saw the address, 7 *Cavendish Avenue*, I said:

"What a coincidence. My surname is Cavendish."

"It must be fate, then, Leslie," she said with a smile. "Don't you think? I'll tell him you'll be over at about six."

It certainly was fate.

My life would never be the same again.

* * *

Queens Park Rangers beat Swindon Town 3-1, kicking off a series of fifteen consecutive matches without defeat. Thrilling as the game must have been, though, I found it impossible to get into the spirit. Was I really going to be cutting Paul McCartney's hair that afternoon? I just couldn't imagine it. In fact, I didn't even dare tell my friends. By the time I got into my Mini and set off towards St John's Wood, I had begun to doubt that my session with Jane Asher had taken place at all. I had to pull out her handwritten note from my pocket, at a traffic light, to convince myself: 7 *Cavendish Avenue*. Just like my surname.

As I turned into the street, I realized there was no need to check the house number. Obviously, it was the three-storey Regency townhouse with the gaggle of girls gathered at the front gates. They all seemed to be wearing the teenage uniform of the day: long straight hair, heavy black eye make-up, miniskirts and boots. Later I would learn that these young fans were known to the Beatles and other regular visitors as the "Apple Scruffs". George Harrison dedicated a sweet little song to them in his first solo album in 1970, 'All Things Must Pass'. As he wrote in that song, these hardcore groupies would stand outside the homes, recording studios and offices of the Beatles, day and night, rain or shine, hoping for any kind of interaction with their adored musicians. Their presence at the gates of Paul's house suddenly brought home to me the kind of privilege I was about to be afforded.

I'd arrived a bit early, so I parked my car and sat in silence, bracing myself for the big meeting. Of course, I'd grown used to rubbing shoulders with celebrities by now, but this was a different league altogether. The Beatles had become an unprecedented global phenomenon. Practically every single they put out became an instant number-one hit. They'd starred in two blockbuster films which more or less invented the concept of the music video. Their latest albums, *Rubber Soul* and *Revolver*, were taking rock-'n'-roll music into new, uncharted territories: the exotic sounds of the sitar, the classical string octet of 'Eleanor Rigby' and the artful lyrics of 'In My Life' and 'Norwegian Wood'. They had even received MBEs from the Queen herself.

Meanwhile, the band had been touring all over the world to sell-out stadium crowds of fans, making headlines wherever they went. That summer, John Lennon's quip to the press that they had become "more popular than Jesus" had set off a firestorm of controversy in the United States. But the truth was, he hadn't been too far off the mark. Fans debated over the philosophical lyrics of 'Tomorrow Never Knows' as fiercely as if they were scripture. Squares cut out of their hotel sheets were being flogged off like holy relics. The hysterical screaming, weeping and fainting of their audiences exceeded the behaviour of even the most fanatical religious devotees.

The real problem was that I belonged to that flock of fanatics. Shirley Bassey was a star, but it was my mother who listened to her songs. The Who were a "happening" band, and I liked their music, but... The Beatles! I'd played their singles so many times that my records were all scratched. There wasn't a lyric of theirs I couldn't recite by heart. Now that they'd stopped touring, the speculation that they might never give another concert, or that they could even break up, was making me anxious. My very hair was a slightly longer and shaggier variation on their early "basin" cut, like that of so many other young people at the time. In fact, it was so obviously a Beatles hairstyle that my picture had been published in a local Spanish newspaper during a summer holiday in Majorca, under the headline "YOUNG MAN WITH THE RINGO STARR LOOK".

All my Sassoon training would have to come into play here. For three years I'd learnt to play it cool around big stars, to make small talk and allow them to relax in the private space of the salon, away from the hungry public eye. Nevertheless, I was human too, and I'd had my moments of weakness. In fact, only a few weeks before, I had made a complete fool of myself in front of my biggest star client.

It turned out that Chris Stamp, the Who's manager, was the brother of Terence Stamp, the famous actor who had recently received an Oscar nomination for his role in *Billy Budd*. Thanks to Chris's recommendation, I also started to cut Terry's hair after hours at the salon. At the time, Terence Stamp was undoubtedly the coolest man in the mid-Sixties. He was suave, handsome, rich and famous, and to top it all, he was going out with Julie Christie, for many the most beautiful English actress of the day. He was also a big Chelsea fan, something I knew well, as football was a topic of conversation I could always rely on for a good chat with my male clients.

One day, I was going to a match at Chelsea's Stamford Bridge ground with a group of my non-QPR friends, when I spied Terence Stamp approaching the gate of the parking lot in his Rolls-Royce.

"Hey," I said excitedly to my mates, "I know who that is!"

The words just spilt out of me – and, to make it worse, I impulsively ran up to the car and banged on the window, shouting: "Hi, Terry!"

At the time, it seemed like the natural thing to do. I'd spent the past hour joking and horsing about with my mates, as far from the world of Vidal Sassoon as I could possibly be. We'd probably had a pint or two in the pub, I was on a football high, and I guess as a result I fancied myself as cool as Terence Stamp himself. For once, I had wanted to impress the gang with my celebrity connections. And why not? Hey, I did know the guy. We'd often chatted about football, and we'd even occasionally had champagne together with his brother Chris, Pete Townshend and Keith Moon.

But then Terry looked up at me through the glass window with a startled expression that quickly soured into *Oh God, not my hairdresser showing off in front of his mates.* I instantly realized what an awful mistake I'd made. To his credit, he did acknowledge me politely, before driving away. My friends were, in fact, impressed. But inside, I felt like a complete prat. For the whole match, all I could think about was how I would ever be able to face Terry again, even if he came back to the salon. He did, in fact, return, and when he did, I apologized for my unprofessional behaviour. But I knew our relationship would never be quite the same again.

It was six o'clock. Time for my private hairdressing appointment at 7 Cavendish Avenue. I grabbed the carpet bag I used as my portable haircutting kit, climbed out of the Mini and headed for the big brick house. The Apple Scruffs eyed me with curiosity as I strolled up to the side gate with as casual an air as I could muster. *Who is this guy?* they must have wondered. And I was wondering the same thing. Who am I to be pressing the bell on Paul McCartney's intercom?

"Hello?"

It was a female voice, but not Jane's. An older-sounding woman.

"Hi, umm… it's… My name is Leslie Cavendish," I stammered. "I'm here for…"

A buzzer sounded, and the heavy gates opened. As I crossed the courtyard towards the front door, circling around a sleek, dark-green Aston Martin, I could feel the eyes of the groupies behind me, following my every step up the driveway.

I waited under the little porch, held up by two white columns, expecting to meet the housekeeper or maid who had picked up the answerphone. But when the door finally opened, there was the man himself, wearing his trademark knitted sleeveless jumper, a welcoming smile spreading across his face.

"Hello, Leslie. Thanks for coming."

I'm not sure what I mumbled at that point as I shook the hand that had penned the notes and lyrics of 'All My Loving', 'Michelle' and 'Yesterday'. I felt light-headed: my entire Beatles-tinted youth flashed before me: the first hearing of 'Love Me Do', my mum's attempts to turn down the volume of 'Twist and Shout' on our Decca player, my twelve-shillings-and-sixpence tickets for the Pigalle Club gig, the evening I watched *A Hard Day's Night* on the big screen, all the times I sang along to 'Drive My Car' as it blasted out of my Mini's radio on my way to work…

Paul led me into the living room, which had a bay window that gave onto the back garden. The first thing I noticed were a piano and two guitars, one acoustic, one bass. *Oh*, I thought, *so this is where it happens*. I felt dizzy again.

Fortunately, Paul came to my rescue.

"So, Jane tells me you're quite good at cutting barnets…"

Barnets. That, of course, was rhyming slang. The amusingly cryptic code, peculiar to the British working class, is commonly associated with London, but thrives in fact in many other cities, including, it would seem, Liverpool. Following its logic, "my old china" is used to mean "my old mate" ("china plate" rhymes with "mate"), whereas "going up the apples" means "going up the stairs" ("apples and pears" rhymes with "stairs"). As for "barnet", the word refers to the London borough which includes Burnt Oak, the very place where I'd lived most of my life. Since the nineteenth century, it's been known for its traditional market, Barnet Fair. And "fair" of course, rhymes with "hair".

I looked up at Paul and noted his faint smile. Suddenly, I realized who he really was. Not some kind of legendary music star that existed only in newsprint – not a hero, idol or demigod: just a nice chappie from Liverpool in serious need of a haircut. And that's where I came in.

"Well, I don't know if I'm that good," I said, "but I'll do my Mae West."

I then asked Paul if Jane was around. He told me she'd gone off for the night's performance of *A Winter's Tale*. Then, seeming to remember something, he disappeared upstairs, saying:

"I'll be back in a couple of minutes. Have a look round."

I didn't need a second invitation. Stepping between a green sofa and a low table covered in an Indian throw, I crossed over towards the bay window, trying to resist the temptation of picking up one of those guitars. The place was seriously untidy. Piles of papers, records, cassettes and books were strewn higgledy-piggledy both on the furniture and all over the floor. I have to say, it didn't look much like my idea of a pop star's house. There was a fireplace with a few knick-knacks on the mantelpiece, family photographs hanging on the walls, a TV set in the corner. It was actually quite homely.

Looking out of the windows, I saw that the back garden was an unkempt jungle of weeds, overgrown grass and wild bushes. Most of the householders on Cavendish Avenue would, no doubt, employ their own gardeners, but Paul's yard was as natural as he was turning out to be. From the undergrowth, several feet high in places, I noticed some kind of large creature emerging – it was a huge English sheepdog.

"That's Martha," Paul said, as he came back down. "She could probably do with a haircut too."

Paul opened the doors to the garden so that the shaggy animal, who would later inspire the song 'Martha My Dear', could give me a good slobber.

"Do you want to come upstairs?" Paul asked. "I think we'll be more comfortable there."

He took me up to the large bedroom, which had two tall rectangular windows and looked like the tidiest place in the house. I set it down to the influence of Jane, who had moved in with Paul just a few months before. You know the story: a bachelor who lives in a bit of a mess, until his girlfriend begins to straighten things out. Indeed, a few months later, the overgrown garden would also be cleaned up under Jane's supervision, and furnished with a circular summerhouse with a geodesic dome. This "meditation chapel" and its circular bed, famously donated by Groucho Marx, would be the only real concession to pop-star eccentricity at 7 Cavendish Avenue. To me, however, the en-suite bathroom Paul then walked into, at the end of the bedroom, was extravagant enough. I'd never seen such a thing before.

"Should we do it in here?" Paul suggested.

It seemed, indeed, the most appropriate place. We grabbed a dressing-table stool at first, but it turned out to be ridiculously short, so we replaced it with a larger armchair that took up a good part of the bathroom. I could tell this was all as new for Paul as it was for me. He'd been on tour now, almost non-stop, for several years, so who knows when and where he'd been having his hair cut.

Paul sat down on what now looked like an oversized throne. All of this playing around with chairs had actually got us a bit giggly. This was starting to feel less and less like a professional visit, and more like a friendly hangout.

I opened up the leather straps of my carpet bag next to the sink and studied Paul's hair as I always liked to do with a new client, running my hand through his brow to find the natural "break" or parting, the place where it falls into two directions, left and right. As I did so, I made him a promise that I would remember many years later:

"You have wonderfully thick hair, just like mine. I can guarantee that you'll *never* go bald."

He laughed. "Well, that's nice to hear."

Satisfied with my inspection, it was time for me to pop the obligatory question:

"So Paul, how would you like it?"

I looked at him in the mirror and he looked back, shrugging his shoulders.

"Just do it as you see it," the Beatle said.

His casual answer took me completely by surprise. We assume these days that major stars will have an army of advisers at their service, who meticulously design their image, including their clothes and hair. I suppose that things weren't quite as planned back then – but even so, I had expected that Paul McCartney would exercise some sort of control over a head of hair that had become an icon of youthful rebellion around the world.

What I hadn't realized, and had no way of knowing, is that the Beatles were undergoing a major change in their career. Since 1962, they had followed the script laid down by their manager Brian Epstein, who had cleaned up their initial scruffiness, convincing them to give up their jeans and leather jackets, wear identical suits and ties, synchronize their bows after each song and refrain from smoking, drinking and swearing on stage. In short, they had spent four years playing the part of a Beatle.

Hair-wise, that role had included their famous inverted bowl-shaped "Arthur" haircut (in *A Hard Day's Night*, a journalist asks George Harrison what he called the style, and that was his answer). The Beatles had initially worn their longish hair greased back, Elvis-style, but in 1960 Stuart Sutcliffe's girlfriend Astrid Kirchherr decided to give him a more modern look – which incidentally covered up Stuart's protruding ears. Later adopted by the other Beatles, it appeared on the covers of their first singles, and quickly became their trademark, to be ridiculed, admired and imitated everywhere. Toy manufacturers sold Beatles' wigs by the thousands, allowing anyone temporarily to don this immediately recognizable cut. But now I could see that Paul's hair was growing longer, growing away from the look we had all come to associate with these world-famous musicians. I soon began to understand why.

"So," I said, getting on with my job. "I hear you've stopped touring for now."

It seemed like a safe question. Everyone was talking about it, so it didn't mark me out as a fawning admirer.

"Yeah, you know," he sighed. "We're pretty tired of all the travelling, the concerts, the hotels... We needed a break."

As I worked on his hair, cutting it "as I saw it", Paul began to paint a picture of life on the road that was both grim and, at the same time, as comical as their crowd-fleeing antics in *A Hard Day's Night*. The Beatles had basically spent the past three years holed up in their hotel rooms, unable to leave except for the concerts themselves, under heavy security. Even the police charged to protect them would often mob them for autographs. Worst of all, they'd been playing the same songs again and again, like trained monkeys, to fans who couldn't even hear the music over their own screaming.

"We had Vox build special speakers for us. The biggest they could make. And it still wasn't enough. So, you know, it wasn't about the music any more. No one cared about the songs. What was the point?"

Paul told me they were taking a three-month holiday, and each of them was doing their own thing. John was shooting a film in Germany and Spain, and George was off to India with his wife, to take sitar lessons.

"I just want to spend a bit of time at home with Jane and Martha," he told me. "Write a bit of music, have my hair cut, that sort of thing."

I smiled.

Now I got it. Paul and the other three Beatles had been desperately yearning for a bit of simple freedom, and they'd finally got their hands on some. Which is why he was relinquishing responsibility over his hair to me, some kid even younger than himself who'd become a qualified stylist only a few months before. What did he care how his hair looked? The point was to feel that Brian Epstein no longer controlled him, nor the millions of screaming fans, nor the weight of the Beatles' role itself. He would probably have been happy to let his hair become as untamed as his garden, as shaggy as Martha's woolly coat – if Jane hadn't stepped in. So I figured it was right to let it grow. This was a man who was enjoying his freedom, his comfy sleeveless jumper, his new-found love, his wild, creative disorder. All he needed was a trim here and there, and he'd look perfectly himself. That's how I saw it.

After my work with the scissors, I washed his hair in the basin, and then we moved into the bedroom to blow-dry it. As he sat on a bed corner, I finally asked him about football.

"So Paul, are you a blue or a red?" I said, referring to the two rival teams from his city.

At first I thought he hadn't heard my question. I hadn't considered that his reaction could have been so muted. Everton had taken the FA Cup in May, whereas Liverpool had won the League. The whole city was football-mad. It was inconceivable that a Liverpudlian like Paul McCartney could remain blasé about the sport.

"So, do you support Everton or Liverpool, Paul?" I asked again.

He raised his voice this time.

"Oh, I'm not really interested in football, Leslie."

I have to say, it was a bit of a disappointment – and a permanent dead end to my favourite topic of conversation with male clients. Sadly – and quite incredibly – I would eventually discover that none of the Beatles cared in the least about the game. Later on, when I tried the same line with John, with George and with Ringo, I met the same bored indifference in each of them. It boggled the mind. The Fab Four... football non-believers! On the other hand, I suppose it may have been a consequence, or even a cause, of their passion for music. Whatever the case may be, back in Paul's bedroom, I feigned indifference to his reply and tried to put it behind me by asking if he was composing any new songs.

As he described his work for the soundtrack of a movie, *The Family Way*, I concentrated on his hair, brushing it upwards with my fingers, as I had done with Jane. There was a natural gap on the left side, so I kept his parting there. His hair was now so long that it flopped over the gap, giving him the gentle, boyish look for which he was to become famous in the mid-Sixties. At Sassoon's, a key principle I had learnt was that, when we had finished styling a male client, it shouldn't look as though he had just been to the hairdresser's. All my art was directed to make it look as natural as possible. Vidal and his assistants had taught me that way, and that's what I always did. Paul would be no different.

I took him into the bathroom so he could evaluate the result in the mirror. It looked good to me, but I was a little apprehensive as to what he might think.

The Beatle turned this way and that, checking out my handiwork. I waited for his verdict.

"It doesn't look as if it's just been cut," he said.

I nodded proudly. Paul's words could have come straight out of Vidal Sassoon's mouth.

"You've got it, Paul. That's the whole idea."

"Is it?" he said, playing around with his new hairstyle. "Yeah, I like it, Leslie. Thanks."

Happy with my performance, I asked Paul for a broom to sweep up the mess in the bathroom.

"Of course, I'll just pop down and ask Mrs Kelly for one," he said. And then he added, "Do you fancy a cup of tea? I'll ask her to make some. And I could play you some of the stuff I was telling you about, if you've got time…"

Oh, did I have time? For a cup of tea with Paul McCartney? And to hear him play a few tunes in his living room? Just the two of us?

"Sure, Paul," I said, hiding my excitement with a showy scrutiny of the job to be done on the bathroom floor. "That would be lovely."

A few minutes later, we took our tea downstairs. Paul then sat at the upright piano and showed me a few of the melodies he'd been tinkering with for his movie soundtrack. At one point, he suddenly interrupted himself, in the middle of a song.

"Come to think of it, Leslie," he said, with an amused grin. "Here's something just for you. It's one of the first songs I ever wrote, when I was still at school. But I was thinking of proposing it for our next album."

Paul's hands began to bounce around the piano, playing a cheerful, music-hall sort of rhythm, and then, after a short introduction, he began to sing along: "When I get older, losing my hair…"

I thought he had to be *taking the mickey*. The old-fashioned ragtime sounded nothing like a Beatles song. It might have been featured on the Perry Como Show. So I laughed along chummily at what I thought was a great joke, suggested by my comment in the upstairs bathroom.

"Sounds great, Paul," I said, when it was over. "Pity you won't be losing your hair."

"Yeah," he said, passing his hand over his thick, freshly cut hair. "Maybe I should change the lyrics…"

Of course, the song did actually end up on *Sgt. Pepper's* and became a classic Beatles tune: 'When I'm Sixty-Four'. But who could have known, at that time, that this rock-'n'-roll band was about to create an album so innovative that it would change pop music for ever?

That first private, post-haircut concert was a surreal experience. There I was, hanging out with Paul McCartney as I might do with Lawrence in front of my Decca record player, enjoying a preview of Beatles songs that hadn't even been released. As I listened to a few other bits of music, sipping on my tea, it dawned on me that this incredible hairdressing gig might not be a one-off. I might have actually gained a new client. Perhaps even four. I lay back in the sofa, listening to the sounds of a future I could never have imagined, even in my most far-fetched teenage dreams.

* * *

Whenever I tell this story, and what came after, people always ask me the same question: "So, did you keep any of his hair?"

The answer is no. Not a single strand.

I admit that the thought did cross my mind, that first time I swept the cuttings off Paul's bathroom floor. In 2016, a single lock of Beatles hair (admittedly, a longish one belonging to John Lennon) was auctioned for £25,000. Even in 1966, however, this exceedingly rare and revered material was worth much more than its weight in gold. As I looked at the wispy tufts on the dustpan, that Saturday afternoon on Cavendish Avenue, and then at my own reflection in the mirror, I saw myself before the final crucible. Would I act like a selfish groupie or treat Paul McCartney with some basic human respect?

In the end, I chucked all of his hair into the bin as what it really was: rubbish. In so doing, I made my choice, and it's one I've always honoured. Call me crazy if you like. To me, it was a basic point of professional ethics, and I've never regretted it. Paul's trust was more important to me than any price I might have been paid for those dead, brittle strands. I'm certain the trust I'd started to earn that afternoon explains why Paul invited me for tea that day and would continue to invite me to many other shared moments, great and small, over the most fascinating period of the Beatles' career. In contrast, Mrs Kelly, the lovely old housekeeper who brewed our tea and served it in china cups in the living room, would try to sell her stories to an Australian newspaper soon after. A few haircuts later, she had been replaced.

Though I didn't go off to the press, I did of course let a few people know whose hair I was now cutting. As soon as I came into work on Monday morning, I made a point of telling Mr Sassoon himself, and he was very pleased. This was an important marketing scoop for his business, and he knew it. Indeed, the news spread like wildfire among the staff and even the clients: Leslie Cavendish, from this very salon, was cutting the hair of a Beatle...

There was one person, however, who was anything but happy with my good fortune. In fact, he was fuming mad. And that was the manager of the Grosvenor House salon, my boss Roger Thompson. Jane Asher had been his client, but – as we've seen – due to his busy Saturday schedule and his usual slowness, she had been tended to by me on that fateful day. As Roger saw it, the most amazing hairdressing opportunity imaginable had dropped into the lap of little Leslie, the nineteen-year-old junior stylist, barely qualified, who had served as his apprentice only months before. And what was worse, Jane Asher herself, from then onwards, would choose me whenever she came in for a hairdo at Sassoon's. It was a humiliating blow Roger would take very badly, and it became obvious to me from his first icy, silent stare. It was he, in the end, who became the Pete Best of the hairdressing world, and the bitterness of it poisoned our relationship from that moment on. For the first time in my life, I had made an enemy.

4

How I Changed Rock-'n'-Roll History with a Single Haircut

All right. I admit that there was that one time when I did keep a lock of Paul McCartney's hair. But I did ask for permission. And, frankly, I think I deserved it. That particular haircut was one of those apparently insignificant everyday events that end up having consequences far beyond what anyone could have foreseen. A suggested change in look, a few snips with my scissors, and pop music was transformed for ever. That afternoon, I changed rock-'n'-roll history – though it would take me another fifty years to figure it out.

The background to this odd tale has to do with the peculiar life the Beatles led at the height of their fame – not by choice, but by the extreme nature of this fame itself. I've just recounted my first visit to Paul's home, and even in that short episode many features of the Beatles' lifestyle – both privilege and curse – stand out. Jane Asher was a well-known actress, of course, but she could still stroll into places like Vidal Sassoon's for a haircut. Her boyfriend, however, might have caused a riot if he'd attempted such an ordinary grooming chore. The visit needed to be organized in private, in the refuge of his own home, away from the adoring fans who, as I've described, went to the lengths of actually camping out permanently outside his gate, on the off-chance they might spot him, exchange a few words or obtain an autograph. As for me, the hairdresser on the job, I felt I needed to control myself and act "normal" before this superstar, otherwise I knew I might make Paul feel uncomfortable and ruin my chances of coming back to cut his hair again. Such was the challenge that was faced by anyone who came into contact with one of the Beatles around that time – and it was a barrier as solid and intimidating as the wall that enclosed the McCartney residence.

I did pass my particular test, of course, and was called back for several new styling sessions during the following weeks. Over the course of that autumn, in 1966, I slowly began to relax in Paul's presence. I won't say that my visits to 7 Cavendish Avenue became anything like mere routine, but after a month or so I was able to work on that legendary head of hair and chat with its owner as if he were any other of my important male clients. The only difference was that I couldn't talk to him about football. Our main topics of conversation were music – Bob Dylan, the Beach Boys, James Brown – his work on the soundtrack for *The Family Way* and my own anecdotes from the salon. In fact, Paul liked to keep tabs on who else was having his hair cut by me.

"Oh, Keith Moon was in the other day," I remember telling him on one occasion. "But he didn't smash up any mirrors or anything. And I've got a new client: Dave Clark."

I thought that would get his attention, and it did. Paul's ears instantly pricked up.

"Ah! Dave Clark... really, Leslie?" he said, fixing me in the mirror with a sly look.

I knew exactly what that smirk meant. Though today people think of the Rolling Stones as the Beatles' main rival, at the time there was no doubt that their closest competitor was the Dave Clark Five. From the moment, in 1964, when the single

'Glad All Over' knocked 'I Want to Hold Your Hand' off the number-one spot in the British charts, the DC5 vied with the Beatles in every possible field. They were invited on the popular Ed Sullivan Show in the US only three weeks after the Beatles made their legendary appearance, and went on to even greater fame than the Fab Four in the States, with sell-out tours and seventeen hits on the Billboard Top 40 between 1964 and 1967. After the Beatles released their film *A Hard Day's Night*, the Dave Clark Five starred in their own vehicle, *Catch Us if You Can*. And of course their haircuts were modelled on the Beatles' own mop tops.

"Yeah, he seemed like a nice bloke, Paul," I told him that afternoon as I blow-dried his hair in the bedroom. "Kept going on about how his band was better than the Beatles."

"Oh really? Is he a musician?" he joked.

Our conversations were very often like that. Just a lot of chummy banter over nothing in particular. Then, after the haircutting sessions, and if he wasn't in a hurry, he'd usually ask Mrs Kelly to make us some tea, as on the first occasion. Sometimes Jane would also join us, if she was around. And of course Martha the sheepdog would always greet me in the garden.

I was amazed, and delighted of course, at how quickly Paul opened up to me in those first weeks. A turning point was when I was invited up, for the first time, to what was known as the "music room" on the top floor. This "holy of holies" for Beatlemaniacs was where Paul composed many of his most celebrated songs on his upright Knight piano, and where it's rumoured Mick Jagger smoked his first joint. Though I don't know if that last story is true, I can confirm that Paul always kept a supply of pre-rolled marijuana cigarettes of the highest quality in his home. In fact, these were soon added to the tea ritual – another surprising show of intimacy, to say the least. I mean, I had only just met the guy. I was merely his hairdresser. And yet, here I was spliffing up with the very bloke who liked to get high with a little help from his friends – just around the time he was writing the song, too…

Needless to say, I have wonderful memories of hanging out with Paul in his music room – though some of them, understandably, have always been a little hazy. A couple of months after I first began to cut his hair, Paul invited the pop-art collective Binder, Edwards and Vaughan (BEV) to paint the Knight piano with the same trippy, bright colours that they had used on the Buick convertible featured on the cover of the Kinks' *Sunny Afternoon* EP. Under the influence of Paul's pre-rolled joints, it always seemed to me that those jagged, layered and intertwined arrows in clashing yellow, pink, blue and green tore downwards through the piano's wood like lightning, or perhaps like the flashes of inspiration that gripped McCartney in the heat of song-writing. A bit later, another influential bit of decoration was added to the room: a painting of a bright-green apple by Magritte with the words "Au revoir" handwritten in white on its skin. Paul loved Magritte's surreal sense of humour, and this gift from his friend, the art dealer Robert Fraser, ended up inspiring the name and logo of Apple Records. You might have seen those famous Beatles' LPs which featured the Granny Smith on one side of the label and the inside of the apple (as if chopped in half) on the B-side.

You might say that I was quickly gravitating towards the core of that inner apple, the closed world of the Beatles that only allowed in a few trusted collaborators – most of them old friends from Liverpool like their road managers Neil Aspinall and Mal Evans. Once I found myself in this position, it was almost inevitable that I would begin to take on assignments that went beyond my initial role as caretaker of Paul's coiffure. One important category of such jobs could be well referred to as "Beatle-smuggling", defined as those schemes and strategies designed to carry a Beatle from point A to point B without attracting hordes of fans, journalists and all-out chaos. The film *A Hard Day's Night* includes a famous scene of Beatle-smuggling: the Fab Four arrive at a train station, jump into a car through one set of doors, escape out the other side and finally board a second getaway vehicle while the first is mobbed by screaming girls. Less commonly remembered is the fact that John Lennon's celebrated "long beard and granny glasses" look was originally worn as a disguise during another Beatle-smuggling episode from *Help!*, the sequel to their first film. Though fictional and caricatured, these movie moments portrayed a part of the Beatles' experience that was only all too real.

One of the most memorable instances of Beatle-smuggling I participated in took place a couple of years after my first meeting with Paul, in the summer of 1968. By then, Paul's relationship with Jane Asher was over, and he had started seeing an American scriptwriter, Francie Schwartz. The breakup with Jane had not yet been made official, but there was a lot of speculation in the press about possible new girlfriends. According to a rumour which has never been fully confirmed or denied, Jane had returned to London early from a trip abroad and found Paul in bed with Francie, in the very same bedroom where I would normally blow-dry his hair. I never did find out if the rumour was true, and certainly never asked Paul himself – one more example of my well-trained discretion. It was a difficult moment for my client, and he had decided to go to ground for the time being.

One evening, I was approached by Chris O'Dell, another American girl who worked for Apple Records and was a close friend both of Francie and of all the Beatles, as well as myself. If the name sounds familiar, it may be because George Harrison wrote a song about her: 'Miss O'Dell'.

"Leslie," Chris said to me that evening, "I've suggested to Paul that we all go out to a club together: you, me and Francie, that is."

"Really? Where did you have in mind?" I asked, rather sceptically. To me, it sounded like a terrible idea. The press was everywhere, looking for a story. If Paul was trying to keep a low profile, going out to a London club sounded like the last thing he should be doing.

"I've suggested the Club dell'Aretusa in Chelsea, and he's agreed."

"Are you sure about that, Chris? Paul hardly ever goes to clubs these days," I countered. He and Jane preferred private parties and discreet restaurants, where there'd be less press attention. "They're too public – now more than ever."

"That's where you come in," Chris said. "We'll go round in your Mini." The smoked-glass windows, she said, would prevent anyone from recognizing the passengers. And who could imagine that a big star would be driven around in a tiny car like that?

"All right, Chris," I gave in. "Sounds cool."

To be honest, I wasn't at all convinced that Chris's Beatle-smuggling plan would work, but it sounded like an amusing escapade, and the idea of a night out with Paul and Francie was too tempting to resist. Chris and I drove to 7 Cavendish Avenue and picked them up as discreetly as we could. As we drew up next to the club, I got out to have a word with the doorman.

"I've got Paul McCartney in the car, with a couple of other friends. Can you arrange for us to have a private table downstairs, please?"

The heavy-set bouncer gave me the once-over, glanced back at my unassuming car, and then his face soured into one of those "whose leg are you trying to pull" expressions London doormen are famous for.

"See for yourself," I shrugged, inviting him over for a closer look.

I nodded to Chris, who pushed open the Mini's sliding window. The doorman stepped closer, grumbling to himself, obviously expecting some kind of joke.

Suddenly, however, the burly man stiffened and went pale as the window was quickly slid shut once again.

"Yes, sir. Of course, sir," he stammered, nodding in my direction with a newfound respect. "That can be arranged."

We piled out quickly, and the doorman escorted us with the skill and discretion of a professional, down to the private part of the club. As we were shown to our table, Arthur Brown's voice boomed over the loudspeakers: "I am the God of hellfire, and I bring you FIRE!" And indeed the red-and-gold dance floor seemed to have burst into flames as the young, shapely bodies jiggled their hips to the rhythm of the new hit single's Hammond organ and beating drum.

"It's the latest dance craze," I informed Paul, who seemed highly amused by their synchronized movements. "The hitch-hike."

We sat down at a table which had been magically reserved for us. Paul had his usual Scotch on the rocks. I ordered a

Bacardi-and-Coke, and the girls had martinis, which were becoming fashionable at that time. Despite my initial worries, everything went down as smoothly as those first drinks down our hatches. Club dell'Aretusa was the kind of place that was accustomed to celebrities, so even though Paul was recognized, nobody bothered us. The sour-faced bouncer appeared to have done a stellar job of keeping out the journalists and photographers. Chris's Beatle-smuggling operation was a success.

* * *

It happened on a windy afternoon in late October, as the leaves rustled by the vinyl go-go boots of the Apple Scruffs on Cavendish Avenue. John and George hadn't yet returned from their travels in Spain and India. Jane Asher and Paul were still at the peak of the romance that inspired such songs as 'All My Loving' or 'We Can Work It Out'.

"I haven't seen Jane for a while," I remarked casually, as we climbed the steps towards Paul's bedroom.

"Me neither, actually," he sighed. "She's been really busy with rehearsals and performances, and now she's going to be acting in a movie version of *A Winter's Tale*."

"Can't you visit her on set?"

"I suppose, but it wouldn't be a very good idea," he said, wistfully. "If I did, the press would be all over me, as usual, instead of talking about her movie. It's time she took the limelight for a while."

I was impressed: I couldn't imagine many celebrities being so considerate. As we lifted his big chair into the bathroom, a routine chore by now, he told me of his plans.

"I'm thinking of taking a few days off in France or Spain. Mal Evans is down there, you know, our road manager.

And we could even meet up with John on his film set in Almeria."

"Sounds like fun."

"Yeah," he said, sitting down in front of the mirror. As he saw himself, he pressed down on his new moustache, as you tend to do when you're not yet used to it. "The only trouble is, these days I can't go anywhere without being mobbed. Being famous and instantly recognizable can be a pain, you know."

He pointed at his own reflection in the mirror, pulled a face of cartoonish excitement and jumped up and down on the chair, as if he was one of his own fans and had just recognized the one and only Paul McCartney. We both laughed, and then a silly idea popped into my head.

"Why don't you go in disguise?" I said, jokingly.

"How?" he asked, looking at me in the mirror. "What do you suggest?"

As I'd just pulled out my scissors from my portable hairdressing kit, I held them up, raised one of my eyebrows meaningfully and sliced the air: *snip, snip.*

"What... cut all my hair off?" He tittered, looking up at himself in the mirror with an expression that was half concern, half excitement.

"Well, not all of it. But I could cut it very short," I said, still in the spirit of fun. As I spoke, I played around with his shaggy hair, which was medium-length by now. "No one would recognize you as a Beatle, would they? I mean, how *could* you be a Beatle without this hair? And with that new moustache you're growing..."

He then swung round, a gleam in his eye, and said:

"Go on then, do it!"

"Are you sure, Paul?" I said.

"Yeah, go ahead, why not?"

I stared down at his famous head of hair. Each of those locks was like a relic to millions of fans. And here was their owner, Paul McCartney, telling me to just chop them all off. It seemed utterly reckless, to the point of sacrilege. And yet, in his own words, *why not*? Why not indeed. His hairstyle was an icon, the symbol for a whole generation even. But as such, it had become an impediment to leading an ordinary life, an immediately recognizable feature that brought on screaming hysterics, public disorder and endless hassle. If I sheared off his hair, he would go back to being someone he hadn't been for a long, long time: an ordinary lad from Liverpool with a slightly goofy smile. Not a Beatle at all.

"All right then," I said, laughing, as if taking up some kind of outrageous bet.

At once, I grabbed a good handful of his hair and raised it high into the air. With my other hand I picked up my scissors, snapped open their sharp blades and proceeded to jam them against the thick bunch of strands.

"Last chance to change your mind..." I warned.

"Go ahead," he said, with a careless wave of his hand.

So I crushed the hair in the scissors' maw and the blades did their work. It was done. There was no turning back.

I looked at Paul. His face was that of a naughty schoolchild skiving from his grammar-school classes as he used to do with John Lennon to make up songs all afternoon. He loved it.

I dropped the chunk of hair on the floor and got to work. I wanted to make Paul unrecognizable, but still give him a proper haircut. Obviously – and despite what some newspapers would later claim – I wasn't going to turn him into a skinhead. Just a regular short back and sides, Penny Lane-barber-shop style, the perfect look for a job interview in the city. Aside from the moustache.

As the floor tiles filled with hair, Paul was riveted to his own reflection in the mirror, grinning the whole time. I was trying to concentrate on my work, but I have to say that every once in a while I too had to stop and stare. It was genuinely shocking to see. The end of an era for the Beatles, for pop music, for youth culture was taking place in that very bathroom, and not only was I a witness to this change, but actually instrumental to it.

"Do you know how many times I've been asked if I'd get a proper haircut?" Paul asked me at one point.

It made him giggle so hard I had to stop for a bit. I don't think I gave him an answer. By that point, I was cruising along: I just wanted to get the thing over and done with.

A few minutes later, I surveyed my work. From a technical perspective, it was impeccable. Here was a young man with his smart new haircut. Like Magritte's shiny green apple, there was no denying its perfection. But I couldn't help feeling a strange sense of guilt. What had I done to Paul's famous barnet? *Au revoir*. It was gone. And nothing could be more surreal than that.

As I brought my portable mirror behind him, so that he could inspect the back of his head, Paul turned this way and that.

"So…" I asked, with some trepidation. "What do you think?"

"Perfect," he said. "Just like you said, Leslie: I'm no longer a Beatle! I could even add a pair of glasses, and no one will be able to recognize me at all. I won't even recognize myself…"

Seeing my client so happy allowed me to calm down a bit.

"Pardon me, young sir," I joked, exaggerating my cockney accent, "but just what are you doing in Paul McCartney's 'ouse?"

Paul stood up, whipped the towel off his neck and gave me a clap on the shoulder while still peering back towards the mirror.

"Oh, this is great, Leslie! I really can go on holiday now. Maybe I could even meet up with Jane when she finishes shooting her movie! Thanks, thanks so much, really."

We both laughed like a couple of truant schoolboys. Underneath, I was still a little shaken by what I'd done, but mightily relieved that Paul seemed so satisfied and grateful.

"Oh!" he then exclaimed. "Let's go give Mrs Kelly a good scare!"

* * *

The disguise really did work. In fact, during his travels in France with Mal Evans, the ruse was so effective that the Beatle was actually refused entry into a club in Bordeaux. He had to break cover and admit who he was to get in.

More importantly, Paul was finally able to go on holiday with Jane Asher. Together with Mal, they spent a few days on a safari through the Tsavo and Amboseli National Parks, following elephants, crocodiles and zebras around in a jeep. Until the three flew back from Nairobi together on 19th November, no one recognized Paul McCartney for who he really was. It was only after they got back to London that photos of Paul's surprising new look appeared in the papers, together with reports that he had enjoyed a holiday in Kenya with Jane. Thanks to my haircut, the trip had remained a complete mystery.

I received plenty of press attention about that "short back and sides". In fact, it was the first time that I was featured in the papers as the Beatle's hairdresser. "THE BARBER WHO MADE PAUL A SKINHEAD!" one of the headlines screamed. So, ironically, by trying to take the spotlight off Paul McCartney, I had gained some for myself. Everyone wanted to know how I had persuaded the Beatle to have his hairstyle changed so radically.

I kept silent, however, and told them that the reasons fell within the bounds of professional secrecy. No matter how good the story was, I felt that my loyalty to Paul was more important, and I'm sure my star client got the message: Leslie Cavendish could be trusted.

As I mentioned at the start of the chapter, there was something else I got out of that particular haircut: a lock of Paul's hair. I was loath to ask, and would have never done so for myself, but as you can imagine, I wasn't the only Beatlemaniac in my family. Since my first visit to 7 Cavendish Avenue, I had come under a lot of pressure at home.

"Listen, Paul…" I said, keeping my eyes on the floor while sweeping away the unusually long pieces of hair scattered all over the tiles of the en-suite bathroom. As I gripped the broom and moved it around clumsily, I could feel Paul staring at me from the door and from the mirror. "I'm embarrassed to even bring up the subject… It's not for me, you know… I would never even think of it, but my cousin Lynn, you see, she's absolutely besotted with you and the Beatles…" Finally, I blurted it out: "Would you mind if I took a bit of your hair? Just a small lock… It would make her so happy…"

"Of course, Leslie." He smiled broadly, and clapped me on the shoulder again. "I understand. Take what you want. I'll sign an album for her too."

After I fished up a few strands of his hair, Paul led me up to the music room and picked out a limited-edition copy of *Revolver*, which was later replaced by another for general release. To this day I've never been sure, but I believe it was his own personal copy. He then pulled the white paper sleeve out of the LP's cardboard jacket and scribbled across the sleeve in his large, messy handwriting:

To Lynn, best wishes from Paul McCartney

Then, as he was about to hand it over to me, he seemed to have another idea and added something right under his name:

(Dave Clark Five)

I laughed at his joke, although at the time it didn't make much sense to me, aside from it being typical of Paul's offbeat sense of humour. He was obviously having a go at me for cutting the hair of his great rival, but perhaps there was more to it than that. I now wonder whether he had been inspired by our previous conversation about giving up his Beatleness and becoming someone else. With his shorter hair, he could easily play around with the idea of becoming someone else – perhaps even one of the more "anonymous" members of the Dave Clark Five.

Lynn still has the album, which she considers her most prized possession. Though probably worth a small fortune – not least due to that cryptic example of Paul McCartney playfulness – my cousin has assured me that she will never sell it.

* * *

I know you're still wondering: how did this haircut, peculiar as it was, change rock-'n'-roll history?

That part of the tale I only discovered recently. For years, I had retold this anecdote as the most radical makeover I ever gave Paul McCartney, as well as the one and only time I kept a lock of Beatles' hair and the explanation for how my cousin Lynn got her autographed copy of *Revolver*.

Not long ago, however, I was surprised to learn that my suggestion to Paul had more profound consequences for the world

The Cavendish family at a bar mitzvah in the late Fifties (left to right):
Uncle Cyril and his wife, Aunt Blanche, my father Alan and my mum Betty,
my granddad Alec and grandma Debbie, and my mum's other two sisters,
Aunt Marilyn and Aunt Gladys.

My bar mitzvah in 1960,
aged thirteen.

Our semi-detached house in
The Chase where I grew up.

The proud captain Cavendish holding the ball for the Chandos School football team in 1958-59, wishing the hoops were Queens Park Rangers'.

Training as a junior under Mark Hilliard at Vidal Sassoon's new salon at the Grosvenor House Hotel in Park Lane, London.

The Four "Muscutteers" (left to right): Vidal Sassoon,
Roger Thompson, Lawrence Falk and myself.

The cutting edge of styling (left to right): Suzanna Leigh, Jane Asher
and Britt Eckland with her little brother Carl.

Keith Moon had a haircut last week by Leslie Cavendish in London's Kings Road. Plus shampoo and dry, it cost him 2 gns. Also in was **Dave Clark** for his weekly hair treatment.

Think he's a pop star? *Looks* like a pop star! He is! He's that good-looking drummer Keith Moon of The Who. This switched-on style was created for us (and Keith) by Leslie, of Vidal Sassoon, 171 New Bond Street, London, W.1. The length is just right and it's easy to manage and keep looking smart.
The Style: Leslie has kept the hair long at the back and fairly short on top. The hair was layer cut and hand dried, and needs trimming only about once a month. Leslie says it is important that men don't look as though they have newly cut hair.

HIS·HERS·HIS·HE

Trimmed

BOTH **RINGO Starr** and **Paul McCartney** had haircuts by **Leslie Cavendish** last week, and Paul has opted for the fringe of the early Beatle days. Leslie also accompanied **Robin Gibb** to the "Top Of The Pops" studio for last-minute snipping before the show. (See page 7.)

Shorn

AFTER months of fuss, **Robin Gibb** has had his hair cut short. He paid two visits to **Leslie Cavendish** in Chelsea Kings Road last week, first time for it to be cut from shoulder to just below ear length. Now after the second visit his ears are showing again. Leslie, who was apprehensive of shearing the controversial head, says it looks "fantastic."

Part of the grooming — Leslie Cavendish tends Robin Gibb's hair

Excerpts from my weekly column in *Disc* magazine and some of the famous heads I styled in the Sixties: Keith Moon, drummer of The Who (top left), and Robin Gibb of the Bee Gees (above right).

Paul on Safari after my "skinhead" haircut (1966).

Styling George Harrison's hair during a recording-session break at Abbey Road Studios.

ONE DAY three years ago one of Leslie Cavendish's clients asked him if he would cut her boyfriend's hair. She was Jane Asher, he was Paul McCartney, and Leslie was a stylist at Vidal Sassoon in London's Park Street. Paul wanted his hair cut on Saturday afternoon, which was when Leslie always went to watch football.

"I'd never cut anyone's hair on Saturday afternoon," recalls Leslie indignantly. "So I went to watch Chelsea, and then went round to cut his hair afterwards."

There can't be many people who put football first and Beatles second, but three years later Leslie is still the Beatles' hairdresser and established by them in his own shop in London's King's Road.

He treats them like any other head of hair with a professional indifference that they admire.

And through cutting their hair and remaining unstartstruck, Leslie has got to know them well

—especially Paul and George. He is the only person outside the music business not in on their recording sessions. He went down to Cornwall with them for "Magical Mystery Tour," and he and Paul have a longstanding arrangement to visit Bloom's, the Jewish restaurant in Whitechapel.

Although the famous fringed mops were the most talked about feature of the Beatles from the beginning, Leslie says they are all quite indifferent about their hair.

"As long as they can wash it and brush it and just leave it as that, they're happy."

"People thought they purposely came on the scene with long hair, but it wasn't true. It was very short at first. The record came out and they never had time to get to the hairdressers.

"It was round the time of 'Sergeant Pepper' that John started growing his hair, and they started growing moustaches. They realised what hair could do to you, and how much it can change you."

As for the hair itself—it goes in the duration with the rest. Leslie has been inundated with offers from fans asking for snippings, and organisations (especially American) who want to raffle it and put it as a prize in competitions.

But in hair as in everything else, the Beatles are four individual individuals. And here's a hairdresser's view head by head.

John Lennon is likely to go bald
says Beatle hairdresser LESLIE CAVENDISH

John Lennon : 'let nature be nature'

Paul McCartney : 'a fascination for ears'

George Harrison : 'thickest head of hair I know'

Ringo Starr : 'a superb grey streak'

PAUL

"I PROBABLY know him the best, since I've been doing his hair the longest. He has it cut every four weeks, and I go to his house in St. John's Wood to do it.

"After the second time I cut his hair I thought I'd never be doing it again. He was going on safari to Nairobi and didn't want to be recognised, so as a joke I said 'How about having it cut to a quarter of an inch all over?' and he said 'O.K.' After the first two lengths I thought 'This is it, I've ruined it'—it was very long at the time.

"But I carried on and when I'd finished there was nothing left. It was as if he'd just been called up to go to Vietnam. Paul couldn't believe it either. It was only after he'd gone and I read in the newspapers he wasn't recognised that I got any satisfaction.

"I went round to his house to cut all their hair last week. For the first time in three years Paul turned round and asked Linda how she liked it— 'Do you want it any shorter here and there?'

"I've never heard him do that before—I thought uh-huh. Then I cut her hair and Heather's. She's an unbelievable little girl, she'll say 'Hey Paul, that's a groovy record you've put on,' and she can't believe all the girls waiting outside the house.

"Paul's got good thick hair that he's wearing off his face at the moment. He's got a fascination for ears—he thinks ears should be shown."

JOHN

"HIS last words to me, about a year ago were 'I'm going to let my hair grow down to my waist.' I haven't cut his hair since—and I don't think anyone else has either.

"But if he lets his hair grow it will get to a certain point and it'll just break off.

"He's got very thin hair anyway, and the way he carries on with it, if he doesn't have it cut it'll break off at the ends and get very weak. Out of the four he's the most likely to go bald, and he could unless he's careful.

"I told Paul this, and Paul just told John 'Oh I expect he'll have it cut.'

"I was more nervous of John

than anyone else at first. But after a while he was just very nice. He never interfered with me cutting his hair. As far as music is concerned nobody interferes with him and if he wants his hair done he won't interfere with me.

"I know why he's growing his hair—he wants to see what happens if you let nature be nature. But he should be careful. If he goes out in the sun it will dry up, and his hair's very dry anyway."

but usually I go round to the Apple offices to do his hair. He asked me to take Pattie to a film a couple of weeks ago when he couldn't go.

RINGO

"I HAVEN'T done his hair since he got married, because his wife Maureen is a hairdresser I think.

"I got to know him on 'Magical Mystery Tour.' One evening we went to a pub owned by Spencer

Davis' road manager and a short mile from where we were having a big sing-song with The Troggs playing 'Knees Up Mother Brown' on a piano, and Ringo plucking away at an old mandolin with just one string. After about two hours he said 'Hey do you know, think I've worn my thumb out, and it was pouring blood.

"Ringo's hair is nearly grey—he's got a superb grey streak down one side. Funnily enough I've got a small part in his film 'The Magical Christian' as a mad hairdresser."

— Caroline Boucher

GEORGE

"I DIDN'T really meet George until this last year. He's got the thickest head of hair I think I know—there's no danger of him going bald.

"He rang me up one day and said he'd found a bloke—Jackie Lomax—and he wanted me to go down to the studios and design a hair style for him. We tried all sorts of things, but in the end decided to leave it long. After all that's Jackie isn't it? And anything else wouldn't have been....

"I did George's hair when he was in hospital recently, and that's when we decided to have it off his face.

"He called into the shop the other day to have it cut again,

LEAPY LEE —SO HAPPY WITH HIS NEW 'GAFF'!

LEAPY LEE'S going to be very proud of his roses this summer—and his immediate plans include a tennis court on the lawn and a donkey in the orchard!

Yes, that IS the Leapy Lee of "Little Arrows" and "Little Arrows", whom we all know and love, the...

...charming wild and not lovely kid.

And now, thanks entirely to the phenomenal world sales of "Little Arrows," Leapy is at last able to leave the dodgy life behind—and has just moved into his very first home, a £28,000 house in the Sunninghill area of Ascot.

"I really can't believe it —but wanna see round the gaff?" were his first cheery words when I popped round for fresh stew and a chat last week.

Leapy moved in to the new county the day before Easter, has already had breakfast on the terrace, bought a motor-mower and is looking forward to apple-picking time. In fact, the transformation is incredible.

But then Leapy has always been a dedicated family man —his two young daughters, Loretta and Kearey, mean the world to him, and just to see them with colour in their cheeks makes up for all the possible loneliness of isolating himself in the country while after years of city life.

"If it weren't for the kids I'd never have moved here ... but just look at them. They've never had it so good. They come—never (and a garden at all—never lived in a house, and they can't believe it either."

The garden comprises three-and-a-half acres of lawns, rose beds, kitchen garden, apple orchard and copse, and the donkey, when it arrives via Shelly's (Mrs. Leapy Lee) parents from Ireland will not only keep the kids happy, but keep the grass down as well.

The house is still sparsely furnished—"I'm broke again...

...of course. Every penny went on it"—but thanks to the kind previous owner, is wall-to-wall carpeted throughout with four bedroom, two bathroom, kitchen, dining room, sitting room, study, wash-house, and two garages.

And the moving-in presents are typical of Leapy's mad friends ... an old upright piano from Jess Conrad, now a greyhound called Flicker—"never won a race in his life, and even runs away from me"—from Troy Dante.

"It's all just like a dream. I mean, one hit record can pay for all this? It's not true. I'm sure it won't last and I'll be back in Paddington (or worse) before long."

But that's just Leapy the eternal pessimist, the man whose inward morbidness belies his laugh-a-minute exterior.

If anyone deserves stability, a good home and some measure of security, it's him ... just don't run up any bills, mate!

— DAVID HUGHES

The article that made me the official Beatles hairdresser (above). Two of many articles that appeared in the press around the time I was styling the Beatles' hair (below).

Sam Meets The Goodlookers

THE BARBER WHO MADE PAUL A SKINHEAD!

HOW would you like to have Paul McCartney's head in your hands once a week? All right, hands down everybody! This privilege belongs to Leslie Cavendish, the lucky guy who cuts Paul's hair.

I was cutting Jane Asher's hair one day, when she suggested I cut Paul's boy—so I did," he said.

He's been attending to Paul's mop ever since. He's been hair-dressing for about seven years now with Vidal Sassoon, but for the past year he's had his own place under a boutique in the King's Road.

"Once Paul asked me to cut his hair on his lunch-date produce problems. I just cut it sitting on a bench...

SUPER JOBS
meet LESLIE CAVENDISH SHEAR GENIUS TO THE BEATLES

LESLIE CAVENDISH is a classy name. And Leslie Cavendish is a classy hairdresser and a very successful young man.

Among his clients he numbers Ringo Starr, the Bee Gees, the Beatles, Keith Moon, Tony Curtis, Peter Sellers, Peter Cook, Peter Asher, Jackie Lomax, Sandie Preston and two destinies from Brockton.

Two destinies from Brockton...

The Magical Mystery Tour coach party, with me sitting second right from
George Harrison with a cigarette in my mouth, before I quit smoking.

Waiting for the Magical Mystery Tour coach to arrive in Allsop Place,
talking to Daniel Lacambre, one of the film's cameramen (above).
Who's the fifth Beatle trying to muscle in on the fish-and-chips,
next to a slightly bewildered Paul McCartney? (below).

The invitation card to the party for the premiere of the *Magical Mystery Tour*
film at the Royal Lancaster Hotel, London (21st December 1967).

of the Beatles and for pop music in general. Specifically, I can claim that my haircut led directly to the creation of one of the most legendary pop albums of all time: *Sgt. Pepper's Lonely Hearts Club Band*.

For those readers who were not around at the time, a word or two needs to be said about *Sgt. Pepper's*. Today, of course, we take this album for granted as a cornerstone of pop music. Its cover, featuring the Beatles themselves dressed as an Edwardian-era military band, surrounded by an odd assortment of famous people in cardboard cut-out form, is as iconic an image of the 1960s as the peace symbol itself. One of the best-selling albums in history, it is almost impossible to grow up in Western society, even fifty years later, without becoming familiar with its songs, which include 'With a Little Help from My Friends', 'Lucy in the Sky with Diamonds', 'When I'm Sixty-Four' and 'A Day in the Life', as well as the title track itself. *Rolling Stone* magazine has ranked *Sgt. Pepper's* number one on its list of the "500 greatest albums of all time", and the *Oxford Encyclopedia of British Literature* considers it "the most important and influential rock-'n'-roll album ever recorded".

Even at the time, however, it was hailed as a ground-breaking work. For the first time, an LP was published not as a mere collection of singles, but as a cohesive unit of songs that blended into each other without breaks, from Paul's introduction of Pepper's fictional band to the final piano chord that closes 'A Day in the Life'. In fact, none of the album's songs had been released before its launch – an unprecedented move only the Beatles could have risked. *Time* magazine described it as "a historic departure in the progress of music" – which indeed it would prove to be. Its innovative instrumentation, startling sound effects and lush production took the music world by storm, setting the stage for future sound experiments that would blast open the way to other genres such as hard rock, punk and new wave. Praised by critics and fans alike, it was the first rock LP to receive the Grammy Award for Album of the Year, along with other accolades. *Sgt. Pepper's* has been credited as marking the beginning of the album era, of art rock and of the recording studio as a compositional tool itself.

Perhaps the single feature that stands out about *Sgt. Pepper's*, however, was the thematic concept that brought it all together. The recording is considered the first ever "concept album", and the concept behind it was the colourfully clad military band the Beatles impersonated on the cover and in the music itself. The idea was a radical one: forget everything we've done before – the Beatles, the Mersey beat, the mop tops; forget John, Paul, George and Ringo; now, on this album, we're someone else entirely: we're "Sgt. Pepper's Lonely Hearts Club Band". In fact, it was this set of alter egos, led by band leader Billy Shears (played by Ringo on 'With a Little Help from My Friends') which justified the stylistic experimentation that characterized the album. From then on, the Beatles wouldn't be the Liverpool lads everyone had heard on stage and in their early three-minute rock-'n'-roll singles. In fact, the Beatles would never tour again, because – among other reasons – their new studio-created songs were impossible to play live. In a sense, the old pop group really was gone for ever.

As for Paul's haircut on that windy autumn afternoon, it had been radical enough to merit a few newspaper articles, but at the time I had no idea it would have deeper consequences. I knew the Beatles were planning a new album, and indeed Paul had played me a few early versions of its songs. During the recording sessions I later attended, and in my conversations with my client at home, it became clear to me that this project represented a complete makeover for the band. And over the following decades, I came to learn how the idea of *Sgt. Pepper's* had originally come about. But I never suspected my unwitting role in the whole business.

The anecdote has been retold in various places, including Barry Miles's official biography of Paul McCartney. It seems that Paul was having his in-flight meal on an airplane, together with the Beatles' road manager Mal Evans, when they started playing around with words, as they often liked to do. Mal brought out the little salt and pepper sacks from his food tray and held them up.

"S and P. What's that mean? Salt and Pepper."

Whereas McCartney, playing with the sounds, came up with a variation:

"Sergeant Pepper."

Later on, he melded together Sergeant Pepper with the idea of a Lonely Hearts Club, an early kind of dating agency, and so the Beatles' alter-ego group was born.

But it wasn't until I was preparing these memoirs and reread this passage in Barry Miles's book that I noticed the flight details of that particular trip during which Paul and Mal came up with the concept: Nairobi to London, 19th November 1966. If it hadn't been for my suggestion to Paul, he would have never gone on holiday with Jane in Africa, he would have never been on that plane with Mal Evans, and the whole shenanigan with the salt-and-pepper packets would never have taken place.

Of course, the Beatles' eighth album would have been a masterpiece regardless of my haircut. I myself had witnessed Paul choosing and composing some of the album's songs before the "Sergeant Pepper" concept had even been invented. The band had taken three months off to relax and find new sources of creativity, such as George Harrison's dabbling in Indian classical music. They were inspired by the Beach Boys' *Pet Sounds* and the Mothers of Invention's *Freak Out!* Thanks to their earlier successes, they had practically limitless studio time and resources to experiment with, and they were bent on creating something truly groundbreaking, building upon their earlier innovations on *Rubber Soul* and *Revolver*. I had nothing to do with any of that.

Nevertheless, like the proverbial butterfly who influences a future hurricane by flapping its wings, my humble snipping and styling had contributed to shaping the future of music. If it hadn't been for my haircut, the album would have had a different title, and certainly a different concept to tie the songs together – including its iconic pop-art cover.

Turning it over in my head, I've even wondered whether the concept itself, the very idea of adopting another identity, of ditching "the Beatles" and being someone else, might have been inspired or reinforced by that conversation in Paul's bathroom and his long stares into the mirror. *Just like you said, Leslie: I'm no longer a Beatle!* I don't know. It sounds crazy even to me. Maybe I smoked one joint too many, and now I'm just imagining plasticine porters, tangerine trees and a girl with kaleidoscope eyes. Do I really want to take any credit for the Beatles' most acclaimed album? Wasn't it enough to shear off Paul McCartney's famous hair? Then again, no one's ever come up with a definitive answer to the question: just who was Billy Shears?

Snip, snip.

5

The Ups and Downs of Dating a Movie Star

Until then, I had scrupulously observed Vidal Sassoon's rule. Apart from the odd fling with our Tuesday-night models – who weren't paying customers, after all – I had successfully resisted every temptation to get romantically involved with our clients. But that fateful autumn of 1966, I decided that Bob Dylan was right, that times were a-changing, particularly for me. Against all odds, I was now a qualified hairdresser, working at one of the most fashionable outfits in London, and with celebrity clients that included Paul McCartney. Who could stop me now? You should have seen me pop out of my cool Mini in the mornings, as smart in my suit and tie as Michael Caine in *The Italian Job*, and strut into the Grosvenor House salon while whistling tunes from an upcoming Beatles album that no one else had yet heard. Oh yeah, I was feeling quite the Sixties Man. Vidal Sassoon could stuff his rule.

Suzanna Leigh was just then becoming the first British actress to break into Hollywood. Her first major role had been as one of the three airline hostesses Tony Curtis tried to juggle in *Boeing Boeing*, an American bedroom farce billed as "the big comedy of nineteen sexty-sex". She had also just co-starred in a film with Elvis Presley: *Paradise, Hawaiian Style*. Both of these films were pretty awful, to be honest, but Suzanna was certainly making a name for herself. And there was a reason why casting directors from across the ocean had noticed her, something that struck me from the first time she stretched out in my chair to have her golden hair styled and flashed her green eyes at me through the brightly lit mirror.

I think it was a combination of her natural elegance together with the unrelenting determination with which she kicked, clobbered and ju-jitsu-chopped three of her brawny male adversaries in an episode of *The Persuaders* that attracted me to Suzanna. I once asked her how she landed her first role in America, and her story confirmed my impression of the feisty, independent spirit that animated her eyes. Apparently, she was working on a set in Paris when she heard that an important Hollywood producer, Hal Wallis, was casting in London. Suzanna wasted no time. She told the TV show's director that she was feeling unwell, ran off the set, caught the first plane to London, rushed in a taxi to the Dorchester Hotel, found out what room the producer was staying in and knocked on his door. When he opened, she announced: "I'm the one you're looking for!" And sure enough, she was.

Understandably, I felt a little intimidated by this stunning woman. As I worked on her hair, Suzanna would tell me about her exciting nights out with her friends Charlotte Rampling, Susan Hampshire and Susan George, all of whom went on to enjoy stellar movie careers. They would often hang out at Annabel's, the most fashionable club at the time, where they met the likes of Joel Lerner, heir to the Marks & Spencer empire, and Alan Sievewright, the famous opera producer. I hardly knew who half of these people were, but I was in awe of her, and her continuous name-dropping only added to her aura.

At that time, my sparring partner at the salon was Jean-Claude, a French stylist who was very much a ladies' man. He and I spent a great deal of time comparing the relative merits of the female clientele, but once I began to work on Suzanna's hair, I only had eyes for her. Eventually, my constant blabbering on about this one client exasperated my friend.

"Why don't you just ask her to go out wiz you, if you are so keen?" he said to me one day.

"Don't be daft," I said. "I'm only her hairdresser! Why would she come out with me? You should hear her go on about her nights out on the town. She only mixes with the rich and famous. Plus, she's older than me. How could I possibly ask her out?"

"In France we 'ave a word for people like you, Leslie. It is *lâche*."

"Meaning?"

"Coward," he explained, rolling the R with a grimace. "Go on, ask her. She can only say *non*."

At first, I tried to ignore Jean-Claude's suggestion, but eventually my infatuation won out, and I made up my mind to take action. Instead of the direct French method, however, I decided to adopt a more subtle approach. I began my campaign by making a point of asking Suzanna, each time she visited the salon, where she would be going that week. My hope was that these questions would appear completely disinterested, and that at some point I might find an opportunity to suggest a casual date. Unfortunately, her answers didn't seem to leave any openings for me.

"Oh, I'll be attending the premiere of *Kaleidoscope*," she'd tell me with one of her graceful hand movements. "Haven't you heard? It's a new film with Warren Beatty and Susannah York."

I was on the point of giving up when one day my long-awaited opportunity presented itself.

"So, Suzanna," I said as I began trimming her hair, "what are your plans for this evening?"

"Oh, not much tonight, Leslie," she said. "I'll just be staying at home."

"In that case…" I said, hiding behind her head, "would you fancy going out for a drink?"

"Where do you have in mind?"

"I'm not sure," I said casually. "Where do you live?"

"Not far. Near the Spanish Embassy, in Belgravia."

"Oh I know that area very well," I said, lying. "I'll come round to pick you up later. Seven o'clock?"

She agreed and gave me her address. After she was gone, I spent the rest of the afternoon asking around for the name of a possible venue, and finally decided upon a traditional English pub. Later, I discovered that it wasn't the sort of place Suzanna would normally go to, but she was gracious enough not to complain. As I sat across the wooden table from this glamorous woman, I felt like I was starring in a movie myself, and that some of the pub-goers around us had recognized Suzanna and were following every bit of our dialogue as it unfolded.

"So… um, what was it like, working with Elvis?" I asked her, as I sipped my drink.

She told me everything about her time in Hawaii – how great it was to work in a proper Hollywood movie, and how charming Elvis was in person. For a while, I managed to keep the focus off me and just basked in her bubbly personality, but then Suzanna turned the tables and said:

"So, Leslie, enough about Elvis… tell me about Paul McCartney. What's he really like?"

"Paul?" I said, as if he were one of my mates. "He's a nice guy. Not a pretentious star type, you know?"

"Not pretentious like me, you mean?" Suzanne teased.

"I didn't mean that at all!"

But then she burst into laughter, and somehow that seemed to set the tone for the rest of the evening. When I accompanied her back home, crossing under the arch into the elegant Belgravia Mews South, and we reached her doorstep, she gave me her phone number, and I kissed her on the cheek.

I felt pretty confident, therefore, when I asked her out again – and sure enough, she said yes.

"Why don't we go to a restaurant?" she suggested.

"Yes, that's fine by me."

"Good. We'll go to San Lorenzo in Knightsbridge. I often go there. My friend Mara owns it. Do you know it?"

"Yes, of course," I lied. "Great choice."

The second date went as smoothly as the first. I felt a little less comfortable in that classy restaurant, where she seemed to know everyone, and loved to show it. But who was I to complain? Before I knew it, we were going out to San Lorenzo on a regular basis. And, dared I say it? She *seemed* to be my girlfriend. And not just any girlfriend. She was gorgeous... she knew Elvis... she'd kissed Elvis. And she'd kissed me.

* * *

In movie terms, I suppose you could say the short-lived affair between Leslie Cavendish and Suzanna Leigh started out as a lusty teenage romance, quickly turned into a comedy and ended tragically – as such things often do.

One thing is for sure: Suzanna liked things to be done on her terms. In fact, my relationship with her was very much a sign of the times. During the 1960s, the status of women experienced a profound change in Britain and the US. Vidal Sassoon's gamine haircuts, short and easy to care for, were designed for a new generation of independent women who were joining the work-force and wanted to be treated on an equal footing with men. The birth-control pill had been available for married women since 1961, and by 1967 it was beginning to be prescribed for unmarried women as well. The Abortion Act was also being debated openly, finally being passed on 27th October 1967. Women were gaining more control over their sexual lives than ever before, and the feminist movement, fuelled by the publica-tion of Betty Friedan's *The Feminine Mystique*, was becoming a political force to be reckoned with.

So it's not surprising that I was beginning to meet so many self-assured women who understood that they didn't need men to define their lives. Around that time, I shared a conversation with Pat Booth, one of David Bailey's models, and later a soci-ety photographer herself. We had met at a mutual friend's flat, where a small crowd of party-goers were having a drink. Pat was a devout Roman Catholic, but her language could be pretty rough. At one point, she suddenly said to us:

"You know what? I can't stand it when I hear people say a man fucked a woman. Why don't you ever hear that a woman fucked a man?"

One of Pat Booth's closest friends, Suzy Kendall, was going out with the great – but pint-sized – comedian Dudley Moore, and towered over him in both stature and determination. Pat, Suzy and Suzanna herself were very much women of their time: self-assured, sexually confident and independent-minded.

Nevertheless, Suzanna was perhaps taking things a bit too far. After a while, I began to feel that my new girlfriend wasn't just asserting her independence – she was in total control of every situation. Even worse, she often seemed to ignore me, particularly in public, as if she were embarrassed to be going out with this young hairdresser. We always had to go to San Lorenzo, her favourite restaurant, where people would be greeting her all the time, and take no notice of me. "Hello, darling!" some theatre producer would say, and Suzanna would go over and talk with him for a while, forgetting to introduce me and leaving me alone at the table. Then someone else would say "Hello, darling" and she'd be off again. At first, these awkward moments were just an annoyance I dutifully put up with. Eventually, however, the feeling of humiliation built up. Having been raised with a conventional view of male-female relations, I decided I'd had enough of all this "women's liberation" foolishness. It was time to take charge.

"I need to be the *man* in this relationship," I told myself. "I won't be treated like a plaything."

The next time we went to San Lorenzo, I was feeling much more assertive. Until that point, the waiter had always given Suzanna the menu first, asked her what she wanted and ignored me completely. This time, however, I cut in from the start:

"Excuse me," I said, grabbing the menu. "I'll take that."

Unfortunately, it turned out to be the wine list, not the menu. This was a problem. Food I could deal with, but wine was not my thing.

"Would you like a bottle or a carafe, sir?" the waiter asked.

I don't think I heard him properly, and said: "Er…. I think… umm… I'll have a… bottle of carafe, please."

"Yes, sir," the waiter said, flashing me a disdainful look, "but which would you prefer? A bottle or a carafe?"

"Oh, a bottle, of course."

"What wine would you like, sir?"

"What would you recommend?"

"May I suggest the Beaujolais Nouveau, sir? It's fresh in from France."

"Fine."

When the waiter returned with the wine, he offered the taster to Suzanna first – as usual. Again, I wasn't going to stand for such humiliation, so again I asserted myself:

"Excuse me." I thrust my glass in his direction. "I'll taste it, thank you."

He poured a little wine into my glass. I took a sip, swilled it around in my mouth as I had seen other people do and then said, full of confidence: "I'm sorry, but it's a bit cold."

"But sir," the waiter said, "Beaujolais Nouveau should always be served lightly chilled."

"Excuse me," I said. "I've drunk a lot of wine in my time, and I can tell you that red wine should always be served at room temperature."

At that point, I felt a sharp kick under the table. I turned towards Suzanna, bewildered. She was fixing me with an icy stare.

"Whatever…" I said, finally giving in.

My plan to take charge had backfired. The evening's atmosphere had been ruined – and from then on I decided to let my lady take the order as usual, for everyone's sake.

My self-esteem continued to suffer at times, but things ran much more smoothly between us. To be fair, Suzanna and I got on quite well when we were on our own. We very much enjoyed each other's company, and we went to a few parties together. But it grated me that she would never publicly acknowledge me as her boyfriend – she never took me to premieres, for example, preferring to be seen on the arm of one of her better-known friends. Deep down, at the bottom of my heart, I was always looking for proof that she really was mine.

One evening, we were lying in bed together when I asked her if she'd ever had sex with the legendary Elvis "The Pelvis". I was sure what the answer would be, but I was in for a surprise.

"Actually, no, I never did, you know."

"Oh, come on, Suzanna." I turned towards her, trying to gauge her expression. "You've got to be joking! Everyone knows what he's like. He's gone to bed with all of his leading ladies!"

"Well, not with this one," she insisted, with an enigmatic smile. Was she teasing me? "I'm not saying he didn't try, but I swear to you, I never did."

"You resisted Elvis Presley?"

"I resisted his charms, yes."

I fell back on the pillow.

"I wouldn't have had time for Elvis," she explained, "even if I'd wanted to."

"What do you mean?" I asked, leaning up on one elbow.

"I was having an affair with someone else..." She then lowered her voice, as if anyone else could have heard her in the privacy of her room. "Richard Harris."

"Richard Harris?" I said. "Do you know who else is a client at Vidal Sassoon's?"

"Who?"

"His wife."

"What?" Suzanne jumped up on the bed, very agitated. "Elizabeth?"

I got some kind of bitter thrill seeing her react like that. "Yeah. Does she know about you and—"

"She does! Oh God, Leslie... You... You have to make sure we're never in the salon at the same time!"

All I could do was fall back on my pillow and laugh. At myself, at Suzanna, at Richard Harris and even his poor wife Elizabeth. Our relationship was turning into a *Boeing Boeing*-style comedy, that was for sure – with me playing Jerry Lewis rather than Tony Curtis. From then on, in addition to other humiliations, I had to stay on my toes at the salon, making sure that Elizabeth Harris and Suzanna Leigh were never in for a treatment simultaneously – or things would get ugly.

*　*　*

Apart from a few dinner parties at home, there was only one time that Suzanna did invite me out with a few of her high-society friends – and it turned out to be another comic disaster. In the summer of 1968, she was acting in a Hammer film production – not the usual horror flick, but a bizarre fantasy-adventure story set in a "living hell that time forgot" and featuring mutant crustaceans, a fanatical sect of Spanish conquistadores and smuggled cans of highly explosive chemicals: *The Lost Continent*. One of her co-stars was Tony Beckley, who was becoming a regular client of mine thanks to her recommendation. One day, the cast were filming in a 175,000-gallon tank that had been constructed for the movie. Suzanna didn't normally like me to watch her being filmed, but on this occasion she made an exception so that I could see what it was like to work in this enormous partly flooded set.

You might suppose that giant rubber crabs and scorpions, killer seaweed and a doomed ship full of screaming passengers would make for a memorable excursion to a film studio – and you'd be right. But the real action took place after the cameras stopped rolling. Tony and Suzanna had decided to celebrate all of that serious splashing-about with a dinner party at an upmarket restaurant in Belgravia. Everyone was invited to bring friends. Tony brought his partner Barry Krost, who was also a client of mine. I called Lawrence Falk, my old school chum, who was by then well established as one of London's top hairdressers. Lawrence was on the verge of setting up his own salon, Crimpers, which would come to rival Vidal Sassoon's. He came with his girlfriend, Gillian, who was also one of Suzanna's friends and was becoming well known herself for her growing modelling agency. The guest list was completed by film director Peter Collinson and Jeremy Lloyd, a writer soon to make a name for himself by penning a string of successful TV comedy series. So it was a proper celebrity party, and I was especially happy that Suzanna was beginning to relax when she was out with me. It was a jolly occasion, and the wine flowed freely. Then, things began to get out of hand.

Tony, who was feeling pretty uninhibited by then, was telling us about the West End production of *Funny Girl*, starring Barbara Streisand. The show had been a huge success in the States, and had now crossed the Atlantic to London, where it was also selling out on a regular basis.

"Some friends of mine went to see the show the other night," he said merrily. "But when they got there, they were told that Streisand wouldn't be appearing that evening, and that an understudy would take over. So, after the show, they went straight to the box office to ask for their money back. I don't blame them, do you? I would have done the same thing. If you pay to see Streisand, why should you be forced to watch a bloody understudy?"

Normally, such a comment wouldn't have made anyone bat an eyelid. What Tony didn't realize, however, was that the understudy in question was an up-and-coming singer and actress called Lisa Shane, who was married to Peter Collinson, the film director sitting across the table from Tony. All of a sudden, this friendly London dinner party seemed to have been transported to a weird and violent Lost Continent. Peter stood up, slowly and deliberately, like an enraged Spanish conquistador preparing to deliver his most melodramatic line:

"And what does an ageing, bloody B-movie poof know about show business?" he snarled.

Tony, his face as red and frightful as a mutant crab's, jumped to his feet, picked up his dinner plate, and hurled it in Peter's direction. Peter ducked, allowing much of the *bœuf bourguignon* to splatter over Lawrence and myself. A proper food fight ensued, turning our elegant table into a mayhem of red-wine sauce and meat chunks. Waiters scattered like well-trained extras, fellow diners gaped in unscripted disbelief, and Suzanna screamed as loudly as if ensnared by a dozen strands of mutant kelp.

Before everything ended as explosively as in the film (spoiler alert: the illegal cargo of dangerous chemicals goes *boom*), Barry restrained and gradually calmed down his partner. Actors do their careers no good by attacking film directors, and Barry knew that. Meanwhile, at the other end of the table, I noticed Jeremy Lloyd sitting quietly while he ate his meal unfazed. I gaped at him, astonished by his sangfroid.

"I was hungry," he shrugged, when he noticed me.

I'm not at all surprised that he became one of Britain's most successful comedy scriptwriters.

In the meantime, Barry rushed over to the manager, apologized profusely, settled the whole bill and offered some extra money for the damage. I also heard that he later bought Peter Collinson a Cartier watch as further compensation for his partner's behaviour. The strategy certainly seemed to work. Collinson's next film turned out to be none other than the classic caper film full of Morris Minis, *The Italian Job*. And guess who secured a supporting role? Tony Beckley.

* * *

This uproarious monster-movie moment perhaps foreshadowed the final turn my romantic comedy with Suzanna would soon take – towards more dramatic territory. The shift in tone began, in fact, when Suzanna was cast for a cloak-and-dagger thriller called *Subterfuge*, alongside Joan Collins. When the filming got underway, she practically disappeared from my life, in theory due to her busy work schedule. I would try phoning her again and again, and even slipped a few messages through her front-door letterbox, but to no avail. For the first time, strange suspicions began to worm themselves into my head. "An Amazing Nightmare of Deception!" screamed the poster for *Subterfuge*, perfectly reflecting my rattled state of mind. Suzanna's backstage stories about Elvis and Richard Harris poisoned my heart with suspicion and jealousy. In *Subterfuge*, Suzanna played the villainous femme fatale. What was she playing at in real life?

Finally, one cold wintry afternoon, having not heard from her in such a long time, I became positively paranoid. I was convinced that she must be seeing someone else. And I decided to do something about it – immediately.

In a rage, I rushed to her house in Belgravia, resolved to catch her out. Yes, I was sure of it, she was with him right now, in the very bedroom we had shared so many times. I stormed into the Mews, stalked up to her front door and rang the bell. There was no reply. However, when I flipped up the lid of the letterbox,

I could hear the sound of a man and woman talking. And they were certainly not discussing the weather.

Consumed by jealousy, I banged on the door like a madman, with my finger jammed into the doorbell all the while. Whatever was going on up there, I was going to put a stop to it. In the end, a top-floor window opened.

"Hah!" I gloated, preparing myself for the scene.

The woman's head that popped out of the window wasn't Suzanne's, however. Her long, dishevelled hair was black. Her striking face was completely at odds with the one I had expected. It took me a few seconds to recognize her, but when I did, there was no doubt about it. The woman was Joan Collins! And she glowered down at me as only Joan Collins could.

"Is... umm... Suzanna there, please?" I bleated, stumbling backwards in disarray.

"No! She's not here," Joan hissed back at me. "Now bugger off!"

"But... but..." I protested weakly.

"Get lost, whoever you are!"

I looked around the empty mews in a state of shock. What was Joan Collins doing there? And where was Suzanna?

When I finally got in touch with my missing girlfriend, I discovered that she had lent Joan the house while they were filming together. Her dark-haired co-star, another of those freewheeling Sixties women, was secretly meeting one of the crew members there. Sorry I disturbed you, Joan!

My pathetic fit of jealousy was the final scene in *Paradise, Belgravia Style*, the tragicomic romance of Leslie Cavendish and Suzanna Leigh, the North London hairdresser and the glamorous superstar. Once Suzanna heard about my loutish behaviour from Joan, she was so outraged that she broke up with me and – as Vidal Sassoon would have predicted – never stepped into the salon again.

At that age, it was hard for me to accept it, but the whole thing was obviously doomed from the start. Being introduced to that fashionable atmosphere of London *luvvies* was an eye-opening experience for me. Deep down, however, I had known the truth from my first conversation about her with Jean-Claude: we belonged to very different worlds. It wasn't too long before I could regard the whole thing philosophically, and even appreciate the funny side of our unbalanced relationship. Eventually, I also came to learn the difference between a bottle and a carafe, the finer points of treating a lady and – oh yes – that Beaujolais Nouveau should be drunk slightly chilled.

* * *

I received an unexpected perk from my affair with Suzanna. Thanks to her movie connections, I'd already obtained several new and interesting clients, including the two great comedians Dudley Moore and Peter Cook, who were at the height of their success with their TV sketch comedy *Not Only... But Also*. Around that time I would visit the BBC studios to cut and style their hair for the show, a job both wonderful and challenging, as the zany pair were always joking around in the most hilarious fashion, forcing me to interrupt my work so that I could pull away my sharp scissors while I laughed, or my client laughed, or we both cracked up with laughter. Without a doubt, Moore and Cook were two of the funniest men I've ever met.

Even more meaningful to me, however, was the call I got, a few months after Suzanna and I split up, from her ex co-star Tony Curtis, who was in London for the premiere of his film *The Boston Strangler*. Thanks to her recommendation, I ended up cutting Curtis's hair at his suite in the Dorchester Hotel, with spectacular views over Hyde Park. I had never been in a full-sized hotel suite before, and was amazed at the kind of luxury movie stars like Curtis enjoyed. While I was trimming his hair, I reflected on the strange irony of it. During the 1950s, when Curtis was at the height of his fame, the distinctive hairstyle he had adopted was known as a "Duck's Tail" in the US and a "Duck's Arse" (DA) in Great Britain, because of the way it was swept back into a kind of ridge. It was also called, more simply, the "Tony Curtis". This greased-back look became popular with rebels and nonconformists, including Elvis Presley and other early rockers. As a result, the initial hairstyle worn by the Beatles in Liverpool was none other than the Tony Curtis. And now here before me was the very man…

Like Diana Dors and Jayne Mansfield, Tony represented a bygone age. His chiselled, matinée-idol looks and neat hair were falling out of fashion in favour of a more feminine, softer style. This barber-shop job wasn't the kind of thing I'd normally be called out for. And yet, it gave me a certain thrill to work on Tony's hair, as if I'd gone full circle somehow. I finally managed to impress my mother too. Forget Paul McCartney. For my mum, Tony Curtis was another thing altogether: a proper movie star.

6

Official Hairdresser to the Beatles

At the same time as a glamorous movie actress was introducing me to the Sixties' sexual revolution, my relationship with the Beatles took a new and unexpected turn. Oddly enough, it was my grandmother who broke the news.

As I've mentioned, my maternal grandmother Debbie lived with us at home. She was a lovely old lady who seemed completely detached from worldly affairs. To the day of her death, she never once asked her husband or her daughter if they'd had a good day at the shop.

"Vot did you eat today?" would be her question, inevitably followed by a shake of the head and a few words of dietary advice, based on the philosophy that "more is better".

As for her thick Russian accent, she'd picked it up from her family and friends in the East End of London, as she emigrated when she was just a baby, around the turn of the century.

One evening, I got back home from the salon and found Grandma sitting in the special reclining chair my parents had bought for her. I was about to give her a kiss, but before I could, she said:

"Somevon called you. I zink he was zat Beatle. Paul McSomezing."

"Paul McCartney?"

"Zat's ze name!"

I was surprised to say the least. Why would my celebrity client call me at home? How did he even have my number? It was normally Neil Aspinall who would fix our appointments over the phone. Moreover, the Beatles' old school friend and road manager always called me at the salon, not at my house in Burnt Oak. Was it something urgent?

"What did he say?" I asked Grandma.

"He vonted to know if you voz here," she explained. "I told him you veren't home yet. He asked me who I voz, so I told him I voz your grandmozer and, you know vot, vee had a nice little chat. Vot a nice yong man! Zen he said: 'Voud you tell Leslie I called?'"

The idea of my grandmother, who had been born in the nineteenth century, having a "nice little chat" with Paul McCartney, was almost impossible to conceive. I thanked her anyway, ran to the phone and called Neil Aspinall at the Beatles' offices, hoping I wasn't in some kind of trouble with my favourite client.

"Oh, thanks for calling, Leslie," Neil said. I could hear a lot of other voices in the background, as if he was in the middle of a big meeting. "Listen, would you mind coming into the office tomorrow?"

Neil said he wanted to settle my bill for my styling services to Paul. The fact was, I'd never actually asked Paul for any money. I always assumed I'd eventually get paid, but frankly, that was the last thing on my mind during my gigs at 7 Cavendish Avenue. Neil and I agreed on a time, and he gave me the address of NEMS, the company Brian Epstein had founded to manage his bands, and which by now had become a musical empire. Then he added, almost as an afterthought:

"Oh, and bring your scissors with you."

Feeling mightily relieved, and more than a little giddy with suspense as to whose hair I might be cutting at the Beatles' offices, I went back to the living room, where my grandmother continued to rest in her recliner.

"Do you realize," I said to her, "that you spoke today with the most famous man in Britain?"

"Who?" she asked in wonder. "Oh, you mean zat Beatle, Paul McVotever? Such a very nice man, Leslie…"

I shook my head in wonder. I had tried explaining to her a few times that Paul McCartney was a client of mine, but I'm not sure it had registered. If I'd told her he'd invited me to a proper Friday-night dinner with soup, lokshen and gedempte chicken, it might have been a different story.

"I do like some of zeir songs, you know," she then added. "Ze only zing I don't understand is… Vhy don't zey get zeir hair cut?"

I didn't bother to explain.

* * *

The next day, I entered the Beatles' offices on the fifth floor of Sutherland House, at 5 Argyll Street, for the first time. It was an old-fashioned sort of office space with many rooms full of boxes of files and a lot of very busy-looking employees. Managing the biggest band in the world obviously required a great deal of paperwork.

As Laurie, a short-haired receptionist, accompanied me through the suite of offices, I kept looking out for glimpses of my long-haired idols, or of the great Mr Epstein himself, but they were nowhere to be seen. Laurie took me to the press office, which was crowded with people all chatting into phones. Neil was waiting for me at the desk of press officer Tony Barrow, who was out that morning. The Beatles' old friend and collaborator went through all the times I had cut Paul's hair and then asked me:

"So, Leslie, how much do we owe you?"

I finally had to face a tricky question I'd been putting off: *How much should I charge a Beatle?*

My normal fee for a men's haircut, blow-dry and styling was two guineas (or £2.10). To put this into context, the average weekly wage at that time was about £14 a week, so my services didn't come cheap. It was obvious, however, that enormous quantities of cash were flowing though the Beatles' bank accounts, and that I could have probably charged what I liked. In fact, I later came to realize that plenty of people were ripping the Beatles off. They were an easy target, not only because they weren't interested in money, but also because the management of their growing empire wasn't terribly well run.

In the end, I made up my mind that honesty was the best policy. I could have done with some extra money, of course, but I wouldn't have felt comfortable hiking up the price. So I charged my normal fee, and didn't exaggerate the number of haircuts I provided. Over the years, I could have made a small fortune out of the Beatles, but, looking back now, I'm glad I didn't. The truth is that I would have cut their hair for nothing.

Once that was settled, Neil unexpectedly asked me if I would cut his own hair. To be honest, it was a little disappointing. Neil was a lovely man, and moreover an ardent Liverpool fan with whom I could chat about football, but as you can imagine, I had hoped the request to bring my scissors had to do with the styling needs of John, George or Ringo. What I didn't realize, though, was that my first visit to the NEMS office had a larger significance. On that day, I was formally welcomed into a closed world very few people ever accessed. All of a sudden, I wasn't just hairdresser to Mr McCartney. I was working for the Beatles.

The change was noticeable the very next time I visited Paul. He seemed very pleased that I'd been over to the offices, and told me Neil had spoken highly of me. As usual, I asked him if he would be recording that evening. The Beatles had been hard at work on their new album, spending long nights in the EMI studios at Abbey Road, crafting what would turn out to be *Sgt. Pepper's Lonely Hearts Club Band*. By then, I had already gathered that it was going to be a different sort of album.

"Yes, we've got an interesting session tonight, Leslie," Paul said. And then his face suddenly lit up with an idea. "Actually, rather than telling you about it, why don't you come along?"

"Ah... um... to the EMI studios?"

"Yeah. It'll be fun, you'll see," he said. "I'll tell Neil you'll be on tap in case anyone needs their hair styled."

"On tap..." I repeated, keeping my sharp scissors well away from his head in case I fainted. "Um... great Paul, thanks... It'll be great to see you work and... cut anyone's hair... or whatever's needed."

*   *   *

When I reached the recording studios for the first time, on a cold February night, I felt like I was attempting to penetrate Fort Knox. One of the heavy-set guards at the reception area stopped me at the door as I walked up the steps from the street. He looked like he was well used to swatting away annoying Beatles fans.

"Can I help you, sir?" he asked in a flat tone.

"Um... yes..." I stammered. "I'm a guest of Mr McCartney. My name is Leslie Cavendish. I'm his... hairdresser."

He gave me a look that suggested such a thing was impossible. Then, without a word, he turned to a telephone and dialled a number.

"Hello? Neil?" he spoke into the receiver. "There's a bloke out 'ere who says he's Paul's 'airdresser, and that you're expecting 'im. Leslie Cavendish."

I was let through. The guard escorted me through a maze of corridors and courtyards. It was all completely silent. Paul had asked me to come around after 6 p.m., so the whole place appeared deserted. Finally, the guard pulled open a thick metal door, and there, in a cloud of menthol cigarettes, I saw a group of people crouched over an enormous table full of switches and buttons.

"Hi Leslie," Neil Aspinall greeted me, standing up and stretching to shake my hand.

As he introduced me to the others in the booth – producer George Martin, fellow road manager Mal Evans, sound engineer Geoff Emerick, who was smoking the menthol cigarettes, and his assistant – out of the corner of my eye I checked out the enormous, brightly lit studio on the other side of the glass partition. To my surprise, there were about ten musicians in there, but they seemed to be holding classical string instruments: violins, violas, cellos and a large harp. What the hell were they all doing in there? Was I in the right studio? Where were the Beatles?

As soon as the introductions were over, the four men returned to their conversation with the harpist, Sheila Bromberg, and the lead violinist, Erich Gruenberg. I was curious to know more, but didn't feel I could interrupt the proceedings with my questions. My professional sixth sense advised me to stand back in the least conspicuous corner and simply watch.

Suddenly, Paul McCartney walked into the studio, looking giddy with pleasure. And right behind him was John Lennon, sporting a moustache, roundish glasses and a flowery shirt. It was an electric moment – I felt as if George Martin had plugged me into his machinery.

I'd seen Lennon once before, of course, at the Pigalle Club. But three years later, this was another man, the one who'd caused worldwide scandal by saying that the Beatles were "more popular than Jesus". The yeah-yeah-yeahs had given way to stirring, soulful Lennon masterpieces such as 'In My Life' or 'Norwegian Wood'. And now I was eavesdropping on him behind the scenes, together with his song-writing partner and friend, the two geniuses at work. But working on what? Were they now moving into classical music? Scanning mentally through their discography, the violins, violas and cellos from 'Eleanor Rigby' came back to me. *Oh, yeah, they've done this before.*

I watched Paul and John move their arms about excitedly as they spoke to the string section. It reminded me of my father's antics in front of the telly during classical-music concerts on the BBC. And the group of musicians, I noticed, had smiles on their faces. Of course… they were as awed to be here, playing with the world-famous Beatles, as I was. Playing, in fact, was the word, because the two wannabe conductors were in a very playful spirit, interrupting and contradicting each other all the time.

A few moments later the two Beatles left the studio and burst into our small room.

"Oh, hi Leslie," Paul said. "John, this is Leslie, my hairdresser. Go on, John – get your hair cut, will you?"

My hands flew instinctively to my portable hairdressing kit, but it turned out to be only a passing McCartney joke.

John said hello absent-mindedly, and then both of them sat down at the controls while they sent George Martin downstairs.

"Don't do anything I wouldn't do," George warned, as he left the room.

Paul and John laughed maniacally and clawed their hands over the mixing board in a mock-threatening way.

During the recording, it was George Martin who actually did the conducting. The music that gushed through the speakers knocked me out. I'd never heard such melancholy strains. If this was the new Beatles sound, I was in.

The classical musicians all seemed very patient as they repeated the score again and again for several hours, while Paul and John gave them directions from the booth and tried different effects. Eventually, however, Erich Gruenberg's patience ran out. After the umpteenth take, he put away his violin, raised his eyes towards the booth and declared in his Austrian accent:

"It is twelve o'clock and we must go home, because we are working in the morning."

Paul's reply was typically laconic: "Well, I suppose that's that, then."

Not everyone could afford to stay up all night like the Beatles. In fact, I left with Erich, Sheila and the others.

If you're a fan of *Sgt. Pepper's* – and, since you're reading this book, I bet you are – you will have already figured out what I heard on my first night at Abbey Road: the string section for 'She's Leaving Home', one of the saddest and most stirring songs the Beatles ever recorded, and also one of the few in which none of the Fab Four played any instrument.

* * *

Paul kept me guessing how it all might fit into their new album. I had to wait until June to hear 'She's Leaving Home' in all of its glory. In the meantime, my visits to the band's offices and recording studios became more regular. Leslie Cavendish was soon a common sight in these places, ready to whip anyone's hair into a fashionable shape at a moment's notice with the instruments in his carpet bag. Considering the amount of press attention the entire Beatles entourage was exposed to on a daily basis, and how hot and sweaty the studio could get after a few hours of work, having a dependable stylist around came in quite handy. And as you can imagine, I was only too happy to fulfil that requirement.

To be honest, in that first year, most of my styling was done at the offices, initially at Argyll Street and a few months later at the 94 Baker Street headquarters of the Beatles' new company, Apple Corps. I did occasionally bring out my scissors and blow-dryer in one of the green rooms at Abbey Road, but my hairdressing role was mainly a handy excuse for me to sneak in there and gape at the proceedings.

Aside from my first visit, most of the sessions I witnessed were a bit more conventional, with one or more of the Beatles wearing headphones and singing what actually sounded like pop songs, or playing instruments normally found in rock bands. What perhaps wasn't so conventional was the way in which John Lennon and Paul McCartney would always be fiddling around with the controls, having figured out that the recording studio was a kind of instrument in itself.

"You don't want to do that," George Martin would protest.

"We just want to hear how it sounds, you know," Paul would then explain.

"It'll sound awful," George would say.

"Good!" John would reply mischievously. "We just want to hear how awful it sounds."

* * *

The second Beatle whose hair I cut was George Harrison. I remember feeling a bit intimidated that first time, for several reasons. As I've described, my sessions with Paul were informal affairs at his home, which included a moment for playing music and sharing a hot drink or a spiced-up cigarette. Paul himself, of course, loved to chat and joke around while I cut his hair. That's just the way he was. When I was summoned to cut George Harrison's hair, however, in the midst of the hustle and bustle of the Beatles' offices, it was inevitably a much more serious thing, professional and to the point. In fact, I did the job in the boardroom where all the important meetings took place. I also quickly understood that this Beatle was a quiet sort of chap, a far cry from McCartney's extroverted chumminess. In fact, after we were introduced and he sat in one of the chairs around the long wooden table in the middle, George hardly spoke a word to me, closing his eyes and drifting off into his own thoughts. I tried not to take it personally.

There was another intimidating aspect of the task, however: the very nature of George's hair. The moment I ran my fingers through it, I was in awe. It was at least twice as thick as Paul's. *This really is Beatles hair*, I thought, overwhelmed once again with such a responsibility. Fortunately, I was in an otherwise empty office, my client had his eyes closed, and there wasn't any mirror for him to supervise my work. So I screwed up my courage, raised my scissors and went for it.

Though it was difficult for me to gauge George's opinion of the end result – little more than a polite word of thanks – it turned out he was quite satisfied. In fact, like Paul, he eventually became a regular client of mine, and I was privileged to care for his double-thick Beatles hair for several years. His behaviour during that first session, and subsequent ones, reflected that dreamy side of George Harrison that attracted him to Eastern mysticism. There was nothing personal in his silence towards me. He simply loved to sink into the deep relaxation that many people experience when someone is caring for their hair.

It was precisely around that time that George wrote the music and lyrics to 'Within You without You', his most important contribution to *Sgt Pepper's*. This spiritual anthem for the Summer of Love, with its exotic sitar sounds, was rooted in the Hindu philosophy George had encountered in India while studying with Ravi Shankar. If the Beatles' guitarist was hoping to spread these teachings to the West with his hypnotic tune, he certainly succeeded. 'Within You without You' almost single-handedly sparked the late Sixties' fashion for Indian music, art and spirituality, inspiring hordes of long-haired backpackers to seek out wise bearded men near the Ganges, or at least local meditation centres. In fact, if you've taken a yoga class, you probably have this Beatle to thank.

Perhaps George was exploring higher states of consciousness during my hairdressing sessions, zoning out from a reality he had begun to understand as illusory and seeking the peace of mind he spoke of in his lyrics. In any case, he clearly treated them as opportunities to chill out from the everyday hassles of work. Who knows? Perhaps, while I was snipping and comb-ing on that first day in 1967, he was being visited by Sarasvati, Hindu goddess of music and the arts, and granted a few ideas for his influential song.

* * *

Cutting John Lennon's hair was, again, a radically different experience. The first time took place just as the *Sgt. Pepper's* recordings were coming to an end. By then John knew perfectly well who I was, but he hadn't yet seemed tempted by my services – alas! Then one day, out of the blue, the most legendary of all the Beatles walked into the boardroom just as I'd finished cutting Mal Evans's hair. He circled around Mal's newly groomed head, admired the layering and neatly cropped sideburns and said to me:

"Very nice, Leslie, very nice indeed. Would you come into my office and do mine, please?"

As you can imagine, I freed my agenda for this long-awaited opportunity.

John's office was as large and impressive as the boardroom itself. When I came in, he was sitting in a leather chair, speaking into the phone with great earnestness. I skulked timidly at the door, but he waved me in, talking all the while. If I hadn't known this young man was a freewheeling pop star who loved to get stoned and basically lived at night, I could have easily mistaken him for a stressed-out businessman. In fact, as if he were too busy to stop his conversation for a haircut, he signalled to me to begin my work. John Lennon was what we would now call a multitasker.

I really sweated through that haircut. Not so much because I was in the presence of John Lennon, or because I feared his opinion. The haircut itself wasn't particularly challenging either. His hair was getting longer, but the look was still relatively conventional for the times, and so my job was pretty straightforward.

The problem was more a life-and-death sort of thing. As I've already described in a previous chapter, cutting hair involves the skilful manipulation of sharp scissors in the proximity of vital parts of the human anatomy. Nipping the skin is a common occurrence, and even the most experienced hairdresser can make a more serious slip – such as when Stephen chopped off his client's earlobe right in front of me, in my early days at Sassoon's. What you really want to avoid, though, is jabbing your blades into the jugular vein.

So one of a stylist's greatest nightmares is dealing with a client who won't keep his head still. John Lennon, as I learnt that afternoon, was perhaps the worst I have ever had to handle. As he happily conducted what turned out to be an extended interview with an important journalist, I concentrated on trying not to deprive the world of one of its greatest musicians by stabbing him in the neck. Whenever I could find an appropriate break in the conversation, I tried to get him to stop moving:

"Could you please keep your head still, John?" I'd ask, again and again, as patiently as I could.

John would briefly acknowledge me, nodding his head as if he'd understood, but the mere fact of nodding demonstrated he hadn't quite got the message. In any case, he would instantly forget I was even there and carried on obliviously, quaking with laughter, shaking his head and arguing vehemently with great sweeps of his arms. I kept visualizing the goriest scenes imaginable over that paper-filled desk of his, and the accompanying headlines in the next day's press: BEATLES' HAIRDRESSER DECAPITATES LENNON!

But that was John. We both survived the test, and I went on to carry out many more death-defying hairdressing stunts over the next couple of years. He always seemed happy with my work. Or perhaps he didn't give it that much importance – certainly not the kind of transcendental significance bestowed upon it by his legions of fans... In any case, he never stopped the normal flow of his hectic lifestyle to make a space for his styling sessions. Somehow, I had to work around whatever else he happened to be doing, a challenge that forced me to become a daredevil hairdresser worthy of the travelling circus I'd heard him singing about in the studio, with men and horses, hoops and garters, and a hogshead of real fire.

One of the most memorable of these sessions involved a certain very charismatic Japanese lady John met in his office while I was cutting his hair. At the time, I had no idea who she was, but of course Yoko Ono would go on to become Lennon's lover, muse, wife and inseparable companion, leading to the breakup of his marriage with Cynthia Lennon and, according to many people, to the breakup of the Beatles themselves.

I was very struck by this small but feisty woman from the moment she walked through the door, dressed all in black. She wasn't conventionally attractive, but there was something about her that arrested your attention – which in my case was not a good thing, considering the scissor somersaults I was performing around John's restless head.

Even at the time, I was conscious of witnessing a momentous encounter. For the first time since I had known him, John Lennon wasn't talking about the Beatles or about music. Their conversation swirled around weightier topics: art, life and truth. I later learnt that John had visited an exhibition of hers at the Indica Gallery and had been intrigued by her quirky interactive pieces. One of them required the visitor to climb a stepladder and peer through a spyglass at a distant spot, which turned out to spell out the word "yes". Another was a white block into which people were invited to hammer a nail, co-creating the work of art. When Yoko and John met, she apparently handed him a card on which was printed "breathe". And yet, she took his breath away.

When I saw them together that first time, he kept asking her about the meaning of her odd creations, and she did her best to explain. Frankly, I couldn't grasp half of what Yoko was going on about, but then again, neither could John. In fact, he was becoming increasingly exasperated with her:

"I don't understand what you're trying to say!" he'd complain, shaking his head dangerously. "I just don't understand!"

"You don't understand because you don't listen," Yoko would answer playfully, as if he were a stuck-up little boy – which perhaps he was. Amazingly, this only seemed to turn him on more.

John was normally the dominant character in any conversation. And yet here, for the first time, I saw this fierce little lady completely in control of their dialogue. It was as if he'd finally met a woman who wasn't drooling for a Beatle, but simply engaging with him as a person. The scene was so fascinating to watch that I had to slow down my normal working pace. In fact, a styling job that might have taken half an hour stretched to over twice as long. They weren't just talking. Their interaction was like a work of performance art, baffling and yet, at the same time, powerfully arresting. They were hammering nails into each other, right before my eyes. They were breathing their most precious breaths. They were peering through spyglasses and finding "yes" inscribed on each other's hearts.

I have to admit: I was embarrassed to be there. Like a lot of performance art, it made me feel queasy. And yet, at the same time, I was mesmerized. It was one of those situations where the hairdresser becomes invisible to his client, who ends up revealing much more than he might have intended to. A year later, when John left his wife Cynthia and took up with Yoko, I was not at all surprised. John Lennon had clearly met his soulmate.

* * *

I worked on Ringo's hair less often than the others. His wife Maureen happened to be a hairdresser, so most of the time she cared for his increasingly shaggy mane. In addition, Ringo wasn't present as often during the recording sessions. With the exception of his lead vocals on 'With a Little Help from My Friends', he wasn't given a lot of space on *Sgt. Pepper's*. Paul and John's innovative vision was taking the Beatles away from the sounds of a rock band, the drummer's traditional kit remaining unused during many of the songs. So when I did see him around, I got the impression he was feeling a little excluded.

In comparison with other big-name pop drummers, Ringo Starr had always been a relatively unassuming presence within his band. His basic, solid, boom-whack beat gives many classic Beatles tunes their backbone, and often an original and instantly recognizable signature, but he never pushed himself to the forefront. Can you remember him ever playing a long drum solo? He was a sharp contrast to the "wild man of pop", Keith Moon of the Who, and to Charlie Watts of the Rolling Stones, whose drumming was a major feature in all their band's tracks. When the Beatles stopped touring and began experimenting in the studio with string sections, calliopes and sitars, Ringo was being pushed even farther into the background by the band's leaders.

In the public eye, of course, he was "good old Ringo", the cheerful, witty and bubbly Liverpudlian who stars in both of the Beatles' films and seems the most comfortable during their endless press interviews. This was something of an illusion, however. He could certainly be funny and light-hearted, and I did find him the sharpest of the four, but he was also somewhat aloof, perhaps as a reaction to his increasingly marginal role in the band. He was the only Beatle – or at least that was my impression – who didn't want you to forget that he *was* a Beatle. So, although I did get closer to him after the breakup of the band, at the time of *Sgt. Pepper's* I found him the most difficult to approach.

One illustrative anecdote stands out in my mind from that period. I remember sitting in the control box at Abbey Road one night while Ringo was drumming out a rhythm in one of the booths of the studio. At one point, Paul McCartney, who was up in the box with George Martin and the rest of us, took off his earphones, ran down to Ringo's booth and grabbed his drumsticks.

"Look, I don't want it like that," he told his fellow Beatle, shooing him off the drummer's seat. "I want it like this!"

And then Paul proceeded to illustrate what he was after, incidentally demonstrating what a brilliant and well-rounded musician he was.

While Paul played the drums, however, I noticed that Ringo was seething with anger.

"Get out!" he ordered, red-faced and shaking his finger at me and the others in the booth. "Clear the studio!"

Everyone except for George Martin and the remaining three Beatles left the control box in a hurry. As for me, I decided it was time to go home for the night.

I don't know about the others, but I really felt for Ringo. As I drove back home, I recalled the many times at the salon when my boss Roger would walk up to my chair as I was finishing a styling job, pull out his scissors and make a show of correcting me in front of the client and my peers. I have no doubt these little episodes of public shaming were purposeful. I had been Roger's junior apprentice only months before, I was still only nineteen years old, and yet already I was getting more press attention than he was. Worst of all, I had "stolen" his client Jane Asher, and as a result Paul McCartney. Roger Thompson should have been the Beatles' official hairdresser, not upstart Leslie Cavendish. So every time he corrected my haircuts, he was both putting me in my place and getting his revenge.

In Ringo's case, I'm just as certain Paul meant no harm by his behaviour that night. Taking over his companion's drum kit and belting out the rhythm was simply the easiest way for him to show Ringo what he wanted. Nevertheless, it must have been humiliating for the drummer to be treated that way in front of the others. I can't imagine Mick Jagger going up to Charlie Watts and saying: "Charlie boy, hand over your sticks – I'm going to show you how it's done." This unintentional peek into the private life of the Beatles helped me to understand why Ringo might have carried around a chip on his shoulder in his relationship with outsiders.

*　*　*

As for me, I have to admit that my early success was getting to my head. How could I resist? Working at one of London's most fashionable salons, seeing my name in the papers, hanging out with the biggest stars in the world... it was all a bit too much for a teenage kid from Burnt Oak. True, I was still living with my parents. But it was the only smear on my otherwise perfect Swinging Sixties image, and it certainly didn't stop me from getting a little cocky, particularly when sitting behind the wheel of my flash Morris Mini. Its gleaming black metal shell made me feel invincible, assuring me, for example, that certain unconventional traffic manoeuvres were reasonable exceptions to the legal code for the likes of Leslie Cavendish.

One rainy morning, I was dashing through the wet streets of North London on my way to an early appointment at the salon, spraying the pavement with arcs of rainwater. As I reached Staples Corner Junction, a busy intersection on the Edgware Road, I came up against a queue of ten cars waiting to turn at the crossing. I wasn't going to allow such a trifle to make me late for work. So I proceeded to skip the queue by overtaking it on the wrong side of the road.

As destiny would have it, however, the second car in the queue belonged to the Metropolitan Police. I was startled by its flashing lights and blaring siren as I came alongside it. Grinding my teeth, I pulled over and waited for the officer to reach my window. When I slid it open, the sound of pouring rain filled the interior of the Mini, and I pulled back to avoid the big drops bursting on the window sill from spraying my elegant Sassoon suit. The policeman slowly lowered his head to my level. He didn't look happy in that rain.

"Good morning sir," he said with strained politeness. "Do you realize you were overtaking a line of cars on the wrong side of the road?"

"I'm so sorry," I said, fully confident that an apology and explanation were all that was needed to be on my way. "I was late for work, you see. I have an important appointment—"

"Would you mind stepping out of the car, sir?" he interrupted me gruffly.

This officer clearly did not understand the trendiness of my car, the quasi-celebrity status of its owner or the importance of my mission.

"I do mind, actually," I said, starting to feel all hot under the collar of my nice, dry, pressed shirt. "It's pouring down with rain. I'm wearing a suit. I work as a hairdresser at Vidal Sassoon's. I'm meeting an important client there. If I get out now, I'll be cutting hair all wet."

The policeman's face ditched its official veil of politeness.

"If I'm out in the fucking rain getting wet," he growled, "then you can fucking well get wet!"

That did it. I didn't care what happened. I wouldn't stand for such treatment.

"I am not getting out of this car," I declared.

It wasn't until that moment, when his hands clenched around the ledge of the driver's window, that I noticed how large and meaty they were. For a moment, I imagined myself being grabbed by the lapels of my suit and yanked out bodily into the street. To my great relief, however, his brawny hands relaxed, pulled away, wrote me a ticket and handed me the soaking piece of paper. But before storming off into the rain, he lowered his big head again through my window and anticipated his revenge.

"You're going to get done for this, son," he said, flicking a bit of rainwater onto my suit for good measure.

He wasn't fooling around either, though when I got the summons for Hendon Magistrates' Court and saw the date, I wondered whether it contained another veiled joke: 1st April. I phoned up the Automobile Association for some advice, and they told me I wouldn't need a lawyer, as I'd never had any previous traffic violations.

"You should expect a fine and three points off your driver's license, nothing more," they assured me.

When I turned up in court, however, I could see the police officer was angling for more: twisting the facts, exaggerating my admittedly insolent behaviour and making me out to be a prime example of everything that was wrong with youth nowadays – an example that required exemplary punishment. I felt everyone in the courthouse, from the judge to the cleaner that leant on his broom in the corner, was looking at my shoulder-length hair and casting a severe verdict on my whole rebellious, pot-smoking, good-for-nothing generation.

This would probably have been a good time to prove them wrong with a show of contrite meekness and exquisite good manners. Had I had a lawyer, I'm sure he would have counselled me in this direction. In the event, however, my cocky nineteen-year-old swagger kept bursting through, adding further damning evidence to the policeman's accusations.

"That's not right!" I protested at one point, interrupting his testimony.

I got a warning from the judge. My turn would come, it was explained to me. When I finally got into the witness box, I tried to set matters straight at once.

"What the policeman said just now... that was all a pack of lies!"

Contempt of court, I was told. *Just answer the questions.* So I answered them, holding my tongue as best as I could. *Was I driving on the wrong side of the road?* Yes. *Did I refuse to get out of the car?* (But... the rain... my suit!) Yes.

The gavel went down: *three months' suspended driver's licence.*

"You can't do that!" I baulked.

"If you say another word, young man," the judge warned me, with no evident sign that it was a further April Fools' joke, "I'll make it six months."

Ooh, that hurt. Three months without my sleek little black Mini! How was I to get to and from work, the Beatles' offices and Abbey Road? By trolley? The worst part, though, was yet to come. As I walked out of the courtroom in an incredulous daze, the police officer sidled up to me, dropped his voice to a whisper and flicked his fingers in my direction, as if to splash a bit more rainwater on my suit:

"Told you I'd fucking get you!" he sneered.

*　　*　　*

The three-month suspension was a tragic blow: to my cool image, of course; to my intimate relationship with my prized wheels; but also to my daily routine. The prospect of travelling between the West End and Burnt Oak without a car, particularly at night, seemed like an unbearable drag. So, for the first time, I began seriously to consider moving away from my parents' house and closer to the salon.

Sassoon's outfits were in Mayfair, an exclusive area far beyond my means, and too sedate for me anyway. Where I really wanted to live, where any Sixties Swinger like myself *had* to live, was in Chelsea. The old bohemian quarter, once the haunt of painters like Turner and John Singer Sargent, was now becoming the rebellious, utopian, peace-loving heart of the emerging pop culture that was taking the world by storm. The King's Road and its environs were teeming with groovy bars and clothing boutiques such as Granny Takes a Trip, with its beaded-glass entrance curtain, Wurlitzer jukebox and pop-art shopfront murals. Fashionable didn't begin to describe these streets. Chelsea was the sacred ground from which British flower power emanated.

Just imagine: within the space of about half a mile square, you could knock on David Bowie's door on Oakley Street, say hi to Mick and Keith of the Stones along Cheyne Walk, watch Eric Clapton pick up his milk on Old Church Street and have tea with Marianne Faithfull on Danvers Street. This was all hypothetical, of course, but not as fanciful as it might seem, considering I was already smoking weed with Paul McCartney. The more I thought about it, the more I desired a pad in the neighbourhood where everything was happening. Chelsea was my natural habitat.

Digging through the rental ads in *The Sunday Times*, I found an apartment in Meriden Court advertised for £12 a week. Nowadays, that sounds like the price of three beers in a Sloane Square pub, but in 1967 it was a fair bit of money. Nevertheless, I worked out that, with tips, I could just about cover the rent.

The place was a tiny little one-room studio flat. But the moment I signed the contract, I realized the policeman's April Fools' joke had really been a blessing in disguise. At last, I was living on my own, and in the trendiest spot in the city, in the country, in the world! Nothing could stop me now – once I got my Mini back.

7

Summer of Love, Summer of War

Early in 1967, the *San Francisco Oracle*, an underground newspaper with an eye-popping psychedelic design, called for a "gathering of tribes" that would take place in Golden Gate Park. The purpose of this unprecedented meeting was to precipitate a new world order, no less:

> A *new concept of celebrations beneath the human underground must emerge, become conscious and be shared, so a revolution can be formed with a renaissance of compassion, awareness and love, and the revelation of unity for all mankind.*

The idealistic call was astoundingly successful. Around 30,000 youngsters – hippies, anti-war campaigners, equal-rights activists, ecotopian pioneers, experimental artists, guitar-toting poets, drug-fuelled truth-seekers and wide-eyed loafers – converged on the city for the first ever "Human Be-In". This wasn't simply a rock festival, though the Grateful Dead and Jefferson Airplane did play there. It was conceived as a communal ritual that would bring about a transformation in human consciousness, from materialism to simplicity, from conformity to rebellion, from violence to peace and love. Shutting down the Vietnam War? Turning nuclear missiles into ploughshares? That was just for starters. To facilitate this spiritual awakening, Beat poet Allen Ginsberg chanted mantras, underground chemist Owsley Stanley distributed about 300,000 tabs of LSD, and ex-Harvard psychologist Timothy Leary led the collective trip as a modern shaman, dressed in a flowing robe with flowers in his hair. It was here that he urged the masses to "turn on, tune in, drop out", providing the new slogan for our generation.

The Human Be-in, however, would be only the prelude to a wider movement that spread around the world like polka-dotted hallucinogenic mushrooms, culminating a few months later in what came to be known as the "Summer of Love". The greatest ever hippy gathering took place around the Haight-Ashbury district in San Francisco, which was flooded by 100,000 turned-on, tuned-in dropouts who participated in massive outdoor concerts the likes of which had never been seen before. London, however, was a close second, with events like the "14 Hour Technicolor Dream" in Alexandra Palace, a "Legalize Pot" rally in Hyde Park and nights at the UFO Club, where Pink Floyd made their name. As for the Beatles, they managed to provide the soundtrack to the Summer of Love without a single live appearance. The album they had been working on for so long, *Sgt. Pepper's Lonely Hearts Club Band*, was released on the first of June, and then played almost non-stop on radio stations worldwide. A few weeks later, they released an additional mantra for the spiritual revolution, live on TV for a global audience of 400 million people: 'All You Need Is Love'.

I was more than ready for the flower-power revolution. Each drag on the joints I'd share around a circle of colourful cushions tasted of that coming utopia in which everyone would get along, regardless of their race, sex, religion or background.

"Peace, man," I'd say to the total stranger who handed me the rolled-up cigarette, as if all barriers between us had been wiped away for ever.

"Yeah," he'd answer with a generous smile, his bleary, blood-shot eyes gazing at me with total earnestness. "You said it: peace."

It was as easy as that! After thousands of years of imperialism, exploitation, violence and greed, my generation was finally going to put a stop to all of the madness, once and for all.

On the fifth of June 1967, however, just four days after the debut of *Sgt. Pepper's*, my innocent little hippy world was turned upside-down. I remember walking into the salon early in the morning, merrily whistling the tune of 'Lucy in the Sky with Diamonds', when I was struck by a front-page headline at the top of a newspaper in the reception area: WAR BREAKS OUT IN THE MIDDLE EAST. The tangerine trees and marmalade skies suddenly burst into flame and disappeared in a cloud of smoke. Like all of my Jewish family and friends, I had over the past few weeks been following the tension that was growing between Israel and its Arab neighbours. Egyptian forces had been massing on the Sinai border, and when President Nasser decided to close the Straits of Tiran to Israeli shipping, the situation reached its breaking point – Israel had warned for years that such a move would constitute an act of war.

Now, as I picked up the newspaper, I saw that the inevitable had happened. The map of Israel pictured on the front page was punctured by arrows which showed the small country attacked from all sides, by Egypt, Jordan, Syria and Lebanon. As my eyes took in the scene, the familiar sounds and smells of Vidal Sassoon's glitzy establishment seemed to melt away, and something inside me snapped.

To this day, I can hardly explain it. Though I've always been proud to be Jewish, I was certainly no Zionist, nor had my family ever much practised the rituals of "our" people. Apart from my grandmother, who would light a couple of candles before the Friday-night meal, we didn't keep the Sabbath. My father, who was a communist, quoted to me from Marx's *Das Kapital* rather than the Torah. At most, he'd take us to the synagogue for Yom Kippur, earning us the title of "once-a-year Jews". Of course, I wasn't able to avoid my bar mitzvah at age thirteen – that was the bare minimum required in our community. I was however thrown out of my preparatory Hebrew classes for not concentrating, and when the moment finally came to stand before the whole synagogue and sing several verses from the Torah, it was one of the most terrifying ordeals of my youth. Years later, in my new life as a groovy Chelsea swinger, my Jewish roots seemed practically irrelevant to my everyday existence.

Nevertheless, that morning at the Grosvenor House salon, when I saw those thick, black, aggressive arrows raining down on Israel from all sides, I felt like they were pointing straight at me. All the shame and anger and feelings of injustice which had burned inside me during my schooldays, when the bullies would insult me and Falky as "Jew boys", were suddenly rekindled. The scar on my lip, where that brute Ollie had pierced me with his shirt-pocket biro as he gripped me in a headlock, seemed to come alive with fresh pain. With every line I read from that news story, my dormant Jewishness bubbled up further, until it finally exploded. Suddenly, Israel wasn't a faraway country any more. My people were in mortal danger, and I had to do something about it. Something more than chanting peace slogans in front of an embassy or waiting for humanity's spiritual awakening to come about while I passed around another joint.

So, a few days later, I found myself at a recruitment office that had been set up in Russell Square, together with several of my Jewish football mates. We were told that we couldn't sign up as a soldiers, but that volunteers were needed to replace the reservists who worked in the kibbutzim, and who had gone to war. It was only at that office, when I picked up the pen to sign up as a volunteer, that I realized how reckless my plan was. Aside from the physical danger I might be putting myself in, taking off to Israel meant risking everything I had built up for myself in London. It meant leaving the salon and all its clients from one day to the next, with no idea when I'd be back. Most worryingly, it meant severing, for an unspecified time, my precious connection to Paul McCartney and the Beatles. Years of work building up a reputation and client list, and now I was planning to throw it all away. Was I really prepared to do that?

Yes, I was. My mind rebelled at the idea, but by then I was learning to turn off my mind, to relax and to float downstream, as John Lennon had sung in 'Tomorrow Never Knows'. My life in Chelsea, my new pad, my Mini, my celebrity clients – what did they really matter, after all? Weren't they just materialistic fluff, the very wall of illusion my generation was fighting against? It was time to surrender to the void and find out if it really was shining. So, with a shaky hand, I filled out the form as quickly as I could and signed at the bottom.

* * *

I didn't bother asking my boss, Roger. I knew he wouldn't be pleased. Or perhaps he'd be too pleased, seeing my defection as an opportunity to steal back all my clients, Paul McCartney in particular. So I went straight to Mr Sassoon. Vidal wasn't just Jewish himself, as we've seen before, but I knew that when he was my age he had joined the Israeli Defence Forces during the 1948 Arab-Israeli War. When I informed him of my decision, the great stylist was more than happy to extend me an indefinite leave of absence. Indeed, it was an emotional moment. He shook my hand, wished me luck and looked upon me like a proud father.

That was the easy part. The real challenge was holding on to Paul McCartney despite my absence. Out of the four Beatles, he was still the only one whose hair I was cutting on a regular basis. Who was going to take care of that job? I could hardly bear the idea of anyone else digging their fingers through his hair, in his private bedroom. Worst of all, Roger Thompson. But someone was going to have to do it, and obviously I couldn't propose a poor replacement. It would reflect badly on me – and besides, it might lead to Paul finding his own stylist. I could have chosen many highly accomplished hairdressers, of course – indeed, much more accomplished than me. The problem was that a skilled replacement might end up taking my place for good.

In the end, I hit upon a devious plan. It involved a colleague by the unusual name of Harley Muse. Harley was undoubtedly an excellent hairdresser, but he was seriously lacking in personality. Knowing Paul, I figured that he would be satisfied with Harley's work, but probably bored stiff during his sessions. With a bit of luck, that would be enough to miss me while I was gone. I recommended Harley to Paul, crossed my fingers and hoped for the best.

My arrival in Israel was quite a shock for a sensitive lad like myself. By the time I got there, the "Six-Day War" was already over, and Israel had emerged victorious. Nevertheless, as I and a few other volunteers were taken on a bus to Kibbutz Mahanayim in northern Israel, the grotesque aftermath of modern warfare was visible everywhere. The place was close to Nazareth and the Golan Heights, an area along the border with Syria that had experienced some of the heaviest fighting. As we zoomed past the blackened, bombed-out tanks and other twisted hulks of military hardware, we were provided with all the evidence we might have possibly wanted of the horrors of war. What really appalled me, though, was the smell of the place: the sweet odour of burnt flesh.

For the entire summer of 1967, I was practically cut off from my previous existence. Kibbutz Mahanayim, a communal farm with spartan living arrangements, was about as far from the swinging scene of Chelsea as you could possibly get. Gone were the elegant stone houses, the trendy bistros, the gaudy threads, the Minis and Aston Martins. Whatever hippy revolution was going on in the rest of the world, I was completely oblivious to it. LSD? Forget it. There wasn't even a joint in sight. As for the pop music that had become a soundtrack to my life, it vanished from one day to the next. *Sgt. Pepper's* wasn't being played by the local radio stations, and we sang our own songs nightly around the campfire.

And yet, to my growing surprise, I came to realize, day by day, that I had come to the very place the stoned-out hippies had been trying to recreate in their Human Be-Ins. As I worked in the fields, washed dishes and got to know my fellow kibbutzniks, each contributing his or her own efforts to the collective good, I began to feel part of something greater than myself. It wasn't a party, to be sure. While the flower-power revellers at the Monterey Festival were running around holding hands in spaced-out fairyland, I was picking oranges in the hot Mediterranean sun for twelve hours. But at the Kibbutz Mahanayim, equality, simplicity and sharing weren't just philosophical concepts or song lyrics about a future new age. They had been put into practice for decades. Decisions were taken together, meals were eaten together and even children were reared together. Men and women took part equally in cooking and cleaning, and we were all treated the same, no matter what our nationality or skin colour. No one owned anything individually – not even their clothes. And all of it seemed so simple, so natural and so obvious that it made you wonder why things should ever be otherwise. So there was little need for me to travel to Haight-Ashbury or the UFO Club. I'd found my own Summer of Love.

Eventually I became the resident hairdresser, working in the most beautiful outdoor salon imaginable, right by the swimming pool. Under the bright-blue Israeli sky, surrounded by lush vegetation, I cut and styled the hair of my fellow kibbutzniks, as if I'd opened up a new branch of Sassoon's in this paradise. If I needed to cut someone's hair wet, I'd simply ask them to jump in the pool. And of course, there was no need for blow-dryers in the Middle Eastern heat. I've never had a better setup.

After a couple of months at the kibbutz, many of the reservist soldiers returned, so we volunteers were no longer needed. Before heading back home, I took off to the south of the country with my friend Leon, who had also come with me from London. We ended up in the resort town of Eilat, which wasn't quite the luxury place it is today, but exciting enough with the lights of Aqaba in Jordan sparkling across the bay. It was strange to think that Israel's enemies of recent months were just a short stretch of water away. The picturesque scene only drove home to us the absurdity of war.

Leon and I enjoyed exploring the town and diving around the coral reefs for which Eilat is famous. But the memory that stands out from that trip was of a musical nature. One morning, I was strolling past the rear of the local concert hall, when suddenly the sound of a single violin reached my ears. A simple melody at first, composed of notes clean like the sky overhead. And then, a wondrous musical pattern, as varied and colourful as the fish darting around the nooks and crannies of a brightly lit coral reef.

I was rooted to the spot. I'd never heard anything like it. Who could play such wonderful music? Then, as I lifted my eyes upwards, I found its source: a middle-aged man dressed in casual clothes, with a pair of horn-rimmed glasses perched on his head, moving his bow dextrously over the strings of his instrument. Evidently, he was rehearsing for a concert. I listened for as long as I dared without disturbing him, and then walked away in a daze, feeling like my consciousness had been expanded by some powerful hallucinogen. I had to find out who that man was.

Around the front of the theatre I found my answer. There, on a poster announcing a benefit concert for the soldiers in the Six-Day War, was the round-faced man I had just seen, pictured here in an elegant dinner jacket: Isaac Stern. That very night, he was to play something called the Mendelssohn Concerto with the Israel Philharmonic, directed by Leonard Bernstein. The concert was sold out, but I decided that I had to see this man play again, and I needed to look up that Mendelssohn chap in my father's record collection. In fact, for the first time in my life, I understood the passion with which my father had flung around his arms to "direct" his orchestras on the telly. There was a whole world of amazing music out there that had nothing to do with electric guitars... How could I have not realized it sooner? Had my experience with the string section at Abbey Road unlocked my ears to these sounds? Might the Beatles have broadened my musical boundaries? To this day, I don't have the answer to that question. But whatever the case may be, my chance encounter with Isaac Stern sparked off a lifelong passion for classical music.

* * *

When I came back to London in late August, my worries came flooding back. During my time in Israel, I had bombarded Paul with postcards, hoping they would keep my client from forgetting about his *real* hairdresser. I sent him news of the kibbutz and the aftermath of war, of diving in Eilat, and of my encounter with a star violinist. From my Mediterranean paradise, I naively expected Paul McCartney to read every one of my cards, possibly putting them up on the mantelpiece in his living room. As soon as I landed at Heathrow, however, reality set in. How many fan letters had he once told me the Beatles received every day? Hundreds? Thousands?

The first thing I did was to visit Harley Muse at his salon.

"How did you get on with Paul?" I asked with some trepidation. Despite not being the most entertaining company in the world, he was a talented hairdresser. What if Paul had decided he preferred Muse's style?

"Oh, I saw him a couple of times," Harley replied in his usual monotone. "It went well, I think."

His answer sounded promising, though I couldn't be certain. Harley wasn't prone to enthusiasm, so perhaps he was hiding something. I phoned Neil Aspinall and let him know I was back, and that if Paul wanted a haircut, to please let me know.

"Thanks, Leslie, yeah, I'll tell Paul," he said, a bit distracted. As usual, I could hear a whirl of voices around him. "Welcome back. Um... speak to you later."

That's when I really started to sweat.

Over the course of that week, I think I must have heard *Sgt. Pepper's Lonely Hearts Club Band*, and the extra single, 'All You Need Is Love', about a hundred times. I myself played it obsessively, astounded by the rich layering of sounds, the eccentric instrumentation, the wild and dreamy lyrics. Each time I reached the screeching orchestral build up and apocalyptic piano chord at the end of 'A Day in the Life', all I could do was turn the vinyl record back to Side A and listen to the whole thing all over again. But it wasn't just me. Billy Shears, Lovely Rita and Mr Kite were being sung about everywhere: in shops, cafés, anyone's house you cared to visit. Not to mention the scandalous and hallucinogenic 'Lucy in the Sky with Diamonds'. The Beatles seemed to have taken over the world. And all I could think was: "Have I blown it just at the height of their fame?"

Finally, I got a call from Neil.

"Hi, Leslie," he said casually. "Paul needs a haircut. Are you free this week?"

I certainly was. Excited, but still uncertain as to whether I had my old job back, I arranged for a visit a few days later. When I arrived at the house on Cavendish Avenue, I looked out for any sign of my postcards on the mantelpiece. Unsurprisingly, there wasn't any.

Then, as soon as I was able to muster the courage, I asked Paul if Harley had done a good job.

"He was OK," Paul shrugged. "He didn't have much to say, though. Just got on with it, really."

What a relief – my plan seemed to have worked perfectly. As I began to cut his hair, trading my adventures in Israel for his holiday stories from Greece, we both relaxed into our old routine. The one and only Billy Shears was back.

* * *

Shortly after I got back from Israel, Paul, John, George and Ringo travelled to Wales for a week of meditation with the Maharishi Mahesh Yogi, a diminutive and white-bearded sage George Harrison had met during his travels in India. As the spiritual exercises were getting underway, however, their mind-expansion was brutally interrupted by a call from their friend Mal Evans: Brian Epstein, their long-time manager, had died from an accidental overdose of alcohol and sleeping pills. In shock, the four musicians returned to London at once.

Epstein had launched the Beatles in their early stages, polishing up their act and landing them their first gigs and record deals. During the years of Beatlemania, he had managed the insanity as the Fab Four toured around the world, mobbed by hysterical adolescents, journalists and photographers. He had become a celebrity himself. However, after the Beatles' last concert at Candlestick Park, Epstein found it difficult to adjust to his newly diminished role, which may have contributed to his increasing drug abuse. During the recording of *Sgt. Pepper's*, he checked into a rehabilitation clinic, but was unable to curb his addictions. His final, tragic overdose was already being announced in the press as the beginning of the end for the Beatles.

The next time I saw Paul, I gave him my condolences. He seemed very affected by the loss, less chatty and more distracted than usual. Sensing his mood, I got on with my work in silence. To be honest, my own mind was a little troubled, and with news

I couldn't quite share with him, of all people. Vidal Sassoon had started up a swanky salon in New York a couple of years before, on Madison Avenue, and I'd been offered a place there. It was an once-in-a-lifetime opportunity, of course, but it meant risking my relationship with the Beatles a second time. Should I call up Harley Muse again and travel to the Big Apple? I could already see myself styling Bob Dylan's wild curls and travelling to San Francisco with flowers in my hair. On the other hand, I was loath to leave Paul and the others again, even temporarily.

After our subdued styling session, we settled down in the music room for a cup of tea and a smoke.

"Leslie, listen," he said at one point, passing me his spliff. "I've been turning an idea around in my head these past few days. I think we all need to get away from London for a bit, you know, do something different, forget about everything. Not just the band, but Mal, and Neil, and all the others."

"That sounds like a really good idea, Paul." I took my first drag. "Like a retreat or something?"

"Yeah, in a way. I was thinking we could all just get into a coach and drive off."

"Where would you go?" I asked, melting into my armchair as the cannabis kicked in. I could almost feel the music wrapping its tendrils around my body.

"Actually, the idea I had in mind wasn't about going anywhere in particular. It was more the idea of the coach trip itself. We could just travel around and see what happens – spontaneously, you know. And get it all on film, for a kind of Beatles road-trip movie. We're inviting a few actors along as well. So... we're going to need a hairdresser for the cast and crew."

I coughed out a lungful of smoke. Behind my closed eyelids, brilliantly coloured fields of geometric flowers exploded.

This made me wonder if I had also hallucinated those last few words.

"Are you inviting me to join you, Paul?" I finally managed to wheeze.

"Yeah." He smiled. "D'you want to come along? We're calling it the 'Magical Mystery Tour'. It's the title of a song we've recorded."

That set me off giggling. Touring around the country on a bus trip with the Beatles? Who could say no to that?

"Ah… yes, Paul," I stammered out, overjoyed. "I'd love to join you."

The words were only just out of my mouth, however, when the consequences of this impulsive decision rose up around me.

"Smashing, Leslie…" Paul's voice came from somewhere.

I sat up and tried to clear my addled head.

The New York offer. Had I just turned it down? And that wasn't the worst of it. How was I to ask Vidal to let me take another leave of absence from the salon, after I'd just come back from Israel? Volunteering for the Jewish cause was one thing, but taking off on a hippy bus trip with the Beatles was quite another. I couldn't even imagine popping the question.

"How long were you planning on… er… travelling on that coach?" I asked Paul, passing the joint back.

"Oh, we'll see," he answered vaguely, inhaling deeply through the cigarette. "That's part of the magical mystery, I suppose."

That night, when I got home, I couldn't fall asleep. I was in a state of mental turmoil. I'd screwed up big time. Paul McCartney had signed me up on his little film excursion. I couldn't back out now, could I? No, of course not. This was Paul McCartney we were talking about. But there was no way Vidal Sassoon was going to let me go on such a lark. Let alone Roger Thompson, my boss. Oh my, Roger was going to rub his hands with glee at this. Here was his chance to get rid of me for ever, poisoning Sassoon's ear with all the venom he could possibly muster. Leslie Cavendish was going to throw away his job, his reputation and his livelihood on a stupid stoned-out whim, ha ha!

On the other hand, though...wasn't a coach trip with the Beatles worth risking one's job, reputation and livelihood for? My mind still buzzing with cannabis, I couldn't really tell. I thought I was going crazy – my head twisted into a vortex, my heart filled the room with its rhythmic pounding. And then, suddenly, like a shamanic vision, my mother's face appeared to me, glowing out into my consciousness, gaining in brightness, shining with white, pure, unquestionable light. Everything else seemed to fade away.

"Don't worry, Les," Betty Boots said, winking at me slyly as I began to doze off at last, completely exhausted. "I'll ring the salon, tell them you've fallen ill, that the doctor says you need at least a week to recover!"

"Oh..." I whispered in amazement, as I toppled backwards into an infinite void and my vision receded away into the distance. "Great idea, Mum."

In truth, my real mother took a bit of convincing. During my entire school career, I'd never skived off a single day of class, let alone involved her in such a scheme. But that was the best plan I could come up with, and so I pleaded with her until she had to agree. There was no way I was going to miss the Beatles' Magical Mystery Tour. Whatever the hell that was.

8

The Magical Mystery Tour

If you've ever seen the *Magical Mystery Tour* movie, you'll have to agree that it's one of the oddest collection of images ever committed to celluloid. The Beatles' two previous films were certainly offbeat, but at least they had a script, and were directed by the talented Richard Lester. This third attempt was more of an experiment, made up as they went along, and with as many directors as pointy-hatted wizards (five: all four Beatles plus Bernard Knowles). I won't bother telling you the plot, as there's not really much of one. The surreal hotchpotch brings together a guitar-playing walrus, a group of white-clad "eggmen", an army sergeant screaming nonsense, a sleazy striptease show and a waiter who shovels a ton of spaghetti onto a plate. Objectively, it looks like someone's home movie of a coach trip to the seaside got spliced together with a few rejected Monty Python sketches and the most outlandish art-film freak-outs imaginable. You'd almost have to assume that those responsible were tripping on acid, and perhaps even trying to set off a psychedelic reaction in the brains of the unsuspecting British public on Boxing Day, during the Christmas Holiday Special on which it first aired. You wouldn't be far off the mark.

Paul McCartney's idea for the Magical Mystery Tour was inspired by a similar outing organized by Ken Kesey, author of *One Flew over the Cuckoo's Nest*. In 1964, Kesey had travelled across America in a bus painted with bright trippy colours, together with a group of friends who called themselves the "Merry Pranksters", meeting up with the Grateful Dead, Allen Ginsberg and the Hells Angels, among other counter-culture figures. Like the Magical Mystery Tour, the bus outing was documented on 16-mm film, though the footage wasn't released for another four decades. And yes, Kesey and his Pranksters were dropping acid tabs every step of the way, as well as introducing others to the drug.

Lysergic acid, or LSD, was an important influence on the Beatles around that time, as it was for the whole hippy movement. That summer, Paul McCartney had not only admitted to having experimented with acid, but actually extolled its virtues live on British television. As for John Lennon, he would later recall that during those years he must have taken around 1,000 tabs of the stuff. Whether 'Lucy in the Sky with Diamonds' was or was not intended as an explicit acronym – incredibly, it has been consistently denied by the band's members – the dreamy, hallucinogenic lyrics of the song certainly reflected their powerful experiences with this mind-altering substance.

Together with the transcendental meditation they had begun to practise under the guidance of the Maharishi Mahesh Yogi, LSD was being used by the Beatles not just for recreation, but as a tool for overcoming the ego, sweeping away cultural constraints and prejudices, and exploring the nature of consciousness and reality. Psychotropic drugs and Eastern spiritual disciplines were twin methods for effecting the "awakening" of humanity heralded by New Agers, and often mixed together. The lyrics for the Beatles' song 'Tomorrow Never Knows', in fact, were adapted from Timothy Leary's book *The Psychedelic Experience*, which describes LSD as a chemical short cut to the profound, life-transforming insights of experienced Buddhist meditators.

Personally, I never really got into either, much as I wanted to experience the whole hippy consciousness-expansion "Age of Aquarius" trip. I tried going to a few meditation classes at the Maharishi's TM Centre in Belgravia, the very same George Harrison had been attending. Together with incense and Indian sitar music, Transcendental Meditation had become the new fashion, and I was convinced that, here at last, I was to find inner peace. I'd been talking with Paul McCartney about books like *Siddhartha* and *The Prophet*, and as a result was feeling spiritually hip already, practically ready for enlightenment.

After just a few minutes of sitting cross-legged, though, I started to get fidgety. My back and inner thighs complained, and I found it difficult to concentrate on the teacher's instructions. In the end, I think I left the place more frustrated and stressed out than I'd gone in. Maybe I was too impatient. I don't really know. In any case, after a few sessions, I decided a good game of tennis was a much more effective chill-out remedy for Leslie Cavendish.

As for LSD, I only tried it once. I was curious to become "experienced", as Jimi Hendrix so subtly put it, so when a friend of Lawrence offered me a tab one evening at home, I decided to give it a go. Initially, it was a bit disappointing. We walked down the King's Road together, but the cafés and shops didn't seem any trippier than usual. I figured that nothing was happening. Then, I returned home on my own and played a new experimental album I'd recently bought, *Indo-Jazz Suite* by John Mayer and Joe Harriott. That's when I noticed that I'd fallen through some kind of rabbit hole. The exotic saxophone tune pouring out of my stereo began to whirl around in an undeniably peculiar way. Giggling like a child, I watched the liquid sound pluck shapes and colours out of the walls and furnishings.

Was it enjoyable? Sure it was. In fact, it was more than that. It was the very psychedelic experience everyone had been raving about. Strawberry fields for ever! After five minutes, though (or was it three hours?), I'd had enough. I mean, how many strawberries can you eat in one sitting, no matter how sweet and luscious, before they start making you ill? And yet, the bloody things just wouldn't stop coming: strawberries, plums, snowflakes and SPIDERS. How long was this twisting, squirming craziness going to last? Surely not another six... eight... ten hours? I would have given anything to make it stop: my Mini, my job, my McCartney gigs. But there was no stopping the insanity. There was no controlling it whatsoever. If it hadn't been for my trusty Mothers of Invention record *We're Only in It for the Money*, which gleefully satirized the whole hippy thing and brought me back down to earth, I think I might not have made it through the night. Thank you, Frank Zappa! The next morning, a friend of mine knocked on my door.

"Christ, Leslie!" he exclaimed upon seeing me. "What have you been up to?"

I felt like I had died and come back to life. Which is pretty much how Timothy Leary describes the LSD experience. From then on, I decided that cannabis was hallucinogenic enough for me, thank you very much.

In any case, the Magical Mystery Tour was, without a doubt, a far-out trip in more ways than one. Songs such as 'I Am the Walrus', 'Blue Jay Way' or 'Flying' seem crafted for stoned-out hippies watching lava lamps. And when the Beatles sang that it was "coming to take you away", everyone knew what they were talking about. Everyone who was switched on to the tripped-out hippy vibe, that is.

So here's the funny thing: during the actual Magical Mystery Tour I went on, there were absolutely no illegal drugs on board that I was aware of. There may have been a bit of pot-smoking in the hotel rooms, behind closed doors. I certainly doubt anyone was tripping on acid. Aside from Lennon, maybe. Perhaps the band was being particularly cautious, after the high-profile arrests of Donovan and the Rolling Stones that year, but the Magical Mystery Tour was actually an astoundingly tame and innocent outing, a far cry from the Merry Pranksters' acid-soaked extravaganza.

Still, it was a heck of a ride.

*　*　*

For me, the tour began early on a Monday morning, just as I was supposed to be starting my working week. Though it was already mid-September, the day turned out bright and warm, as if the Summer of Love had been extended just for us. I showed up at the meeting spot, Allsop Place, near Baker Street Tube station, feeling as guilty and excited as a truant schoolboy. An odd assortment of characters were already assembled on the pavement, and as more passengers arrived, it only grew odder. Aside from the Beatles' Liverpool friends and close collaborators like Mal Evans and Neil Aspinall, there were a few people with lights, tripods and cameras, a four-year-old girl holding hands with a white-haired woman, a stern-looking Scotsman, a very fat and jolly lady, and a dwarf. The Scotsman, I later learnt, was Ivor Cutler, an eccentric poet and deadpan humourist who was to play the part of Mr Blood Vessel in the film; the jolly fat lady was Jessie Robins, who was to play Ringo's Auntie Jessie, while the dwarf was George Claydon, the photographer for the tour.

I asked Neil where the Beatles were, and he explained that we'd be picking up John, George and Ringo from their homes in Virginia Water, Surrey. As for Paul, he'd rushed off on a last-minute errand to buy the driver's uniform.

"Everything's a bit last-minute," he added, with the resigned air of someone used to managing chaos.

"Oh yeah?" I said.

"You may have noticed there's no coach."

"I had, actually. When's it due?"

"It's being redecorated. We're waiting for the designers to finish."

That was the first inkling I got of the kind of improvised madness that would ensue over the following week. As we waited for the bus, I gathered that some of the actors and film people were more than a bit unsettled by the lack of planning. They had been hoping for some kind of script, but when Paul finally arrived, all he brought was a single sheet of paper with a big circle divided up like a pie chart, with numbers in each section and a few words or doodles scribbled all around. In the number-four slice, for instance, there was a little smiley face. Cute, but not very reassuring.

We decided to head over to a nearby café used by London Transport staff. Over a cup of tea, I discovered from one of Paul's old friends that, at his old school, the Liverpool Institute, they used to hold an annual event known as the "mystery tour". Each year, the older boys who were just transferring into the Sixth Form, aged fifteen or sixteen, were treated to a coach trip, its destination a mystery. These mystery tours always ended in Blackpool, but the myth of the unknown adventure persisted.

"So is that where you're taking us, Paul?" I asked the Beatle, who was dutifully signing some autographs for the amazed clientele. "To see the Blackpool lights?"

"I don't know..." he teased, raising one of his eyebrows. "It's a mystery!"

The coach rolled into Allsop Place about two hours late, but it certainly made an impression. Freshly painted in yellow and light blue, with rainbow-trailing stars and the words "Magical Mystery Tour" in nice, rounded letters you could almost hug, it seemed like the kind of fantastical vehicle that might take you flying over the moon. We all piled inside enthusiastically, and then, as we were setting off, Neil gave each of us five pounds (a bit less than £100 in twenty-first-century money), to cover our food-and-drink expenses on the way.

Filming got started almost as soon as we picked up the remaining three Beatles. Miranda Wright, who played the winsome hostess, introduced various sights around the countryside, while the rest of us were supposed to look like happy tourists. This didn't take a lot of acting skill, of course, and I was particularly thrilled, because Shirley Evans, who happened to be a client of mine at the salon, had chosen to sit next to me on the bus. Shirley was a larger-than-life character, an accordionist with a stunning personality and a figure as wavy as her thick auburn hair. She'd become famous on variety shows with her unique playing style, both flamboyant and sexy.

"Can you believe it, Leslie?" she kept saying to me. "We're on tour with the Beatles!"

What I couldn't believe is how Miss Evans had suddenly become my new best friend. My imagination was already running wild over the keys of her accordion. The Magical Mystery Tour was getting off to a very promising start.

* * *

Things didn't quite go as planned, however, either for me or for the Beatles. Shirley Evans turned out to have a husband, Reg Wale, and ended up keeping me at arm's length during the entire trip. Furthermore, the random, spontaneous surprises that Paul had hoped to film during the tour were also foiled at almost every stop. Though a few interactions were recorded with gobsmacked punters at the Pied Piper Restaurant in Basingstoke, where we had lunch on the first day, by the time we reached our hotel in Teignmouth, Devon, word of the Beatles' "secret" project seemed to have leaked: hundreds of local teenagers were waiting for their idols in the rain. After an impromptu press conference that first night, the colourful coach was trailed everywhere by a cavalcade of fans, journalists and photographers. And it was that press attention which led directly to the biggest, most random and spontaneous surprise of the entire tour. At least for me.

The following evening, after a memorable dinner of mussels and chips, I rang my mum from the Atlantic Hotel in Newquay to tell her about the day's adventures. On the way to the Widecombe Fair, the coach driver, Alf, had tried to take a secondary road to avoid the Beatlemaniacs, but got stuck on a narrow bridge and had to reverse for half a mile. The Beatles had an argument, and the film crew decided to roll the cameras as their tempers flared, John Lennon's in particular – footage which never made it into the film. But when I began telling my mother the story, she interrupted me.

"Have you looked at the papers today, Les?" she asked.

"Oh, no, mum," I said. "We haven't had time for that. There's too much going on here…"

"Well, you should," she continued. "There was a special feature about the tour in the *Daily Express*, with plenty of photos."

"Really? Am I in any of them?"

"Well, yes, you are…" she said. "There's a picture of Paul McCartney chatting with a strange-looking man, and you're right next to him. And there's another one showing you with Paul and a policeman. It's definitely you, Les!"

"Wow, Mum, that's great," I said. I wasn't as thrilled as she seemed to be. I'd already had a few features in the press about cutting hair for the Beatles, so it was just one more bit of publicity. "Thanks for spotting it."

"The thing is," she then said, with a stern, parental I-told-you-so sort of tone, "I'm afraid someone else has spotted it too. Your boss, Roger."

I felt chilled to the bone. "What?" I spluttered.

"He's seen the pictures, and he's been on the phone to me, asking where you are."

"And what did you…" People were staring at me in the hotel's reception. I lowered my tone of voice. "What did you tell him?"

She didn't answer my question. What was the point? Roger had seen exactly where I was. He knew I'd lied.

"They want you back at the salon right away, Les," my mother said. Her heavy sigh blew over the receiver. "I think they might sack you, otherwise."

After I hung up, I couldn't join the others at the hotel bar. I felt the beer in my belly churning awfully with the mussels and chips. I stumbled back up to the room I shared with John Kelly, the tour's photographer, and lay down on my bed in a daze. As the seaside wind battered on the exposed hotel windows, I considered my options. I could take the first train back to London the next morning and try to save my job. But how could I pull out of my commitment to Paul and the other Beatles? I'd already started to tend for their hair, in preparation for the various film scenes. There's no way I could abandon them halfway through. Nor did I want to, either. I was on the Magical Mystery Tour! I was making history! On the other hand, I couldn't jeopardize my steady income and my reputation as a stylist. The occasional haircutting gigs with Paul McCartney and his bandmates weren't enough to pay my rent.

Then, just as I was beginning to regret the day I'd decided to charge the Beatles my normal styling fee, I remembered the NEMS office in which I'd taken that decision and, by association, the man who founded NEMS and launched the Beatles, Brian Epstein. Death certainly has a way of putting problems into perspective. One day you're here, the next you're gone. I looked out of the window into the black Cornish night, towards the raging sea. What did I really want to do with my life? What more could I possibly want? Wasn't this it?

If Vidal Sassoon didn't want me in his salon, I'm sure I could find some other outfit that would hire the Beatles' stylist. In any case, what did it matter if I returned the next day or at the end of the week? The damage was done. So I decided to quit moping, forced myself off the bed and rushed back down to the bar. If the Beatles had decided to go on a silly bus tour in the face of Brian Epstein's death, I certainly wasn't going to spoil the fun over a stupid row at work.

* * *

Thus, with my uncertain future hanging over me, I proceeded to make the most of the trip. Fortunately, I had plenty of distractions. For starters, there was the filming itself. As the production's unofficial stylist, I'd occasionally be called over to make sure the actors' hair looked all right on camera, often having to work in quite challenging conditions: outdoors, on windy fields and beaches, and without a proper hairdresser's chair, sink, dryer or other essential equipment. It was a good thing I'd had two months of training at my makeshift kibbutz "salon". When I wasn't needed, I'd tag along with my mate John Kelly while he took photos of the production.

One thing I hadn't counted on was that I'd have to *act* in this Beatles movie. *Excuse me? I'm in the next shot?* Oh yes, Leslie – all forty-three passengers are also characters in the film. And you're up!

Though some of the more complicated scenes were shot after the bus tour, including the music videos for 'Fool on the Hill' and 'I Am the Walrus', I did participate in plenty of silliness. In one of my first onscreen moments, I was asked to watch a conversation between Ringo and the lady who played Auntie Jessie. I wasn't given much direction, except that I should react normally. "Normally" for me, in front of a film camera and next to Ringo Starr, would have meant shaking like a leaf. But I knew what they meant, and in the end it turned out to be easier than I expected. When the camera started to roll, the two began to argue so furiously that I really did think they were having a row. I didn't have to act at all!

One of the strangest moments happened during the filming of a chaotic scene in which I and many other members of the cast kept climbing in and out of a tiny tent set up in the middle of the countryside. At one point, as I crawled out of the canvas, I noticed George Harrison sitting cross-legged in a cornfield, meditating peacefully in his oversized blue jacket, not too far from our film set. The contrast of our rowdy tent shenanigans with his transcendental chill-out moment was as surreal as anything in the film itself. I certainly couldn't have managed such a feat.

Another distraction for me during my week on the Beatles bus was little Nicola, the four-year-old I'd noticed on the first day. She was there with her mother and grandmother, Pam and Amy Smedley, who were family of the casting director. Nicola joined the tour only because Pam was unable to find a babysitter for her at short notice, during the school holidays. Nobody seemed to mind at first, nor did Nicola appreciate that she was about to become part of musical history. However, there's an old saying in Hollywood: "never work with animals or children" – and over the course of the week, our amateur crew of film-makers came to understand why.

To be fair, Nicola was a lovely child with incredibly cute, rounded cheeks, and a bright and cheerful presence on the bus. But she was just a child, after all, and occasionally became restless in the enclosed space. Though John Lennon shares a sweet moment in the film with Nicola, who plays with the white feather in his bowler hat and receives a balloon from the Beatle, the truth was that he often became quite impatient with the girl's antics. For some reason, she seemed to have become John's newest adoring fan, and kept trying to play with or around him. Once, he angrily ordered me and Ringo to quit playing a fun little game we'd started up with Nicola and a football (admittedly, the ball had struck his precious Beatle head). On another occasion, when she woke John up from a nap by pulling out his feather, he turned to me, his temper just barely under control, and said through a crooked smile: "Leslie, could you *kindly* keep that child under control?" From then on, I was designated "Chief Child Minder", a job which incidentally provided me with my greatest starring role in the film.

We shot the scene at Smedley's fish-and-chip shop in Taunton, owned by Nicola's grandparents. In this episode, I hold Nicola up to the counter, surrounded by all four Beatles, while wait-ing to be served. A bit later, and somewhat bizarrely, you can also see Nicola behind the counter, straining on her tiptoes to serve us the fish and chips herself. Unfortunately for me, the sequence wasn't included in the final cut of the movie, but these days you can watch it online. Just search for "Magical Mystery Tour Fish and Chips".

As for the Beatles themselves, it's obvious that, for many of us passengers, hanging out with them in such an enclosed space was a privilege and constant thrill. No one pestered them on board, of course, as their ubiquitous fans did at every stop – we had all been chosen as trustworthy travel companions. In our mobile backstage, we dealt with them simply as fellow human beings, and I think everyone appreciated that the band members were undergoing a trying time in their professional career.

I got the impression that the Magical Mystery Tour was Paul's project, his particular way of dealing with the challenge of Brian Epstein's untimely death, and trying to keep the Beatles united. Ringo seemed the only one to share his enthusiasm, however. After the tense moments I'd witnessed on the *Sgt. Pepper's* recordings, the band's drummer seemed transformed by the opportunity to star in this new Beatles film. A moment which stands out for me was the morning Ringo and I went down to Porth beach to watch Paul larking around on a tandem with George the dwarf. The two Beatles were in such a cheerful, playful mood, you would have never guessed that their manager had died only a couple of weeks before.

John and George, however, were clearly disengaged from Paul's film-making experiment. George Harrison seemed to have chosen a different way of coping with the uncertainty of the Beatles' future: retreating to an alternative plane of consciousness. Whether sitting cross-legged in a field, or simply zoning out in the bus, he looked pretty detached from the production of the film or the school-outing atmosphere. By then, he was reaching the high point of his passion for Eastern mysticism, and I got the feeling he would have rather been back at the Maharishi's ashram instead of travelling around Devon and Cornwall on a crowded bus.

As for John, he spent much of his time napping or looking distracted, and I've already mentioned the grumpiness that would occasionally flare out into angry outbursts. Unlike Paul and Ringo, who mixed with all of us more freely, John hung out almost exclusively with an odd character sporting a big blond moustache called Alexis Mardas. This Greek artist (and possibly con artist) presented himself as a kind of electronics wizard, promising the Beatles to build them a 72-track studio, among other far-out innovations. To fulfil such promises, "Magic Alex" had recently been named the head of Apple Electronics, the technology branch of the new corporation they were beginning to set up. Mainly though, he seemed to have become John Lennon's latest guru. Apparently, John would spend hours tripping on acid and looking into the "Nothing Box", a plastic cube with randomly flashing lights Magic Alex had designed. Mardas was also responsible for Paul's "holiday" with the other Beatles in Greece that summer. He'd convinced them to buy a Greek island, and then brokered the deal with the country's government.

Among other bizarre ideas Magic Alex supposedly proposed to the Beatles, such as building a flying saucer or manufacturing invisibility paint, it has been said he offered them a system that would create a force field around their homes. I don't know if those rumours are true, but during the Magical Mystery Tour I got the impression he was definitely trying to create a force field around John Lennon, so that no one else could get too close. Reflecting back on it now, I think it's ironic that Lennon was often considered to be the most dominant of the four Beatles. To me, he always seemed under the spell of some "guru" figure or other: Magic Alex, Yoko Ono or the Maharishi Mahesh Yogi – first admired on the Magical Mystery Tour as the "Fool on the Hill" and later criticized in the White Album as "Sexy Sadie". Each of these figures has received some blame for the Beatles' eventual breakup, but perhaps the real cause, or part of it, was John Lennon's fascination for charismatic characters, who would lead him in new and unexpected directions. The question is, though: would their world-changing music have ever been possible without such a tendency?

* * *

Ironically, the musical memories I have of the Magical Mystery Tour have nothing to do with any Beatles songs at all. There was plenty of raucous singing on the bus, and we all joined in enthusiastically, but the tunes were mainly old music-hall classics such as 'Toot, Toot, Tootsie!' or 'When Irish Eyes Are Smiling', accompanied by Shirley Evans's accordion. In fact, after the bus tour, Paul and John were inspired to write a song for her, appropriately named 'Shirley's Wild Accordion'. On the recording, which unfortunately never made it into the film or the album, Paul can be heard shouting: "Go on Shirl!" – something he also used to shout on the bus during the boisterous sing-along sessions.

Perhaps the most memorable musical moment was provided by Spencer Davis, whose group had recently published the hit single 'Keep on Running'. The Beatles knew Spencer, and he happened to be on holiday nearby, so he invited us to come down for the evening to a pub owned by his family. Though the cast and crew were exhausted from the hard day's filming, a few of us made our way from the Atlantic Hotel to the nearby Tywarnhayle Inn. Spencer had told the pub regulars to expect a surprise, but he didn't give them any details, so when Paul McCartney and Ringo Starr suddenly strode into the place, the entire pub fell quiet – and then, a few seconds later, it erupted into a great, noisy hullabaloo.

Paul bought a pint of beer and made straight for the piano. Plonking the beer down on top of it, he announced that he was now the resident pianist. With that, he kicked off the evening with a rendition of 'Knees Up Mother Brown'. Ringo quickly joined his fellow Beatle, playing an old mandolin he found lying in the corner, which only had one string. At first, the pub-goers just listened in stunned silence, but soon all inhibitions were put aside and an enthusiastic chorus ensued. Apart from 'Yellow Submarine', which Paul refused to play, we must have sung every song in the books. It was only when Ringo drunkenly announced that he had worn his finger away to a bleeding pulp on the mandolin that we all decided to lurch back home. It must have been at least 2 a.m., and I expect the Tywarnhayle Inn had never seen such a "lock-in".

*   *   *

Our Magical Mystery Tour ended on Friday 15th September, and our return trip was as jolly as our departure. There was plenty of beer on the coach, and Shirley led us in a few final rousing sing-alongs. Eventually, though, we dropped off George, John and Ringo at their homes in Virginia Water, and the coach headed into London. As we hit the familiar traffic of the capital, the magic and the mystery soon faded away, replaced by the reality of the city's straight roads and vertical tower blocks. As I peeked out guiltily through the glass windows, I felt myself sinking into my seat. I was in deep trouble, and there was no more escaping it. The Summer of Love was over for good.

I called first thing in the morning. It was a Saturday, and I heard the buzz of the hectic salon in the background as soon as Stephen Way, the deputy manager, picked up the phone.

"Hello," I said, hesitantly. "Um… it's Leslie here. I'm back."

"Ah, Leslie," he said, a bit tersely. "I have a message for you from Roger."

"Oh, I see," I said. "What is it?"

"He says you're sacked. I'm sorry, Leslie… but, you must understand. You took time off without permission, and that kind of behaviour can't be allowed at the salon."

My nightmare had come true. I was out of a job. I mentally waved goodbye to my swinging Chelsea life, my professional standing, most of my celebrity clients, perhaps even the Beatles.

"Wait… Stephen…" I added before he could hang up. "Could you book me an appointment with Mr Sassoon? I need to talk to him."

As soon as I received the confirmation that Vidal had agreed to meet me, I jumped into my Mini and rushed over to the Bond Street salon. Vidal was waiting in his office, impeccably dressed as always, in his dark suit. He stood up with a pained expression, like that of a doctor forced to repeat a hopeless diagnosis. But before he could speak, I took the initiative.

"Mr Sassoon, when I asked you for permission to volunteer in Israel, you promised to keep my job open, and you were true to your word. Now, as you know, my work with Paul McCartney and the other Beatles has brought us excellent publicity in magazines and newspapers. When journalists ask how to quote me,

I've always told them to write 'Hair by Leslie at Vidal Sassoon'. I could easily have said 'Hair by Leslie Cavendish' and take all the credit, but I didn't. I've always been as loyal to you as you have been to me."

Vidal remained silent, so I continued.

"Now, I know I've made a mistake, and I'm sorry. I was afraid to ask for an additional leave of absence. It was stupid of me, but I didn't know how else to act. In any case, that's not why Roger wants me out. He resents me because I took over doing Jane Asher's hair, and subsequently Paul McCartney's and the Beatles. I'm convinced of it."

Vidal still didn't say a word.

"And let's face it, Mr Sassoon," I concluded, "we have plenty of new clients, pop stars and actors, thanks to the publicity I've brought in. So… would you please reconsider giving me another chance?"

Vidal had been listening intently. At last he spoke, in his usual whisper.

"I tell you what I will do. I will have a word with Roger, and let you know."

I left the salon in a daze, drained as if I'd spent the entire week cutting hair non-stop, twenty-four hours a day, instead of touring on a coach with the Beatles. I couldn't imagine Roger changing his mind, but at least I was satisfied that I'd done all I could. I was ready to look for new employment, if that was what was required.

On the following day, and to my great surprise, Roger called me. He must have been seething with rage, but his tone was cold and flat.

"Hello, Leslie. You can come back to the salon."

He was never to forgive me.

* * *

Magical Mystery Tour premiered on television on 26th December 1967, as that year's BBC Christmas Special. A few days before it aired, a launch party was held at the Royal Lancaster Hotel, to which I was invited along with all the rest of the Beatles-styled "merry pranksters". The invitation had such a trippy design, however, that I failed to notice an important written instruction among the streaming rays, whirling curlicues and flowers.

The day of the party, Paul called me over to 7 Cavendish Avenue so I could style his hair in preparation for the event. We were both quite excited at the prospect of seeing the edited cut of our late-summer outing on the big screen, and while I worked on his hair, we reminisced about the bus getting stuck on the bridge, the accordion sing-alongs, Nicola's antics and other stories.

Later, as we hung out in his living room, the Beatle asked me a surprising question.

"So, what are you wearing to the launch party, Leslie?"

I was a little taken aback. Paul had never shown any interest in my clothes before.

"Er, I haven't thought about it," I said.

"Well you'd better think quick!" he chuckled, confusing me even further. "Jane and I are going as the Pearly King and Queen."

The Pearly King and Queen? Why would Paul?... Unless?... Oh, no.

"You did realize it was fancy dress, didn't you?" he asked.

I clapped my hand over my forehead.

"No," I said. "And I haven't got anything to wear!"

As Paul burst into laughter, Jane walked into the living room. When he told her about my oversight, she suggested an idea.

"Maybe we've got something he could use," she said.

"Yeah, Leslie," Paul agreed enthusiastically, "why don't you go upstairs and have a look in my wardrobe?"

"Really?" I asked, a bit embarrassed.

"Yeah, go ahead," he said, waving me in the direction of the stairs.

"Paul's got plenty of odd stuff up there," Jane said, as she snuggled up to her boyfriend on the couch. The two were just about to announce their engagement, so they were at the height of their romance.

Crikey. It felt odd going up to Paul and Jane's bedroom on my own and pulling open his wardrobe. Jane hadn't been exaggerating either. The rack was full of the most extravagant floral-print jackets, colourful velvet trousers and frilly silk shirts the cream of Sixties fashion designers could cook up while tripping on acid. These were the outlandish clothes Paul would wear to album launches, celebrity parties and other big press events. Along the King's Road, I'd often pass by some of the trendy "peacock revolution" boutiques that exhibited such outfits in their window displays: Hung on You, Granny Takes a Trip and Dandie Fashions. Their freewheeling experiments could certainly be mistaken for fancy-dress costumes.

Suddenly, my hand, absently roving over the shoulders of the hanging jackets, grazed over something that seemed unmistakably familiar: an epaulet with a broad bullion fringe of little silver tassels. I unhooked the hanger from the rack, revealing the sky-blue satin jacket, silver buttons and braided pink macramé rope.

Oh my. It was Paul's *Sgt. Pepper* coat. I got a shiver just thinking about the idea of putting it on.

Instinctively, I looked over towards the door of the bedroom, as if I were about to nick the crown jewels from the Tower of London. Dared I do it? Could I see myself attending the *Magical Mystery Tour* launch party dressed as Paul on the *Pepper* cover? I wasn't sure this was what my client had in mind when he'd said that I might find "something I could use" in his wardrobe. But perhaps I could just try it on? For a few minutes? I was all on my own up there, after all. No one would ever know.

Before I knew it, I'd thrust my arm through the satin sleeve. Wow, that felt good! Then the other. The coat reached down almost to my knees. I did up the buttons, bringing together the five horizontal silver bars across the chest. It was a bit tight on me, but a good enough fit, all in all. By then, I'd whistled my way through half of 'Lucy in the Sky with Diamonds', and I have to say that, as my heart pounded into the chest, I felt like this magical outfit had transported me into a different world – as if, by putting it on, in Paul's own bedroom, I'd stepped into his skin. My hands grabbed an imaginary guitar, left-handed, as Paul was and I'd always been. I shook my head, on stage, making my hair fly around to the rhythm: *Now let me introduce to you the one and only Billy Shears from Sgt. Pepper's Lonely Hearts Club Baaaand!*

Life really could be strange. In that very room, I had suggested to Paul that he go on his trip to France and Africa in disguise. Right on that chair, I'd cut his hair, transforming him into someone else, someone who couldn't be recognized as Paul McCartney. This jacket I was wearing became part of that new disguise. And yet now, by putting the thing on, it was I who became Paul McCartney.

When I stepped in front of the full-length mirror on the wall, however, the illusion was broken. I saw my familiar mug popping out of the gaudy, ill-fitting coat and thought: *What the hell are you thinking, Leslie? You can't bloody well turn up at the launch party looking like that!*

I quickly undid the buttons, took the jacket off and put it back on the hanger. In fact, I decided I didn't want to wear anything of Paul's. That evening, I dressed up in the fanciest outfit I kept at home for special occasions: a double-breasted suit from Paul the Tailor in fashionable Berwick Street, a pink shirt from John Michael, a tie from Turnbull & Asser and boots from Pinet of Bond Street. Not quite as amusing as Ringo and Maureen, who came as a circus master and a Native American squaw. But at least I looked smart and dignified.

Do I regret not having worn Paul's *Sgt. Pepper* outfit to that party? Not really. I'm sure I made the right choice. Nevertheless, I will admit that, occasionally, I still daydream about strutting into the Royal Lancaster Hotel looking like Billy Shears.

* * *

When *Magical Mystery Tour* was aired on Boxing Day, the surreal, hour-long program caused a nationwide scandal, as if the Beatles had been found spiking Santa Claus's mulled wine with Purple Haze. The BBC switchboard was flooded with calls from angry, baffled viewers. "Blatant rubbish!" declared the *Daily Express*. "Chaotic," echoed the *Daily Mirror*. "A colossal conceit," the *Daily Mail* huffed. For the first time in their career, the Beatles had flopped, and Paul even offered a kind of apology on the BBC a few days later: "We don't say it was a good film. It was our first attempt. If we goofed, then we goofed. It was a challenge, and it didn't come off. We'll know better next time."

The movie has improved enormously with the passage of time. In the post-MTV world, the Beatles' surreal video segments seem fun and quirky but familiar. Also, we can now enjoy the Beatles' trippy romp in all of its wild, colourful glory, whereas in 1967 the BBC decided to broadcast it in black and white, colour TV sets still being quite rare. So you might say that the Magical Mystery Tour was so ahead of its time that very few people understood what the Beatles were trying to do. In my own home, the showing proceeded in an atmosphere of embarrassed silence, broken only by Grandma Debbie's reaction each time I appeared: "There's our Les!"

Even on that Boxing Day in 1967, though, I never thought it was so awful, nor did most young people. For us, the establishment's outrage at this "utter rubbish" only confirmed how strait-laced British society was, how conservative and out of touch with themselves, and also how threatened they felt by a wave of change that was inexplicably washing over them, overwhelming even sacred institutions like Christmas, or the crusty BBC itself. The Beatles had become like the "Fool on the Hill": *nobody seems to like him, but the eyes in his head see the world spinning round, and he knows that they're the fools.*

And another thing: didn't anyone notice the excellent hairstyling of the cast?

9

The Real Yellow Submarine

Long before the MacBook and iPhones, when Steve Jobs was still a nerdy teenager, there existed another Apple Corporation, known as the Apple Corps. It was every bit as influential, ambitious and revolutionary as the technological powerhouse from Cupertino would come to be, representing a whole new way of doing business that seemed ready to change the world for ever. But it wasn't based in California. It was in London. And it was headed not by one charismatic leader, but by four: John Lennon, Paul McCartney, George Harrison and Ringo Starr.

In 1967, the Beatles decided to go into business, big time. They were motivated initially by the "taxman" they'd lampooned in the opening track to *Revolver*. The line "there's one for you, nineteen for me" refers to the fact that, in those pre-Thatcher days, the members of the band were paying the 95% "supertax" imposed by Harold Wilson's government. Their accountants advised the Beatles to invest their money into some kind of productive venture, instead of just giving it away to Inland Revenue. Initially, they thought of setting up a chain of shops that would sell Beatles-branded T-shirts, caps and fridge magnets. Such a materialistic enterprise seemed too restrictive for the Beatles, however. If they were forced to set up a business, they figured, why not take the opportunity to set off a new revolution?

Soon, the Fab Four were announcing their vision worldwide, in TV interviews and press ads. They were inaugurating something they called Apple Corps, comprised of Apple Records, Apple Publishing, Apple Films, Apple Electronics and Apple Retail. Through this idealistic new corporation, they would help aspiring artists, poets, songwriters, film-makers and inventors fulfil their dreams. No longer would young, scruffy talent be turned away by the cigar-smoking gatekeepers of big business. Apple Corps would listen to their ideas, finance their projects and bring to the spotlight the marginalized geniuses of this generation. To get the ball rolling, Apple Records put out an ad campaign, calling for all hopeful musicians to mail in their demo tapes. With this open invitation to the world's creative youngsters, the new hippy start-up demonstrated that it wouldn't behave like any other corporation on the planet. "A mix of business and enjoyment", they called it, a "controlled weirdness" and a kind of "Western communism". "We're in the happy position of not needing any more money," McCartney explained during the press launch. "So, for the first time, the bosses aren't in it for profit. We've already bought all our dreams. We want to share that possibility with others." Perhaps they didn't realize how many kids would throw their dreams at them, however. The management of the new start-up was quickly forced to rent out new office space just to make room for the thousands of boxes and padded envelopes that began to flood in through the mail.

I was a frequent visitor to Apple, from its start in a small, old-fashioned office in Baker Street to the lavish headquarters it moved into less than a year later at 3 Savile Row, right between all the fancy bespoke tailors of London. At first, I'd be called up for actual hairdressing work, whether for one of the Beatles or for office staff, who would sometimes sit in a row, five or six at a time, as I worked on their hair. After a while, though, it just became a place for me to hang out after my day at the salon, the perfect chill-out spot in the heart of London, where I could unwind in the company of the grooviest people in the world. Rather than a corporate headquarters, Apple felt more like the "yellow submarine" the Beatles had sung about: a group of friends all having a good time in their own little vessel, surrounded by music and general bonhomie.

The epicentre of what has been described as "the longest cocktail party" in history was undoubtedly Apple's press room, commandeered by the Beatles PR man Derek Taylor. Here was where the endless stream of journalists, artists, collaborators, fans and loafers who passed through the place were treated to copious quantities of Scotch-and-Coke, Derek's favourite daytime tipple, from the well-stocked liquor cabinet. Joints were also on offer, courtesy of a quiet type known as Stocky, who would sit in the lotus position on top of the big grey filing cabinet, to roll what were known as his "Benson and hashish B52 bombers". And if you required an even stronger chemical high, that too could be discreetly procured.

That's not to say that the work didn't get done. Behind Derek's general affability and drinking there lay a shrewd mind and a vast knowledge of the music business, which he'd garnered during his time in Los Angeles doing PR for bands like the Beach Boys and the Byrds. At Apple, his press-office staff must have processed a thousand calls a day. Those phones never stopped ringing, bringing wave upon wave of reporters asking for interviews, businessmen with "irresistible" proposals, penniless artists and assorted nut-jobs who had been contacted by aliens or elves and needed to relay a world-saving message to George Harrison. They didn't just call, either, but often turned up in person at the entrance downstairs, or even managed to get past the overwhelmed receptionists and demanded to see one of the Beatles at once. Derek was a master at fielding this constant barrage, ever the charming host of his never-ending party, however chaotic things got. This is the man who had to face the British press, as Beatles spokesman, during the shock of Paul McCartney's breakup with Jane Asher, the ridicule surrounding their Indian guru, the scandal of John and Yoko's "obscene" nude photos, the humiliating drug busts, the absurd but insistent "Paul is dead" rumours, the growing tensions among the four Beatles and their eventual separation. And yet, he seemed actually to enjoy the chaos – something I was able to confirm when he first invited me to his home in Sunningdale and introduced me to his five (later six) children and his donkey. Derek carried it all off with boundless energy, awe-inspiring grace and an impeccable appearance, the last of which I often contributed to as his hairdresser.

* * *

I have Derek Taylor to thank for introducing me to a lady who was to become a great friend of mine: Chris O'Dell. Like a lot of people at the Apple Corps, this friendly Californian blonde just turned up at the reception one morning, with no money and nowhere to stay. She'd befriended Derek while working for him in Los Angeles, so he helped her out initially by booking her a hotel room, and then asked me if I might put her up at my place for a bit while she got settled in London.

Around that time, in 1968, I'd had one of the luckiest breaks of my life. As you might have gathered, lucky breaks were being tossed at me in that period as regularly as Stocky's B52 Bombers, but this one was the size of the biggest joint I ever saw him roll. Since I'd moved to my tiny Chelsea studio, I'd often go out on the town with my friend Eddie, a dressmaker who was part of the local gay scene, the entirety of which eventually suspected I had become Eddie's new boyfriend. Through Eddie I got to know people like Vicky Wickham, the producer of the iconic TV show *Ready Steady Go!*, and the soul singer Dusty Springfield, who was at the height of her fame at the time. One night, Eddie invited me along to a dinner outing at the Casserole, together with a group of friends including Dusty and her girlfriend Norma Tanega, a singer most noted for her single 'Walkin' My Cat Named Dog'.

At the restaurant, I found myself sitting next to Dusty's brother Tom Springfield, a songwriter whose film *Georgy Girl* had recently become a huge hit. He seemed rather preoccupied that evening.

"What's up with you, Tom?" I asked him.

"I've got so much to do, and not enough time to do it," he confessed grimly. "I'm about to go off to South America to promote *Georgy Girl*, you see."

"Tom, you've really got it, tough!" I said, with a chuckle.

"Yeah, OK." He lifted his hands in self-defence. "But I've got my mother's flat to unload, and we're going away in ten days' time!"

"Unload?"

"I need to sell it. It's in Dover Court."

"I don't believe it, I live opposite there, in Meriden Court," I replied. "And funnily enough, the lease on my flat is up soon. I'd be interested myself, if I had the money."

"Oh, that's perfect, Leslie! Why don't you have a look at the place?"

"Well, fine, but... I wouldn't be able to afford it."

Tom didn't give up. On the contrary, he grabbed my shirt sleeve, almost desperate.

"Look, I'm in a rush, Leslie. Come over in the morning. If you like the place, all I'm asking is that you pay the lawyer's fees and you can have it."

I couldn't believe what I was hearing. "You want to give me your flat for free? Are you joking, Tom?"

It turned out he wasn't. These successful show-business types obviously had so much cash lying around that giving away a flat in Chelsea was, to them, nothing but a huge relief. The lawyers' fees turned out to be £50. And that's all I paid for my first piece of real estate, in the trendiest neighbourhood in London...

So when Derek asked me if I wouldn't mind letting his destitute Californian friend crash in my spare room, I was more than happy to oblige. I was feeling indebted to the universe, and could still hardly believe that I actually owned a flat just off the King's Road. Moreover, Chris O'Dell seemed like the most entertaining sort of flatmate imaginable, and it didn't take a genius to figure out that she'd come down from California with a Summer of Love mentality. While she became a sort of collective personal assistant at Apple Corps, thanks to her amazing organizational skills, fun-loving attitude and astounding tolerance to alcohol and drugs, we became best of friends, and often spent time together as part of the Beatles' entourage, both at the office, in the recording studios and, of course, at home. I can even confess to have joined her star-studded list of lovers – which eventually included Mick Jagger, Bob Dylan and Ringo Starr – for about five and a half minutes.

*   *   *

Chris lived her life intensely, whether on or off LSD – and it was often on. Moreover, she had a knack for getting herself into the thick of things. She happened to be at Trident Studios, for instance, during the recording of 'Hey Jude', and was asked to take up a microphone as part of its boisterous final chorus. She was also on the Apple rooftop during the Beatles' final concert, and even in Ringo's kitchen when George admitted to his bandmate that he was sleeping with the drummer's wife. So it's not surprising that she was also involved in many of my most memorable anecdotes from that period, such as the Beatle-smuggling episode at the Club dell'Aretusa I recounted in Chapter 4. The story that stands out most vividly in my mind, however, had to do with the extended visit of the Hells Angels to the world of the Beatles.

The Savile Row offices were always inhabited by an odd assortment of characters. The more or less official staff included experienced showbiz types like Derek Taylor and Ron Kass, who headed Apple Records, old Liverpool chums like Neil Aspinall (then the managing director of Apple Corps), Mal Evans and Alistair Taylor. There was also the Greek technology wizard Alexis Mardas building a 72-track studio in the basement, the bad-tempered and often dangerously drunk photo coordinator Jeremy Banks, the heavy-set doorman-bouncer Jimmy Clark, an ex-Apple Scruff who had managed to get herself a job in the kitchen, an astrologer employed to tell everyone's fortune – and even, if you can believe it, a resident hairdresser who wouldn't stop jabbering about Queens Park Rangers. Another category was the artists being promoted by Apple Records, such as the stoned-out American hippy James Taylor and the young and innocent Welsh folk singer Mary Hopkin, but also the entire group of devotees from the Radha Krishna Temple, who might be heard chanting mantras up and down the apple-green car-peted steps of the building at any given time. This stable crowd was granted some daily variety by the occasional visitors:

reporters and DJs, both long- and short-haired depending on the media channel, suited-up businessmen, photographers coming in to show off their portfolios to Jeremy Banks, and the continuous catwalk of aspiring artists, poets, hippies, fans and weirdos trying to hustle their way through to the Fab Four. Last, but obviously not least, came the elusive Beatles themselves, who only occasionally set foot in their headquarters – inevitably rousing both staff and visitors into frenzy.

Once in a while, however, there would be a special guest at the Apple offices, not necessarily invited by anyone but somehow accepted into the fold. Usually they were short visits, as when the American actress Lauren Bacall turned up with her children to meet the four famous Liverpudlians – I mean, who could say no to Mrs Bacall and the teenage Leslie Bogart? Some of these special visitors, however, took up residence in the guest room, right above the press office, for extended periods of time. Such was the case of Emily, a red-headed Californian hippy "momma", her chilled-out husband Frank and their four children aged zero to fifteen. While tripping on acid, they had hatched a plan of retiring to the Fiji Islands with John Lennon and Yoko Ono. So they had stopped by London to pick up the famous couple, and wouldn't listen to anyone's sensible explanations about John and Yoko's busy schedule. In the meantime, they made use of the guest room's record player and the tasty food prepared in the kitchen just next door by the two cordonbleu chefs employed at Apple.

It was around that same time, in December 1968, that the Hells Angels descended upon us. This notorious outlaw motorcycle club was rumoured to have been involved in all kinds of criminal activity in the United States. A couple of years earlier, Hunter S. Thompson had published a book in which these "righteous dudes" were portrayed as a gang of lawless thugs who tore around the country raping, pillaging and brawling like a band of twentieth-century Vikings. "People will just have to learn to stay out of our way," one of them was quoted as saying. "We'll bust up everyone who gets in our way." Now, they'd crossed the Atlantic for the first time, and their "way" was going to rip right through the Apple offices.

The first news I had of the Angels was when my little Mini turned into Savile Row one afternoon and came across two impressive Harley-Davidsons hogging up the parking spaces near the entrance, their massive exhaust pipes tilted menacingly at the gentlemen in bowler hats and tailored suits who gaped at this unseemly invasion. When I reached the press office, the ceiling appeared ready to crash down from the loud music, stomping and shouting overhead.

"What's going on?" I asked Derek. "It sounds like a riot up there."

"Oh," he said, shrugging, while holding the phone up to his ear. "It seems George invited the Hells Angels over, while he was recording in California with Jackie Lomax."

"Why would he do that?"

"He never thought they'd take up the invitation. But they certainly did. Apparently, they've caused mayhem on their flight over. They've turned it into some kind of Red Indian powwow. They even brought their machines over."

"I saw them parked outside..."

"We had to pay customs to let those bikes through, if you can believe it. Well, at least George sent a memo to warn us all."

He showed me a copy of George's note, which explained that twelve members of the gang would be stopping over in London on the way to "straighten out" the volatile political situation in Czechoslovakia, where the Prague Spring reforms had been crushed by the invasion of Warsaw Pact troops and tanks. George asked the Apple management to welcome the Angels in, with assurances that, while these chain-toting bikers may look pretty fierce, they were actually a good bunch of lads. Nevertheless, he warned the staff not to let the Angels "take control of Savile Row".

I ran up the steps and found the guest room packed with people dancing, lying on the floor and getting through several crates of beer. The whole place stank of patchouli oil. In the end, it turned out that only two of them were proper Hells Angels: Bill Fritch (aka "Sweet William Tumbleweed") and Peter Knell ("Frisco Pete"), both formidable characters sporting shoulder-length, unwashed hair and outfitted in their trademark black-leather jackets with a winged death's head on the back. They were accompanied, however, by what they called the "Pleasure Crew", sixteen Californian hedonists straight out of Haight-Ashbury: guitars, suckling babies and dazed smiles all round. The crew even included Ken Kesey, whose acid-soaked bus trip had inspired the Magical Mystery Tour, as well as Rock Scully, manager of the Grateful Dead. From what I could see, there was no immediate danger of the building being razed to the ground, but still, I remained wary of this wild bunch during the remainder of their stay. To the dismay of the Apple management, who didn't know how to get rid of them, this visit stretched out to weeks and then months.

Then, one evening, things got a little hairier. Literally. As I approached my apartment after work, I was struck by the sight of two Harley-Davidsons chained to a lamp-post. They bore a worrying resemblance to the outlandish machines I had seen outside the Apple offices – and, in fact, turned out to be the very same.

Oh no, Chris, I thought. *Please don't tell me you've invited the Hells Angels into my flat.*

Sure enough, as I came in through the front door, I was greeted by a wave of patchouli scent and blasts of raucous laughter. Through the haze of smoke I recognized Sweet William Tumbleweed, Frisco Pete, my flatmate Chris O'Dell and a girl called Frankie Hart, who was part of the Pleasure Crew, as well as the girlfriend of Bob Weir of the Grateful Dead. The four of them had settled comfortably into my sofa and armchairs, and appeared to be in a worryingly relaxed state of mind. They all held Budweiser beers in their hands, and Jefferson Airplane's 'White Rabbit' was blasting out of my stereo system at maximum volume. Chris jumped up and introduced me to our guests.

"Hi there," Frankie smiled, giving me the peace sign. "Chris told us you're cutting the Beatles' hair."

"Yeah, that's far out, man," said Sweet William, clapping my hand in his with the force of a controlled punch.

"Wanna beer, Les?" Pete asked me, his thick fingers curling around an unopened bottle of Bud.

Les? I hate being called "Les". I always have done. I am *Leslie*, and only my mother gets to call me "Les". On this occasion, though, I decided to let it pass. Perhaps it was the sight of the "1%" patch on Frisco Pete's leather jacket. As I'd been informed, it refers to a statement once made by the American Motorcycle Association, to the effect that 99% of motorcyclists are law-abiding citizens. The Hells Angels, presumably, belonged to the *other* one per cent. So when Pete cracked open the bottle on the edge of my coffee table, I let that pass too.

I swigged on my lager and pulled up a chair – all the comfy seats had been taken by my unexpected guests. I felt like my flat had been boarded by pirates, and that only thanks to their generous magnanimity was I allowed to stick around and share a drink. How long were they going to stay? I hadn't been in their presence for more than a couple of minutes, and already I was feeling decidedly uncomfortable. As the sinister Jefferson Airplane guitars kept droning and Grace Slick crooned on mysteriously about magical pills and smoking caterpillars, the invading brutes on the couch just smiled at me, moving their big heads to the rhythm, as if waiting for me to say something. But I was at a loss for words. How do you make small talk with a couple of Hells Angels? They probably weren't going to be too interested in the Queens Park Rangers' promotion to the First Division, however unprecedented. No, I simply couldn't imagine myself spending the entire evening in the company of these motorized gangsters.

"I saw your... um... wheels outside," I stammered at one point, trying to act cool. "Great bikes, man."

Chris giggled into a cushion. The new rogue captains of my ship just nodded and smiled, tolerant of me for now, though clearly willing to throw me overboard if displeased.

Fortunately, the alcohol began to kick in. I relaxed into their vibe, and once the marijuana came out, things went a lot more smoothly. I was, after all, a big fan of the Grateful Dead, so it turned out we had a lot to talk about. As we listened to the Dead's latest album, *Anthem of the Sun,* I told them of how Chris had once met the band's guitarist Bob Weir at Apple and brought him home so I could cut his hair. It had been one of my first experiences of working with the very long, shoulder-length style that was becoming so fashionable that year. Unfortunately, during that haircut, I'd started to rave about Jerry Garcia, the Dead's lead singer. Bob Weir had got offended, and indignantly told me that he co-wrote all of the band's music with Jerry. As I finished telling the story, the Hells Angels broke up

Publicity photo for the opening of the Apple hairdressing salon
at 161 King's Road, Chelsea.

The shop front of the Apple Tailoring shop in Chelsea (above).
Downstairs at the entrance of the Apple hairdressing salon (below left).
Partying with John Lennon, Amanda Lear, George Harrison and John Crittle
in our shop after its inauguration at the Aretusa Club (below right).

Relaxing in my Chelsea apartment (above left). On my way to Switzerland with my friend Ellen Sherman and her friend Barry (top right). The "courtesy" card given to me by Frisco Pete (above right). Landing in Ibiza with Chris O'Dell (below left). Snipping the hair of Formula One world champion James Hunt in his villa in Marbella (below right).

Some precious memorabilia from my time as the Beatles hairdresser (clock-wise from the top left): my Dave Clark Five Christmas card (front and inside); Heather McCartney's card, which she drew for me while I was cutting her daddy's hair; Paul McCartney's enigmatic dedication to my cousin Lynn on the inner sleeve of his personal copy of the *Revolver* album; my "Summer of Love" Christmas card from Peter Asher, Jane's brother.

Ernie and his playmate Martha: Ernie fondly embraced by my then girlfriend Louisa Rabaiotti (above left); Paul and his beloved sheepdog Martha at his home on Cavendish Avenue (above right).

At the Mirage Hotel in Las Vegas after attending the Cirque du Soleil's celebrated Beatles show *Love*.

With the cast of the *Let It Be* musical in the cast's dressing room at the Savoy Theatre in London.

Strumming the Gretsch guitar John Lennon used during the recording of 'Paperback Writer', now owned by Jim Irsay.

Leaving after a visit to Abbey Road Studios (above left). Standing at the entrance to Paul McCartney's auditiorium in the Liverpool Institute of Performing Arts, the former school where Paul and George studied in the 1950s (above right).

Sitting outside the Liverpool Art College on Mount Street, where John Lennon studied and first played with Paul and George.

Standing with my childhood friend and fellow "crimper" Lawrence Falk outside
John and Yoko's apartment in Montague Square, London (2017).

into uproarious laughter. *Maybe George Harrison was right*, I thought, feeling pretty stoned by then. *Maybe these rough-looking hulks aren't so bad after all*. I even began to fantasize about joining their Pleasure Crew sometime, on a tour along Route 66, struggling to tame their greasy, undomesticated manes in the shade of rusty desert gas stations.

Only one minor worry occasionally surfaced at the edges of my zonked-out mind. What would happen if a local police officer noticed all of the illegal smoke billowing out of my windows, and the two evil-looking choppers parked near my flat? A couple of months earlier, John and Yoko had got busted by Detective Sergeant Pilcher, the head of the London Drugs Squad, who had previously arrested Donovan and Mick Jagger. What if Pilcher now had his sights set on the Hells Angels?

By then, though, the psychedelic rock was chilling me out; the atmosphere was getting as friendly as that of a Californian Be-In, and any traces of paranoia quickly vanished. In fact, I let my defences melt down a bit too far around my buzzing brain.

"Hey, man, you know what?" I blurted out to Sweet William at one point, with the drawl of an American outlaw, "I've never actually been on a Harley."

As soon as the words had left my mouth, I tried to suck them back in, drawing the bitter pot smoke deep into my lungs and setting off a coughing fit. Why the hell had I just said that? Still coughing, I sat up, fully alert again. Spaced out, but somehow fully alert.

"Are you kiddin' me, Les?" Sweet William stroked his little compact beard and ground his teeth with a pained expression, as if such a virginal state of affairs just couldn't be allowed. "Come on, let's go for a ride. Chris has already been out with us. We had a blast, didn't we, baby?"

"Um... yeah, great fun," she nodded, a bit too emphatically. "You should definitely have a go, Leslie."

I knew Chris well enough by then to suspect that something was up. She loved to pull my leg, but I wasn't about to be taken in. That strangeness in her voice was warning me off. I took a deep breath and screwed up my courage.

"Actually, you know what?" I said, looking into Sweet William's tough-guy face, which showed every sign of having been pummelled by a million miles of wind, rain and desert sun all across the American highway system. "Thanks, but no thanks. It's too cold out there and, well... I'm not quite sure my debut should be on a Harley."

There was a long silence then, filled in only by a cascading drum solo from the Grateful Dead's 'Alligator'. But then, to my immense relief, the Angel let it drop.

"Whatever, man..." he said, making my sofa creak as he collapsed back onto it.

Maybe Sweet William didn't feel like going out into the chilly London air either. Maybe I'd blown my coolness and he decided I wasn't worth his Harley. For whatever reason, I was mercifully reprieved. And it was just as well, because, as Chris later revealed to me in the kitchen, her ride on the back of his bike had been a horrifying experience. They'd both been tripping on acid, and she was convinced at every moment that they were about to meet the real death's head at the end of a fiery crash.

"But they're not on acid now, are they?" I asked.

"Of course they are!" She laughed, bringing out some munchies into the living room. "We took a few tabs before you came in."

My mind spun at the thought of the suicidal ride I'd just managed to avoid. This girl really was consuming too many drugs.

And taking her Sixties experimentation too far. I mean, living life to the full was one thing, but cruising through the streets of London with a tripped-out Hells Angel was quite another. I needed to give her another of my flatmate-to-flatmate talks. But this wasn't the time or the place.

I followed Chris back to the main party. Then, just a few minutes later, she said, in front of the whole crew, as cool as anything: "Do you mind if the guys crash here tonight, Leslie?"

I looked at my flatmate helplessly, and then at the hulking hoods that had taken possession of my couch. What was I to do? Look an Angel in the eye and tell him to leave?

"No, of course, you're welcome to stay," I said.

So we sat around for another while, listening to their fantastic stories of rumbles over pool tables, a dog-eating rival gang and run-ins with the California Highway Patrol. Everyone they talked about seemed to have names like Buzzard, Crazy Cross, Filthy Phil or Charlie the Child Molester. Deep into the night, as they finally grew drowsy, we found them a place to sleep. I spread out my collection of Moroccan cushions around the floor, and Chris and I threw a patchwork quilt over the three of them. They were soon sleeping like babies – and snoring like a trio of Harley-Davidson Knucklehead V-Twin engines.

"How long do you suppose they're going to stay with us, Chris?" I asked my flatmate with grave concern.

"Oh, don't sweat it, Leslie. Not more than a month or two…" She giggled, and disappeared into her room with another lit joint in her hand.

When I woke up the next morning, I was afraid to open my bedroom door and face the sight of those motorcycle gangsters still sprawled all over the floor. To my surprise, though, they were already up and about, helping themselves to some toast and coffee. By mid-morning, they'd grabbed their bikes and roared away towards Savile Row. Just before they left, Pete handed me something I could never have imagined even existed: a Hells Angel calling card.

"Thanks for letting us stay, man," he said, holding the card in the tips of his fingers. "If you're ever in San Francisco, come and visit with us."

As they thundered off on their powerful wheels, I read what was written on the card: "You have been assisted by Pete, a member of the Hells Angels Frisco, California Chapter". On the back of the card was their motto, which read: "When we do right, no one remembers. When we do wrong, no one forgets".

Well, I never did forget the Hells Angels, nor the smell of patchouli oil that lingered in my flat for days after they'd left. Mercifully, however, I can also say that they never "did me wrong". A few weeks later, I heard about the Apple Christmas party, when John Lennon was almost beaten up by a ravenous Frisco Pete, once again high on drugs and booze, over the late arrival of the giant roast turkey that was being prepared in the kitchen. As he screamed and swore at a terrified Lennon, who was dressed in a Father Christmas costume, the husband of Mavis from the press office intervened, and got punched in the face for his trouble.

So, however friendly those dudes might have been most of the time, Hunter S. Thompson wasn't exaggerating: they really did bust up anyone who got in their way...

* * *

Becoming a regular visitor to the Apple Corps had an unavoidable side effect. Once people realized that I was a part of the exclusive in-crowd, I began to get "Beatled" all the time. By getting Beatled, we at Apple used to mean being pestered by the endless stream of fans, musicians, artists, business people and freaks trying to get access to one or more of the Beatles. And it could happen anywhere, at any time. On the steps of the typically crowded entrance, during a haircutting session with the office staff, while having a sandwich in the guest room, or even out on the town along the King's Road, at the Picasso Coffee Bar or the Chelsea Potter Pub.

"Hi, you're Paul McCartney's hairdresser, aren't you? Listen, I've got this farm in Wales. Ley lines running all over it, dig? Spiritual. And I had this vision the other day… You follow me, yeah? Exactly. A big festival, a gathering of the tribes. But with the *Beatles*, can you imagine?"

"Excuse me, yes, you there, do you happen to know if John Lennon is in the office this afternoon? Because I mailed him a demo tape over three months ago, and I haven't heard back from him yet."

"Look, I don't want to be a bother, but could you be a darling and deliver this letter for me?"

"Hey man, d'you know what they were sayin' about Apple, you know, makin' our dreams come true and all that shit? Well, I've got mine, but I gotta talk to George Harrison in person. It's too juicy to put on paper, and he's the only one who's gonna get it, you know, and those birds at reception keep givin' me the run-around. Just tell him to come out for a sec, all right? I know he's in there…"

And on and on it went. Usually, I'd just be polite and explain that I couldn't really help. Sometimes I'd even feel sorry for them. They seemed so desperate – particularly when they'd travelled from California or India or Australia just to meet their idols. At other times, though, they were so pushy or insistent that they ended up getting on my nerves. On one occasion, I got really riled up. It was a long-distance phone call, at the salon, from a fast-talking American salesman type in Los Angeles.

"Hi, is this the Beatles' hairdresser?"

"Sure," I said warily. "What do you want?"

"Great to meet you, son. Listen, I got a fantastic business opportunity for ya. I own a string of hotels where the Beatles have stayed, and I'm selling their memorabilia. Quality material, no bullshit, real stuff from the places where they've been."

"Like what?"

"Well, like if they took a dunk in a swimming pool, we bottle the water and sell it as Beatles water. And we're cutting up the bedsheets they slept in and selling the squares. The girls go gaga for those, hah."

I couldn't believe what I was hearing. Pieces of the Beatles' bedsheets? Did they wash them first? Or were stained squares more valuable?

"So here's the deal. We wanna expand our offering, and what could be better than selling real Beatles' hair? All you gotta do is collect the hair clippings. We'll take care of everything else: packaging, advertising, distribution. We got it all set up. And there's plenty in it for you, of course. Whaddaya say?"

While the excited entrepreneur laid out his plan, I became more and more pissed off. From my first session with Paul, I'd resolved never to pick up any hair cuttings, even for myself. I'd been Beatled by my cousin Lynn into giving her a lock, I suppose, but she was family. Anyway, that had been my one and only exception, and I'd asked Paul for his permission. The idea of selling the stuff behind the Beatles' backs revolted me. How far would these hucksters go? Would they end up fishing in the hotel toilets?

"Enough, man, enough!" I shouted into the phone. "There's no way you're ever going to have a single lock. So don't ever call me again!"

I don't think slamming the phone down into its cradle has ever felt so satisfying.

* * *

I can remember only one time, aside from my Cousin Lynn's request, in which I got successfully Beatled. As on that first occasion, the pressure was simply too much to bear. In this case, it was my old friend Lawrence Falk asking – the very one who had encouraged me to become a hairdresser in the first place. How could I refuse?

In 1968, Lawrence and I were still best mates, and our careers had grown in parallel since we'd chosen our common profession. He'd become so successful as a stylist that he'd taken over Eric's of Baker Street, where he'd been working for the past few years, and turned it into Crimpers, an establishment that – as I mentioned before – became one of the most iconic hairdressing salons in London. Crimpers' radical innovation was to allow men and women to visit the salon together. In fact, the chairs in which clients sat were arranged around wooden tables, as in a café, so that a couple or a group of friends could sit together while they were having their hair done. This revolutionary "unisex" salon became yet another stage for the ongoing transformation in long-held gender divisions and stereotypes. For the first time in Western society, men were to join women in using their clothes and hair to express their personality, and not just their social status. Crimpers, by catering to the pioneers of this new movement, became hugely successful. The place was frequented by top models and movie stars alike, and had even begun to rival Vidal Sassoon's, pitting its "hair sculpture" against its predecessor's "hair architecture".

One day, I met Lawrence in a pub after work and mentioned I'd been at one of the Beatles' recording sessions, where the four were preparing some of the songs for what would be eventually known as their "White Album".

"Hey, Leslie," he said at one point. "Do you think there's any chance of me coming along?"

"No can do," I said regretfully. "They don't like too many people at the studio, especially strangers. I'm sure I've told you before, Falky. Sorry!"

It felt terrible getting Beatled by a friend, and having to turn him down like I did all the others. But what else could I do?

"Oh, come on Leslie, don't give me that..." he persisted. "I know you can swing it!"

Swing it? Lawrence had no idea what he was talking about. In all the recording sessions I'd ever been to, I'd never seen anyone in there who didn't have some kind of role to play – as a musician, a sound engineer, or as part of Apple Records. In my case, I was the Beatles' hairdresser, and even if I wasn't always cutting and styling, everyone knew I was "on call". These sessions were not parties to which anyone could just "invite one of their mates".

The Beatles themselves had stuck to a rule that forbade even wives and girlfriends from attending – though there had recently been one glaring exception. After coming back from India, John had started letting Yoko Ono into the studio. This violation hadn't gone down very well with his bandmates. As far as I know, John didn't even ask them for permission. He just brought his new partner in one day, causing an awkward atmosphere at the studio. No one mentioned it, but it was there like the proverbial elephant in the room. Later, Beatles historians would cite this move as one of the contributing factors to the band's dismantling.

So how could I, with my tenuous hairdressing excuse, even consider bringing along my old schoolmate? It was unthinkable. And yet, Lawrence wouldn't give up.

"Come on, Leslie, just try it… for old times' sake. You owe me, mate!"

I looked down into my beer, ashamed and not knowing what to do. I really did owe him. How many times had Falky stuck out his neck out for me? Back at school, I'd once got into a fight with one of the other boys in Form Nought. On top of my black eye, I ended up getting a caning from the headmaster for misbehaving, but the worst of it was that Lawrence got a caning too, simply because he was the oldest boy present.

I finally raised my hands, conceding defeat. "Fine, you bastard. I'll ask Paul."

"That's better!"

"Don't get your hopes up," I warned him, hoping he wouldn't be terribly disappointed when the inevitable answer came back.

"Bah, I know you can swing it," he said, clinking his pint glass against mine.

For days, I sweated over how to pop the question to Paul. The next time I visited 7 Cavendish Avenue, I was as nervous as the first time I'd met my star client – with the difference that Paul now knew me better, so he could probably notice my embarrassment. At one point, he mentioned the recording session that had been planned for the next evening. I guess my scissors must have started to jitter dangerously around his head.

"Anything wrong, Leslie?" he said, smiling at me.

"Um… ah… no. Well… yes, actually."

I put down my scissors and began to explain my friend's persistent request. Incredibly, he interrupted me within seconds.

"No problem, Leslie," he said, in that chirpy, matter-of-fact way of his. "Bring him along. In fact, I may want your opinion on something."

Bring him along? I couldn't believe it. How could it be? I was delighted, of course, and thanked Paul a dozen times before our session was over. But the more I thought about it, the odder it seemed. Why would Paul allow a complete stranger into the studio?

"I told you you could swing it!" Lawrence shouted with excitement when I called to give him the good news.

That evening, we drove over to Abbey Road, parked opposite the building and walked over the striped lines that would eventually become the most photographed zebra crossing in the world. Even with Paul's permission, it felt very odd to bring an outsider into the proceedings – the atmosphere was tense enough with Yoko around.

"When we go in there," I said to Lawrence, "don't say anything – don't ask any questions – don't… move! Just keep quiet and watch."

"What if I need to go to the loo?" he grinned, seeing how uptight I was getting.

"I'm serious, Falky. If you need to go to the loo, raise your hand and ask for permission. Promise me."

"All right, yeah, I promise."

There was little need for me to repeat my instructions. As soon as we got there, it was obvious that things were not hunky-dory with the Beatles. Their recent month-long meditation retreat with the Maharishi didn't seem to have helped their relationships very much, and the estrangement was definitely having an effect on their work. I don't think any actual recording got done that night. Paul, George and Ringo were rehearsing some new songs, trying different ways of playing and singing them. Meanwhile, John spent most of his time sitting on the floor next to Yoko, chatting privately with her as she stroked his hair. He seemed no more involved in the proceedings than me and Lawrence, who watched the uncomfortable tension building from the other side of the studio.

"Hey John." Paul turned around to face him at one point. "Are you in this band or what?"

It may have been a joke aimed to defuse the situation, but it certainly put into words what everyone was thinking.

The session only lasted until about 3 a.m. Before leaving, George Harrison made some tea for Paul and himself. After handing a cup to his bandmate, he picked up his guitar and, for some reason, began singing one of my all-time favourite Beatles songs, 'In My Life'. At the time, I didn't make much of it, but later I considered that its wistful lyrics may have been a comment on the delicate moment the band was going through.

That song seemed to remind Paul of something. He went over to the piano, put his cup of tea on top and invited Lawrence and me to come closer.

"Hey guys, see what you think of this new song I've composed."

As we came over by the piano, he started up on one of his bouncier tunes, singing with great gusto:

"Ob-la-di, ob-la-da, life goes on, brah! La-la how the life goes on…"

No one outside the studio had heard that whimsical masterpiece, and Lawrence and I were instantly hooked on it, moving our heads and tapping our feet to the rhythm. As you can imagine, we gushed to Paul about what a hit that fun little ditty was going to become. And it wasn't just the moment's excitement.

"That's got to be a huge hit," Lawrence said as we walked back to the car over the famous zebra crossing. "We've already got it stuck in our heads!"

On the way home, we sang it together to keep ourselves awake. It was a fantastic ending to a memorable evening, and I was ecstatic that I'd managed to sneak my best mate into this closed world.

Over the years, though, I've wondered what it all meant. Why had Paul allowed Lawrence, a complete stranger, into the studio? Was he trying to get back at John for bringing Yoko and thus violating their old rule? If so, then maybe all of that Ob-la-di wasn't directed at me and Lawrence at all. Perhaps he was lampooning John's new dependence on Yoko's advice by consulting his hairdresser and the latter's best mate about his latest composition.

Who knows? Who cares? Ob-la-di, ob-la-da, life goes on, brah!…

10

In Business with the Beatles

The most weird and wonderful twist on my helter-skelter ride through the Sixties began in the spring of 1968, as I walked into the Apple press office one afternoon. The cocktail party was in full swing, with journalists and visitors ambling through the smoky room, ice clinking in their glasses.

"Hi Derek," I said, as I spotted the press officer by the drinks cabinet. "Is this a good time for your haircut?"

"It would be," he said, with a funny smirk under his blond, brush-like moustache, "except that Paul and George told me they wanted to see you as soon as you got here. They're in the boardroom."

What could Paul and George possibly want with me? As I walked up the stairs, I recalled a conversation I'd had with Paul a few months before, during one of my visits to Cavendish Avenue. When the Beatles were starting up their corporation, one of the first enterprises they had planned was the "Apple Boutique", a shop that would sell hippy fashion and accessories on the corner of Baker and Paddington Street. Paul imagined that a whole chain of shops might follow, and that the next stage might be to inaugurate a hairdressing salon.

"Would you be interested, Leslie?" he'd asked me on that occasion.

"In… interested…?"

"You'd have to give up your job at Sassoon's, of course," he continued. "But, you know, you'd have your own salon. And we'd back the whole thing. You could furnish it however you liked, make it into a cool place."

"I... I don't know what to say, Paul... I can't believe you'd give me such an opportunity."

"That's what Apple's all about, Leslie... giving people like you the chance to show off their talent, to live out their dreams."

Dreams indeed. When he'd spoken those words, Paul's proposal sounded too good to be true. And in fact, I'd heard nothing else about the matter for over six months. The Apple Shop did open on Baker Street in December 1967, the entire building decorated with an incredible three-storey-tall mural of a shamanic woman towering over the London traffic, surrounded by rainbows, stars and planets. But Paul hadn't mentioned the hairdressing idea again to me, and I didn't dare bring it up myself.

As I walked in, Paul and George were sitting close to one end of the massive central table that took up much of the boardroom, looking at a set of plans laid out on its wooden surface. There was a third person with them I didn't recognize at first, and who made me feel immediately uncomfortable as he stared at me through his tinted sunglasses with a sort of sneer. Sporting a velvet hat, a frilly multicoloured shirt and a textured dark-green jacket, he seemed to be sitting at the very pinnacle of foppish, flower-power fashion. In fact, that's exactly what he was doing. Just before Paul introduced us, I suddenly realized who he was.

"Leslie, have you met John Crittle?"

"No," I said, stretching out my hand. "Pleased to meet you, Mr Crittle."

"John," he said in his Australian accent, barely standing and giving me a limp handshake, as if he couldn't actually be bothered to waste his energies on a vulgar hair-snipper.

I instantly took a dislike to this odd creature of a man. I'd heard he was a close friend of John Lennon, but of course, that wasn't much of a guarantee, as John was also close friends with Alexis Mardas, the supposed electronics whiz who'd promised the Beatles all of those technological innovations.

"Remember what we talked about, Leslie?" Paul asked with his usual enthusiasm. "About the Apple Hairdressing Salon?"

My heart leapt up again. I was right! This was it! But... what did John Crittle have to do with it?

"Well, we've finally found a way. We're going to take over John's shop on the King's Road. You know the one?"

"Sure, yeah." I nodded, still unnerved by the way Crittle was staring at me through his tinted glasses.

Of course I knew the place. "Dandie" was where the Beatles used to buy their wildest clothes, along with Mick Jagger, Procol Harum and much of the fashion aristocracy of the day. Half the wardrobe I'd rifled through in Paul's bedroom, just before the *Magical Mystery Tour* launch, was probably designed by him. Crittle had set up Dandie in 1966 together with Tara Browne, the wealthy heir to the Guinness brewing empire, and possibly the hippest "man about town" of the day. Browne died tragically in a road accident that very year, a fact that some think was obliquely immortalized in the Beatles' song 'A Day in the Life'.

After his death, Crittle bought up Browne's share and managed to turn Dandie into the most swinging tailors in London. I'd been in there a couple of times, out of sheer curiosity, though its flamboyant (and outrageously expensive) silk-frilled shirts and colourful Edwardian-cut jackets were a bit too much for me. On reflection, it made perfect sense for the Beatles to buy the place, as a more upmarket version of their Apple Boutique on Baker Street.

"There's some extra room in the basement," Paul explained, waving towards the plans on the table. "So, I thought, perfect, you know – that's where we can put Leslie's salon."

"Yeah," George added. "I'm sure it'll be more comfortable than the green room at Abbey Road."

"Wow!" I said, full of wonder and joy at the generosity of these incredible clients of mine. For a second, even John Crittle, in all of his arrogant gaudiness, disappeared from view. I looked around at the panelled walls and ornate plaster ceilings of the Apple boardroom, humbled that the Beatles considered me one of their own now – part of the Yellow Submarine's merry crew.

"That's unbelievable, Paul... I don't know what to say."

"Just say yes, and we're in business, Leslie," Paul beamed.

Of course I said yes. What else was I going to say? It really was a no-brainer. The chance to strike out on my own? Backed by the Beatles? On the premises of the most fashionable shop in town? As an actual branch of the coolest corporation on earth? Who could say no to that? Within days, I took Paul's offer, signed the papers, thanked Mr Sassoon effusively for everything he'd given me and quit my job.

The only thing that bothered me was having to set up my salon inside the premises of John Crittle's fancy little emporium. At that first meeting in the Apple boardroom, I'd got the unmistakable feeling that my future business partner didn't want me there at all. As I later discovered, in fact, Crittle had expected to keep the whole place for himself, but Paul had insisted that I came with the deal. So he was stuck with me, and I with him. The Beatles had arranged our entrepreneurial marriage, and now we both had to make the most of it.

I soon set about decorating my ideal salon. Apple Corps seemed to be swimming in money at the time, so I decided to go for it big time. Why not? The salon was going to bear the Apple name. It had to be the ultimate in Sixties trendiness. My first stop was the most chic interiors shop in London, Casa Pupo on Pimlico Road, where I had a wonderful time selecting a set of stylish Italian blue and white ceramic tiles. I remember handing over my outrageously expensive order to the Apple accounts office with some trepidation, and being shocked at how casually it was picked up and filed away with a simple "Oh, thanks Leslie, we'll take care of it as soon as possible". When the boxes came in from Casa Pupo, well, that was when it really hit me: Paul hadn't been joking around. I really was going into business with the Beatles! In any case, my taste must have been good, because those gorgeous floral tiles are still on display at 161 King's Road fifty years later, even though the place is now an art gallery.

Next, I found a magnificent Victorian barber's chair at the Chelsea Antiques Market, one of my regular haunts, and had it upholstered in crushed blue velvet. To this I added a pair of swinging saloon-style doors – and I was off and running.

*   *   *

The shop at 161 King's Road was soon rebranded, with a huge white placard right over the doors, which featured the words "Apple Tailoring (Civil and Theatrical)" in black flowing script. The official launch, held at the Club dell'Aretusa on 22nd May 1968, was the first time that John Lennon and Yoko Ono appeared in public together before the press. But the photos I remember were the publicity stills that John Kelly, my room-mate from the Magical Mystery Tour, took of me with a giant pair of wooden scissors I'd come across in another antiques shop in World's End. As I posed for him in his studio, I felt like I was living one of those out-of-body experiences the LSD crowd talked about. Me, the bicycle-delivery boy from Burnt Oak, getting my portrait taken by the Beatles' official photographer – for a publicity shoot – for my own Apple company! It was as mad as any of the lyrics from the quirky new album the Beatles were working on. But it was also – let's face it – very, very cool. And I understood why Kelly was entrusted with so many of the Fab Four's photographs. I don't think I've ever looked better.

Officially named "Leslie Cavendish's Hairdressing Studio at Apple Tailoring", my salon was much smaller than Vidal Sassoon's, but ten times as groovy: an intimate, exclusive environment. As you came in through the swinging doors that separated the hairdressing studio from the rest of Apple Tailoring, you'd find yourself in a dreamy space pulsating with instrumental music, illuminated by soft blue and white spotlights. You'd be offered a cigarette, sit down on the luxurious barber-shop chair, and then be invited to relax as Mr Cavendish began your makeover, with the assistance of his junior, William Western. The cigarette smoke in the closed basement environment, which sounds like a toxic trap from our twenty-first-century perspective, at the time just added to the cool, spaced-out atmosphere.

Most of my clients were both trendy and well off, like those of Apple Tailoring itself. I was asking the old Vidal Sassoon rate of two guineas (£2.10) at a time when the average wage was £20 per week, a typical house cost £3,800 and a Ford Cortina, Britain's most popular car of the day, went for £750. Occasionally, though, I'd also get requests from clients who, while undoubtedly hip, couldn't easily afford my prices. This led to some interesting and creative deals. One artist presented me with a painting that looked remarkably like a Pink Floyd album cover as his payment – and which went straight up on the wall. I also agreed to cut and style the straggly hair of a young and impecunious musician in return for him playing his guitar at the salon a couple of times a week. Having forgotten the name of the young artist who would play these exclusive gigs at my tiny venue, I've often wondered who he was, and whether he ever made it big. Perhaps I helped launch a major career without ever knowing it.

In addition to some of my old celebrity clients like Dave Clarke and Keith Moon, I picked up a few new ones at 161 King's Road, like Julie Felix, the British folk singer of Native American origin, and a few popular DJs like Emperor Rosko and David "Kid" Jensen. Of the Beatles, George Harrison was the only member who dropped by on a regular basis. Paul's hair I'd always cut at home, John Lennon multitasked and Ringo had his wife Maureen. But George seemed to love the mellow atmosphere of my basement studio. He was especially fond of his manicures with Marion Slade, a young assistant who later went on to co-found the radical feminist journal *Spare Rib*, after joining a couple of punk bands as bass guitarist. I always made a point of creating a pleasant atmosphere, with soft music and subdued lighting, when George came in for his "beauty treatment" with Marion – all very romantic and very much a "do not disturb" type of situation.

Running that Apple-backed salon was an amazing experience. Even while waiting for the next appointment, I might meet Rod Stewart or Brian Jones as they picked out the outfits they'd wear at their next concert or TV appearance. Once, I remember Jimi Hendrix, one of Crittle's regular customers, falling in love with a particular double-breasted velvet jacket in apple green.

"Oh, that's far out, man," he said, caressing the richly patterned fabric. "I'll take that one."

When asked if he'd like it in that particular colour, Hendrix rifled through a whole stack of fifty beautiful velvet pieces that had been piled up on a counter, in every shade imaginable, for him to choose from.

"Just gimme all the colours," he decided nonchalantly.

That's the kind of shopper who came into Apple Tailoring (Civil and Theatrical).

Aside from the pure experience of it, fronting my own Apple enterprise obviously gave me a great deal of exposure. I began to be featured in a regular column on *Disc* magazine, one of the most important pop-music weeklies, with the highlights of that week's celebrity visits to my studio. And of course, I was making good money. My prices were relatively high, I had plenty of clients, and the only rent I paid was a modest one to John Crittle. As for Apple, they charged me nothing, which was typical of their utopian free-for-all approach.

My only reserve was with Crittle himself. The more I got to know him, the less I liked the guy. And I wasn't alone in this regard. There's a rumour that Ray Davies of the Kinks met him at a party and found him so unbearably full of himself that they ended up getting into a fist fight. Later, Davies apparently wrote his song 'Dedicated Follower of Fashion' as a satire of Crittle and all his stuck-up, frilly-clothed clientele. Whether true or not, my business partner certainly was a first-class snob, as were most of his friends. And I soon discovered he was also as shady as his sunglasses.

"Come on, Leslie, let's go for a ride in the car," he'd tell me every so often, frisking his hands together with anticipation.

"The car" was an astoundingly eye-catching 1956 Bentley S1 Sports Saloon, its luxurious curves painted in purple, gold, red, blue, green, black and white. The extravagant design, by the same Binder-Edwards-Vaughan trio who painted Paul

McCartney's Knight piano, included a flaming sun that flashed out from the bonnet, curling its red tentacles around the headlights, and butterfly wings that stretched back towards the boot. It was impossible not to be knocked out by the sight of that Unidentified Fashion Object cruising down the heart of Chelsea. And as you might imagine, Crittle's aim in being chauffeured up and down the King's Road was precisely to provoke this effect on the young, trendy, miniskirted beauties whose hearts inevitably went all a-flutter when the heavenly wheels stopped right next to them and the back window rolled down. After all, who could be in there but John Lennon, Paul McCartney or one of their closest and coolest friends?

Fair enough. Crittle liked women, and he flashed around his wealth to attract them. Not the only one to do so, I suppose. The only problem was that he wasn't actually single, but married to the model Andrea Williams, with whom he was about to have a baby girl, Marnie. What kind of a father was he going to make, always high on drugs and cheating on his wife every other day? And that wasn't the worst of it. Things were to become a bit more – shall we say – unsavoury when I learnt about the trap door in the floor of his shop.

My suspicions had already been aroused when we first discussed the space that would be allotted to my new hairdressing salon on his premises. There was something funny about the way Crittle insisted that he needed a certain amount of room "for storage", but it took him a while to reveal the true reason for his reluctance. One morning, a few weeks after I moved into his shop, he waved me over to a corner of the draughtboard-tiled flooring on the ground floor.

"What is that?" I asked. "A trap door?"

"Yeah," he said, pulling it open. "Have a look."

Downstairs, on the same level as my salon, he kept a small, secret room.

"You naughty boy," I said, when I climbed down into his little private boudoir. He clearly hadn't set up that bed for his baby daughter to sleep on.

"Ah, but you haven't seen the best bit," he said, showing me the big mirror set up on one of the walls.

"Yeah, I saw it," I said.

"No, you haven't," he grinned. "Unless you've figured out what's behind that mirror…"

"Behind?"

It took me a while to get my bearings, to trace my way out from the secret room, up to the shop, across to the main stairs, down into the basement, along the aisles of fancy jackets, brightly patterned cravats and extravagant hats, and finally…

Crittle switched off the lights, turning the mirror into a window with a view into the contiguous room, right where female clients would try on the selection of ladies' clothes downstairs.

"Oh, I see." I gulped down my dismay. This bastard was secretly peeping at the elegant young ladies who frequented his establishment and modelled his clothes, unwittingly, for his private viewing pleasure. It was a relatively secluded part of the shop, so these customers would often think themselves completely on their own as they preened themselves in front of the mirror.

I never got over the giggles of glee that echoed in that squalid little room. All I could think about was that poor baby girl, Marnie, who would be stuck with such a man as her father. As I climbed back out of the trap door, feeling tainted by Crittle's own foulness, I was overcome by the first sense of real disappointment in the whole Beatles project. I'd noticed the lack of financial control at Apple, the rampant alcohol and drug abuse on the premises, and the way a lot of people seemed willing to take advantage of the Beatles' generosity and naivety. But here was my first face-to-face encounter with a close friend and collaborator who clearly wasn't to be trusted. From then on, each time I saw a client walk into the changing room, I felt ashamed to be associated with that despicable man.

As I feared, Crittle turned out to be an utterly irresponsible father, and his relationship with Andrea Williams didn't last. Years later, little Marnie grew up to become Darcey Bussell, one of Britain's most celebrated classical ballerinas. She disowned John Crittle, dropped his last name, didn't give him a mention in her autobiography, *Life in Dance*, and ignored his attempts to contact her before he died of emphysema, thirty years later, in 2000. It's sad to say, but I don't blame her.

* * *

The Beatles decided to pull out of their investment in Apple Tailoring less than three months after its launch. This didn't have anything to do with John Crittle's integrity. They'd simply changed their minds about getting into the retail business. As Paul stated in the official press release on 31st July, the shops "just weren't our thingy". From then on, Apple would concentrate on music and entertainment.

The shops really weren't their thingy. Apple Tailoring's flamboyant outfits (not to mention its prices) scared off most customers. Unless you were someone like Jimi Hendrix or Mick Jagger, you wouldn't be able to afford such whimsical luxuries. The real disaster, though, was the Apple Boutique. I wasn't privy to the details, but from all other accounts, the Baker Street shop had lost enormous amounts of money. The boutique's decor and all of its wares, designed by a Dutch art collective known as "The

Fool", featured expensive silk labels and other extravagances that made little business sense. Worse still, the boutique was plagued by rampant shoplifting. Customers, shop assistants and even the members of The Fool itself would just raid the place for Apple-branded goodies. As a final humiliation, it turned out that the enormous hippy mural on the outside had been painted without proper permission from Westminster City Council, who ordered it to be removed by May. Two months later, the Beatles decided it wasn't worth the bother. They closed the boutique down, together with Crittle's shop and my hairdresser's downstairs – probably the only healthy part of the business.

It has to be said that they did so with astounding generosity. At the Apple Boutique, the Beatles gave away the entire stock for free. First John, Paul, George and Ringo took whatever they wanted, then they invited the Apple staff to do the same, and finally the rest was left for the general public to take home, in a wild scramble that had to be overseen by the police to avoid a riot. In the case of Apple Tailoring, John Crittle and I were allowed to keep our respective businesses, which we continued to run for another two years from 161 King's Road. To the world at large, Apple demonstrated once again that it was no ordinary corporation, but rather an embodiment of the hippy ideal that eschewed materialism and privileged sharing, art and having an all-round good time.

The truth was, though, that the Beatles just weren't interested in business. They only wanted to get on with their music, their art and their cultural revolution, without having to deal with hassles like strategic plans or accounting. At the same time, they had an "I'll get by with a little help from my friends" mentality, even in serious matters of management. And that included getting "*high* with a little help from my friends". Thus, they ended up building an empire that was run by a cheerful bunch of stoners, whose main qualification seemed to be the fact that they were good mates with Paul, John, George or Ringo.

This all became clear to me on one memorable evening in the summer of 1968. Paul had recently broken up with Jane Asher, and though he had a new girlfriend, he seemed heartbroken to me. He'd stopped shaving his beard, hardly ever left the house and began taking more drugs. One evening, Paul held a dinner party at 7 Cavendish Avenue, with John Lennon and several of the Apple executives, including Pete Shotton, John's oldest school friend from the Quarry Bank Grammar School in Liverpool, and their ex-road managers Mal Evans and Neil Aspinall. Another guest was the up-and-coming singer Donovan, who'd visited the Maharishi's ashram at the same time as the Beatles and collaborated on various Apple Records projects. A few months later, Donovan would release one of the all-time greatest hippy anthems, 'Atlantis'. And I was invited along to the party as well, probably because I was one of the few people Paul was seeing during that dark and confused period of his life.

During the dinner, I happened to sit next to Pete Shotton. Pete had played the washboard for the Quarrymen, the skiffle band that was the forerunner of the Beatles, until he admitted to John that he didn't really enjoy playing. This led to Lennon breaking the washboard on poor Pete's head. Nevertheless, they remained close friends, and the ex-Quarryman even contributed some lyrics and background percussion to a few Beatles tracks.

I liked Pete. With his light-red hair and loud laugh, he was a genuine Scouser, the kind of down-to-earth bloke the Beatles had been before they became world-famous. That evening, he told me the story of how his friend John had virtually rescued him from destitution after failing in a number of attempts to start a career. In a few short years, he rose from the breadline to running a supermarket on Hayling Island that John Lennon and George Harrison generously bought for him. Then he was put in charge of the Apple Boutique.

"Which was a disaster, you know," he said, as the pudding was being served.

I did know, of course.

"And now – can you believe it? – they've made me managing director of Apple Corps," Pete continued, elbowing John Lennon in the ribs. "I'm not sure I'm up to the job, you know."

"You'll do fine, Pete," John said. "Remember, we're not business freaks, we're artists. But if it all goes to hell, we'll blame it on you."

"Thanks, John, that's very reassuring," he chuckled.

At that point, someone offered us tabs of LSD as casually as if they were After Eight mints, and the group of Apple artists and executives all eagerly partook of this little "dessert". Feeling like a teetotaller in a brewery, I politely declined mine. Apart from being afraid of repeating the bad trip I'd experienced the first time around, I was the only one in the group who had to get up early the next morning and manipulate sharp scissors around my clients' necks.

Still, it gave me some pause for thought. As I left the party, while everyone else's was just beginning, I wondered whether a serious business could be run this way. What would my mother have thought? I recalled her reaction the day she and my dad turned up at my Chelsea flat unannounced and came across a packet of Rizla rolling papers: "If he wants to be a junkie, let him be a junkie!" The Beatles had left their empire in the hands of those people at Paul's dinner: Pete, Mal, Neil, Chris… They trusted them. They got high with them. It was a great trip, to be sure. But how long could it possibly last? Wasn't it as doomed as the Apple Boutique itself? Or was I being as strait-laced as my mother?

11

Paul Is Not Dead

On the other hand, the Beatles were still as popular as ever. At the end of that summer in 1968, the band released its biggest hit yet, which stayed at number one in the charts for nine weeks. Everywhere you went, you found people chanting it – even my grandma with her Russian accent: "Naaaa-naaa-naaa-nanananaaaa, nanananaaaaa, heeeey Juuuuude!"

And it wasn't just their music that dominated the airwaves. The Fab Four were in the papers and on TV incessantly, accompanying media pieces about their new releases, their recording sessions, their nights out on the town, their clothes, love lives and, of course, their hair. Journalists and photographers followed them like flies. The microphones and photo cameras were always around. So it's hardly surprising that, as an increasingly regular part of their entourage, I too was becoming embroiled in the non-stop media storm. Me and my dog Ernie, that is.

That year, on top of everything else that was happening to me, I had another two incredible strokes of luck. The first was that I won the government's monthly Premium Bond lottery – a £25 prize. That may not sound like much, but back then £25 was worth several hundred pounds of today's money. The second stroke of luck was that I finally fell properly in love, with a blonde Irish-Italian woman called Louisa Rabaiotti. She'd been working as one of Tom Jones's backing dancers, but she certainly wasn't just another long-legged dolly bird. Louisa was funny, assertive, well educated – she seemed to have everything I'd ever hoped for in a woman. In fact, when she moved into my flat in Chelsea, I began seriously to consider ideas that had been foreign to me until that point: marriage, settling down, children. At last, I began to understand the true meaning of 'All My Loving', 'Michelle' and the rest of those songs.

These two happy events led to Ernie's adoption. Louisa wanted a dog, and I was in love, so that's how I spent the lottery money. He was a rare breed, a Ware cocker spaniel – and a beautiful, well-behaved little guy. I named him Ernie because the machine that picked out the winning number in the Premium Bond lottery was called, and still is called, the Electronic Random Number Indicator Equipment, or ERNIE.

Around that time, I would take Ernie wherever I went. Paul McCartney got to know him quite well, as I'd often drop him off at his house on Cavendish Avenue to play with Martha the sheepdog – the two would spend the afternoon frolicking around the garden together while I watched a match at the nearby Lord's Cricket Ground. I'd also take him into shops, restaurants and even, surprisingly enough, into recording sessions. One day, we both visited Olympic Studios, where the Beatles had worked on such classics as 'All You Need Is Love'. There was the usual collection of reporters outside, and one of them shouted to me, "Why are you bringing your dog into the studio?"

"Actually my dog is doing backing vocals with John and Yoko," I shouted back.

Why I said that, I have no idea. I suppose I was in a silly mood. Perhaps I was reminded of Yoko's tendency to wail and whine in the background of some of her more outlandish tracks with John.

Later that day, Louisa and I went out on the town with Larry Curzon, a friendly and assertive American who was in London heading the local office of William Morris Endeavor, the most important US talent and PR agency. I'd met Larry at the Apple offices, where he was trying to convince the Beatles to audition a new band he'd brought together, made up of David Crosby from the Byrds, Stephen Stills from Buffalo Springfield, and Graham Nash from the British band the Hollies. Though he was a typical loud American, we'd hit it off straight away. That afternoon, when I told Larry the story about Ernie and the press, a light seemed to turn on in his brain.

"I've got it!" he said.

"Got what?" I asked.

"We'll plant a story in the *Daily Express*, in the William Hickey column. You know the guy... writes up all the gossip."

"A story about Ernie?"

"Yeah, it's perfect – the singing dog! Hah, hah! I'll tell them I represent Ernie for the William Morris Agency. We'll get them to interview you, take some pictures. Then we'll offer Pedigree Chum a sponsorship deal."

"The dog-food company?"

"You can't imagine how crazy these marketing people go when they smell the Beatles, Leslie! They're already pouring thousands of pounds into the Crufts Dog Show. Imagine how famous they could make Ernie!"

The whole scheme sounded far too eccentric. I couldn't imagine the *Daily Express*, which at the time was a more important newspaper than it is nowadays, publishing such a kooky piece of nonsense. Frankly, I wasn't even sure I wanted to be associated with that kind of story. And I'd seen Larry's ambitious ideas crashing and burning before: incredible as it may seem, considering the future success of Crosby, Stills and Nash, he failed to convince Apple to take on the band.

I was in love, though, and Louisa found the idea of our dog hitting the papers hilarious. So we gave Larry the go-ahead and, to my surprise, a few days later, someone called up to arrange the interview.

"It's the *Daily Express*!" I whispered to Louisa, cupping the phone with my hand.

"Wow!" she cried. "That's wonderful!"

I didn't share Louisa's enthusiasm. Making an offhand, joking comment, to a bunch of reporters on the street was one thing – actually sitting down with a journalist face to face and expanding on that story as if it were real was quite another. I found the whole idea more than a little embarrassing

"Look… why don't you take care of it?" I said, handing her the telephone.

"Of course!" she exclaimed.

Ah, she was happy. That was the important thing. I don't know what new and strange adventure we were getting ourselves into, but she loved me, and with a love like that, you know it can't be bad…

A couple of days later, while I was at work, the reporter turned up at our home with a photographer.

"What did you say?" I asked her when I came home.

"It was so much fun, darling!" she said. "They swallowed the whole thing about his backing vocals with John and Yoko, and about having his own agent! And I made up lots of other stuff too: that we feed Ernie a special diet of smoked salmon, and that we give him regular massages!"

I laughed along with Louisa, but secretly remained doubtful that any of that silliness would make it into the *Daily Express*.

Surely, no self-respecting newspaper would print a story about a singing dog, would they?

The next day, however, there it was, in black and white: the story of Ernie the singing dog and the Beatles, signed by William Hickey. The article read as follows:

Encouraged by the lack of talent to be heard in modern pop singing, the Beatles' hairdresser, 22-year-old Leslie Cavendish, is putting his own singing dog into the business.

It is a one-and-a-half-year-old spaniel, called Ernie because it was bought out of a £25 Premium Bond prize. Ernie has an unusual talent for singing in tune. It is so marked that he has been signed up at once by William Morris, the American-based entertainments agency who handle Elvis Presley, the Supremes and Stevie Wonder.

At the agency, Larry Curzon, a voluble American, is enthusiastic. "Ernie is not really a normal client," he says, "I didn't give him a formal audition, but he has a good chance, I think.

"His record won't get a bad review. After all, who's going to knock a dog!"

Ernie will soon pad off to a recording studio in Barnes, West London. What his first record will be is not yet disclosed.

Until then he is in the care of Mr Cavendish's girlfriend, Louisa Rabaiotti. "I give him smoked salmon and vitamin pills; they're good for his vocal chords," she says.

Sorry for pulling your leg, Mr Hickey! If anyone needed any further evidence that you shouldn't believe everything you read in the papers, there you have it. At least the *Daily Express* didn't print the bit about the backing vocals for John and Yoko. And I was right about the last part of Larry's plan: Pedigree Chum understandably turned us down for a sponsorship deal. This was a mighty disappointment to my dear sweet Louisa, but at least I was able to sigh with relief that the world hadn't gone completely mad.

* * *

By spending time in Derek Taylor's press office, I learnt a great deal about the Beatles' love-hate relationship with the news media. Obviously, the band needed and courted the press and, with the help of Taylor's cunning, were often able to manipulate journalists to their advantage. Giving away the stock of the Apple Boutique, for example, made little business sense, but as a media coup it was pure genius. The most impressive deployment of such tactics, however, took place in January 1969, and involved a secret so closely guarded that even my good friend Chris O'Dell wouldn't let the cat out of the bag.

"What do you mean, you can't tell me?" I asked her, incredulous.

"I'm sworn to secrecy!" she insisted. "Just make sure you're at Savile Row on Thursday, at noon."

"What? Is it a state secret? Is the Queen coming?"

"Just be there, Leslie…" She smiled mysteriously.

I did turn up at the Apple offices, of course, well before noon. As I entered the reception area, it was obvious that some major and highly unusual operation was underway. People were whizzing all around the place, shouting instructions and carting heavy equipment up the stairs. All I could do was make sure I kept out of everybody's way.

I found Chris on the first-floor landing.

"All right," I said to her. "Spill the beans. What's going on?"

"They're going to play up there." She smiled excitedly, pointing upwards with her finger. "On the roof."

"What do you mean, on the roof? Who?"

"The Beatles, they're going to play – live – today!"

I was in shock. Anyone would have been. The Beatles' last live concert had taken place at Candlestick Park, San Francisco, in 1966. Their millions of fans, not to mention a relentless horde of music promoters and venue owners from around the world, had been desperately waiting for a new gig for almost three years. This was big news. It was huge. It was the kind of news you wanted to get up on a rooftop yourself for, and yell it out to the whole world – which is precisely why Derek Taylor had made Chris, and everyone else, swear on their mother's soul that they would keep the secret until the Beatles actually hit their improvised stage.

I made my way upstairs, and got as far as the third floor. Mal Evans had been posted there as the unofficial bouncer.

"Hey Mal, do you think I could..."

"Sorry Leslie, there's just a handful of people allowed on the roof," he explained, holding on nervously to his thick-framed glasses. "There's hardly any space, with all the equipment. But frankly, it's pretty cold and windy out there. You're better off inside anyway."

At the time, of course, I didn't realize that this event was to become the stuff of legend – the Beatles' very last concert. If I had, I might have tried to blag my way up. Would I have managed to gatecrash the Beatles' rooftop gig? Who knows. I'm a pretty good blagger, and by then I knew Mal quite well, not to mention most of the people who would be up there. On the other hand, Mal could be a tough nut to crack. And he hadn't been exaggerating on either point. Aside from the

Beatles themselves, joined on this occasion by their new key-board player Billy Preston, very few people were allowed on the roof: the technical staff, Yoko Ono, Ringo's wife Maureen and a handful of other guests – including, somehow, my good friend Chris, an even better blagger than myself… On the other hand, they were all freezing up there. In fact, Yoko had to lend John Lennon her fur coat, and George wore Maureen's red raincoat.

So I waited where I was, along with most of the Apple staff, and we all gossiped excitedly. What did all of this mean? Was it the start of a new stage in the Beatles' career? Maybe they'd begin touring again. Considering all of the tensions I'd witnessed in the studio, which had led to both Ringo and George Harrison temporarily quitting the band in the past few months, it sounded like a reasonable idea. I hadn't heard anyone talking about such a move, but then again, the Beatles always seemed to be improvising.

Suddenly, the music erupted overhead, setting off cheering and applause all around me. I think we were all blown away by the raw rock-'n'-roll sound that rained down on us. No string quartets here. The Beatles were going back to their roots, and Paul seemed to be yelling as much to the whole of London: "Get back, get back, get back to where you once belonged!" If you've watched the film Let It Be, you'll remember a thickly bearded Paul belting out that song with everything he's got, and Lennon going for a memorable guitar solo while his long straggly locks blew right over his face. Towering over their adopted city, doing what they did best, no one could have imagined that it would be the last time the Beatles played live together.

From the third-floor windows, we peered down towards the street, watching with glee as confused office workers on their lunch break swivelled their heads round, trying to figure out where the raucous music was coming from. Some of the elegant gentlemen coming out of the bespoke tailoring shops didn't seem too happy with the unseemly uproar, but other people, perhaps recognizing who it was up there, began to jump up and clap. Traffic on Savile Row came to a halt, and people began to pop out of every window and rooftop hatch for a better view. We also noticed the various places, both on other buildings and down below, where Derek had artfully placed cameras to record the whole publicity stunt.

After a few songs were played, we watched as a police car pulled up outside the entrance. Soon after, the festive atmosphere on the third floor was dampened considerably by the arrival of Constable Ken Wharfe (later to become Princess Diana's bodyguard) and a fellow officer, who made their way through the crowd in silence, on their way up. We supposed that this disturbance of the city's peace would be immediately halted, or that the Beatles might even be arrested. In fact, that had been part of Derek Taylor's master plan. He couldn't have imagined a more powerful advertisement for the band's upcoming record and film than photos of the four rebellious musicians being carted off to a police station. To our surprise, however, after the end of the song that was being played, the Beatles started up again. It turned out that Ken Wharfe was a huge fan of the band. As Chris told me the story later, he simply went up to his idol, Paul, and asked him how much longer they wanted to play. The officers stayed on for the rest of the open-air show, and seemed to take in good humour Paul McCartney's improvised ribbing during his final performance of 'Get Back': "You've been playing on the roofs again, and you know your momma doesn't like it, she's gonna have you arrested!"

As they finished, John Lennon made his famous joke: "I'd like to say thank you on behalf of the group, and I hope we passed the audition." And that was that. Even without the arrest of the Beatles, the publicity stunt was a huge success, one of the first ever "viral" news stories, before such things even existed. John's sign-off made headlines worldwide, and the Fab Four's surprise concert became an instant legend.

* * *

Derek Taylor didn't always get his way, however. Promoting the Beatles was one thing, getting interviews and press coverage for new Apple artists like Mary Hopkin, Doris Troy or the Iveys (later known as Badfinger) was quite another. Apple Records had promised fame and fortune to the younger generation's most talented musicians, but the press only seemed interested in John and Yoko's "pornographic" new album cover, Paul's wedding to Linda Eastman or George and Pattie's arrest for drugs possession (on the same day as Paul and Linda's wedding – which they missed). Jackie Lomax, a talented and good-looking guitarist, put out a single that was written by George Harrison and featured both Paul and Ringo as musicians, as well as Eric Clapton. Remember 'Sour Milk Sea'? I didn't think so. It's a cracking rock-'n'-roll song, and perfectly in tune with that year's Eastern-spirituality vibe, so it was simply destined to be a huge hit, but... no one seemed interested in Lomax.

Even James Taylor, who eventually did become world-famous, was only another struggling, drug-addicted musician at that point. Derek couldn't get any of the big newspapers or magazines to pay this nineteen-year-old American dropout any attention. I cut James's hair several times at Trident Studios during the summer of 1968, when he was recording such classics as 'Carolina in My Mind', for which Paul McCartney played the bass and George Harrison sang backing vocals. I remember being powerfully impressed by that sensitive kid's soft voice, haunting lyrics and lilting melodies, and also by the huge sandalled feet that jutted out from his body as I styled his long flowing hair. But mainly, he struck me as the epitome of an American hippy, including the tendency to be permanently stoned – and I mean spaced way out there. Unfortunately, this turned out to be a major obstacle to his career. James was hospitalized to recover from heroin addiction just before Apple launched his first album, so that, to Derek Taylor's desperation, he missed his own press launch and was unable to turn up for any promotional work at all. The LP did get some great reviews however. Everyone who actually listened to 'Something in the Way She Moves' felt that a new star had been born. But few people purchased the record, and it would only be after he left Apple Records that James Taylor climbed to the top of the charts.

* * *

On the other hand, the Beatles sometimes suffered from the opposite problem: too much press attention – although of the wrong kind. The media monster was a fickle beast, and could turn on its four favourite pop stars with sudden and violent treachery. The Beatles had first learnt about the dangers of the press in 1966, when John made his notorious "more popular than Jesus" remark. Published originally in a March interview for the *Evening Standard*, the comment caused no fuss whatsoever in the UK. It was only five months later, when the American teen magazine *Datebook* reprinted the interview with Lennon's provocative comment on the cover, that a media scandal erupted. Many radio stations banned the Beatles' music, concerts were cancelled, and demonstrations were held in which outraged teenagers publicly burned their records.

Since then, the band had taken several bashings, including the critical reactions to the *Magical Mystery Tour*, the ridicule surrounding their Indian guru and the mostly negative coverage of Lennon's new avant-garde girlfriend. As a result, Derek Taylor and his staff were understandably wary of the journalists they courted day after day, and worked hard to exercise some measure of control over the Beatles' image. Among other things, they knew that the press considered someone like me, an innocent hairdresser with little knowledge of PR, a weak link in the armour that protected the band – and thus an ideal target.

My first real test arrived one February afternoon in 1969, while I was sitting on one of the white press-office couches, leafing through a copy of *Melody Maker*.

"Hey Leslie, have you got a minute?" Derek asked, waving for me to come over.

"Sure," I said, dropping the magazine and walking up to his desk. "What is it?"

"George is having his tonsils out at University College Hospital," he explained.

"Oh, really?" I said, wondering what this could possibly have to do with me. "Well, I hope he'll be OK."

"Thing is, he's pretty bored over there. He needs something to do."

"A-ha." I nodded, a bit nonplussed. I still didn't get Derek's drift. "What can I do?"

"Well, I thought it might be good if you went over there and, you know... washed and blow-dried his hair or something. Just to keep him amused, you know?"

It was I who was amused at that point. I don't think my hairdressing services had ever been described as entertainment before. But of course I was more than happy to go along with it. How many times had I been entertained by George and his friends?

Before I left the room, however, Derek added something else.

"Listen, Leslie," he said. "Whatever happens, do *not* speak to any reporters. There will be hundreds of them outside, and they will throw a million questions at you. Don't say *anything* about George. Is that clear?"

"OK, Derek, mum's the word."

As I headed for the hospital, I wondered whether Derek's job had made him a little paranoid. I mean, what was there to hide? Then again... perhaps there really was something seriously wrong with George, and the tonsils story was just a smokescreen. What if the Beatle's voice was at risk? What if he might never sing again? Was that the reason for such secrecy?

When I got to the hospital, I saw that Derek hadn't been exaggerating. The place was positively swarming with journalists and photographers. No one knew who I was, however, so getting through the crowd undetected was simple. The security guards posted outside George's room had to check my identity, but Derek must have briefed them, because they allowed me in.

"How you doin', George?" I said cheerfully as I came in.

George nodded to me with a faint smile. His shoulder-length hair fell around his pillow in a mess, and by then he'd started growing a longish moustache and goatee beard. He made hand signals to explain he couldn't talk.

"That's fine, don't worry. I'll do the chatting. Derek told me you wanted your hair done. By the way, he says he's got a Scotch ready for you when you get back. Best thing for a sore throat, he says. Do you think you can get out of bed? We'll have to wash your hair in the bathroom sink."

We set up the impromptu salon, and I got to work. It was something of a shock to encounter a Beatle who was unable to talk, let alone sing, but George had never been much of a talker, so it wasn't that different from our sessions at my Apple salon. The hospital-room chair wasn't as luxurious as my retro velvet wonder, but George relaxed into it and managed to go off into his particular meditative la-la-land. As for me, I decided to take things as slowly as possible, working the shampoo into his scalp with unhurried circular movements, rinsing thoroughly, towelling off his long mane, then blow-drying it carefully, combing his thick hair with my fingers. Even Vidal Sassoon himself couldn't have drawn the "entertainment" out any longer.

"There you go," I said, when the job was finished. "Feeling better now?"

George gave me the thumbs up. I think the poor guy, more than anything else, needed to see a familiar face. As I left the room, I appreciated Derek's good sense in sending me over. I actually felt the warm, inner glow of having done a good deed.

As I came down the stairs, however, I suddenly found myself surrounded by the press.

"How's George?"

"What's happening?"

"When will he be coming out?"

"Are you a friend of his?"

I was a bit taken aback, having forgotten all about the crowd of journalists. What was it that Derek had said? Oh, yeah: say *nothing*.

"Err... no comment," I stammered, remembering what I'd seen people on TV saying in similar situations.

I pushed my way through the gaggle of squawking reporters, shielded behind those two words, which I just kept repeating again and again, as they followed me all the way back to my car, tugging on my jacket and throwing their questions at me.

"No comment, no comment, no comment!"

As I drove off, relieved to have escaped the onslaught unscathed, I reviewed the scene in my head as if I was watching it on TV. It was actually quite amusing to imagine. I felt so important, all of a sudden, keeping secrets from the press, avoiding their questions like a hounded politician. If I were forced to remain in the public spotlight all the time, I could understand what a nightmare it would be. But just for a few minutes, I have to say that it was rather fun.

As for Derek's advice, I understood what he'd meant. Clearly, there was nothing seriously wrong with George. I could have simply said something to the reporters like, "Oh, George has lost his voice, but he seems OK." But who knows what kind of headline that could have made, just to sell more papers? BEATLE GEORGE'S CAREER THREATENED BY VOICE LOSS! It makes me tremble just to think about it.

* * *

My relationship with the media took an unexpected turn thanks to Ray Connolly, who wrote for the *Evening Standard* and happened to be a client himself. Ray interviewed all the top stars and musicians of that period and, in fact, continues to do so to this day. He was great friends with Derek Taylor and used to get plenty of Beatles scoops. One day, however, while I was cutting his hair, he turned to me and said:

"You know what, Leslie? I think it's about time I interviewed you!"

"Me?" I laughed. "That should be interesting..."

"I'm not joking, Leslie. You're a star yourself these days. Come on, you're cutting everyone's hair, you're a part of the fashion revolution – the long hair, all of it."

I think he could tell I was a bit nervous about the idea.

"Don't worry, Leslie," he reassured me. "I'm going to make you look good."

When Ray interviewed me, I was an innocent media virgin, so I spoke to him in a completely unguarded way. Luckily for me, Ray really was to be trusted. In fact, that explains why he was able to get so many exclusive interviews not only with the Beatles, but with all the great names in pop. In my case, his article was a priceless piece of publicity that launched my career as "the Beatles' hairdresser". The headline ran: "DON'T CALL LESLIE A BARBER, HE BELIEVES IN HAIR". In the piece, Connolly stressed the notion that male hairdressers had now become artists, in the same way that Vidal Sassoon and other famous women's stylists were. For the first time, he explained to his readership, men were now seeking out a new level of hair care. And Leslie Cavendish, creator of the Beatles' trend-setting coiffures, was the man to see for it...

It was an unbelievable write-up, from a well-respected journalist, and in the London *Evening Standard*, no less. In fact, I think he made me look better than I really deserved. In all honesty, I can't claim that I'd become a world-class stylist – certainly not in the same league as Vidal Sassoon or Roger

Thompson. As I've recounted, my relationship with the Beatles had to do more with luck, salesmanship and my bullet-proof discretion than my haircutting skills. I'm not even sure how responsible I was for the change in the band's image that took place during the second half of their career. As I began working for Paul and the others, it became clear to me I should let their hair grow – fashions were moving that way – and that this longer, softer look would match the change in the way they were dressing. But by then, the Beatles had taken control of their own image, just like they had taken control of the recording studio in which they crafted their multi-layered songs. My role was closer to that of George Martin during *Sgt. Pepper's*: at the controls, but working closely with these four independent artists.

In any case, I was eternally grateful to Ray. Much of my reputation came from that article, leading to many new clients and untold haircuts.

This first positive experience with the press, however, made me a bit too trusting – a slip that would eventually get me into hot water. I had another hip young journalist among my clients, Caroline Boucher, who also asked me for an interview to be published in *Disc Magazine*.

"Just an informal conversation about your impressions of the Beatles," she explained. "And perhaps something about their hair, its texture, its changing style – that kind of thing."

It sounded similar to my interview with Ray, and Caroline seemed like a nice woman, so I was happy to accept this new offer of free publicity.

We met at the Picasso café on the King's Road, and she took notes as we talked about my work and my celebrity clients. I remember being quite relaxed, and even having a few laughs during the interview. At the end, I felt satisfied that things had gone splendidly, and imagined that the new article was going to be another great boost to my burgeoning career.

During the session, however, she asked me a question which I should have been a little more careful in answering:

"Which of the Beatles do you think will lose his hair first, Leslie?"

At the time, I saw no harm in answering more or less truthfully.

"Well, actually, all of the Beatles have good thick hair," I told her. "I suppose John's hair isn't as thick as the others. That's all I can say."

"A-ha," she nodded, as she scribbled my reply onto her notepad.

Two weeks afterwards, late in the evening, I was at home getting ready for bed when I received a phone call from one of the staff members at the Apple press office.

"What did you tell the journalist from *Disc Magazine*?" she asked me, point-blank.

Instantly, I started to shiver in my pyjamas. What had I said? What could possibly cause the Apple office to call me up at eleven o' clock at night? The entire interview with Caroline Boucher flashed through my mind, a jumble of words that now seemed all wrong, full of terrible meanings and hidden connotations. But I couldn't recall any single particularly awful detail.

"I… um… Nothing! I mean… I don't know what you mean…"

Suddenly, someone else took over the phone at the other end. It was Derek Taylor. So the thing really was serious. I slumped into an armchair for support. I could feel my face and neck becoming hot.

"Leslie," he began. "Some radio stations are spreading a story that Lennon is going bald. Now, as his hairdresser, can you shed any light on this?"

"No Derek," I protested, desperately trying to call up that part of the interview. I vaguely remembered being asked who would lose their hair first, but that I'd answered in a non-committal way. My voice went reedy as I finished my answer. "I certainly haven't said any such thing."

A breathy sigh came over the phone, and then there was a pause. I imagined Derek taking a swig from his late-night Scotch-and-Coke.

"All right Leslie," he said finally. "Fuck knows what they've made up this time. Anyway, we'll have to wait for the new edition of *Disc Magazine*. It's out tomorrow. Speak to you then."

The next morning, I rushed out to buy a copy at my nearest newsagents. There, right on the front page, a headline screamed out:

"LENNON COULD GO BALD! SAYS THE BEATLES' HAIRDRESSER."

Rooted to the spot, in the middle of the newsagent's, my eyes rushed through the article. From what I could see, the text seemed largely accurate. However, Caroline had totally misrepresented my comment about John's hair being "less thick" than that of the other Beatles, exaggerating it to mean that he was going bald. When I spoke to Derek a bit later, he was understanding, but he repeated to me, once again, to be ever on my toes whenever I spoke to the press. And he warned me I might get a call from Lennon.

For the next couple of days, I jumped every time the phone rang. I'd seen first-hand, on a number of occasions, what John Lennon's temper could be like. And it wasn't pretty. Could

I have placed my whole relationship with the Beatles at risk over a stupid comment? It seemed ridiculous, but evidently John must have got angry with Derek. Or else, why would the whole press office be so upset over the whole thing?

Finally, the call came. I was at the salon, and immediately recognized John's voice. I started babbling at once.

"Look, John, I'm so sorry! I don't know why she wrote that. I certainly never said anything about you going bald..."

I went on and on like this, until I ran out of words. This was followed by a long silence, which sounded to me like the calm before a storm. And then John, with a worried voice, asked:

"Am I really going bald?"

So that was it! He wasn't so much angry as afraid that *Disc Magazine* might be right about the fate of his beloved hair!

"No, John!" I assured him at once. "Of course not. Look... I'm sorry. They twisted my words..."

"You don't have to explain how journalists work," John said, with a snigger. "Remember when I said I thought the Beatles were more popular than Jesus? The whole of America wanted my fucking head on a plate!"

I laughed along with him, but it was nervous laughter.

"So I don't need to worry about my hair, then?" he asked once again, only half in jest.

"No, you don't, John, seriously."

"Well, that's good news," John said. "Anyway, you'd better come over to the Apple offices quickly."

"Oh," I said, straightening up again. "Why's that?"

"Before it all falls out!" he joked.

I went over to Savile Row and met John there. Once again, I reassured him that his hair wasn't falling out, and we had a real laugh over the whole silly episode. I did advise him to have his hair trimmed regularly, however, so that it didn't get wispy and break off at the ends. But did he take any notice? No! Together with Yoko Ono, he just let his hair grow and grow – and eventually it did begin to recede.

Now, after fifty years, I can reveal the truth. Back in 1969, I knew perfectly well that John was beginning to lose his hair. During my first meeting with Paul at 7 Cavendish Avenue, I had guaranteed my new client that he would never go bald. In John Lennon's case, I couldn't have made such a promise. Had he lived significantly beyond forty, his hair would indeed have thinned out to such a point that he could have been defined as bald-headed. To be clear: I never revealed my true opinion to Caroline Boucher. What she wrote was her own interpretation, though with hindsight I guess you could say she saw right through me – probably part of her skill as a professional reporter. In any case, it is quite a thought: a bald John Lennon! Then again, it did little harm to Elton John

* * *

Among all of the rumours spread about the Beatles, perhaps none is odder than the conspiracy theory, still popular today on many websites, that Paul McCartney is dead, and has been dead for the past fifty years.

This urban legend was sparked by an article published by Tim Harper in the 17th September 1969 edition of *Times-Delphic*, the student newspaper of Drake University in Iowa. According to this article and a follow-up piece by Fred LaBour in a University of Michigan paper, Paul McCartney suffered a deadly road accident with his Aston Martin in November 1966, shortly after I cut his hair for the first time, and was replaced by a lookalike to prevent a fall in record sales. For some reason, the other three Beatles, Jane Asher and many of their closest friends went along with the crazy, ultra-secret scheme, but then spent years planting subtle and highly cunning "clues" in subsequent songs and records. The "evidence" that has been put forward over the years includes the following claims:

The *Sgt. Pepper's* album cover supposedly represents a funeral, with a wreath in the shape of Paul's guitar. The "Billy Shears" introduced in the title track of the album refers to William Campbell, the impersonator who replaced Paul, after winning a McCartney lookalike contest.

During the second fade-out of 'Strawberry Fields Forever', you can hear John saying "I buried Paul".

The "Walrus" on the *Magical Mystery Tour* is supposed to be Paul, as revealed in the *White Album* song 'Glass Onion'. And the walrus is said to be a symbol of death.

If you play 'Revolution 9' from the *White Album* backwards, you can hear the words 'Turn me on dead man' being repeated over and over again.

The picture of the band walking over the zebra crossing at Abbey Road represents a funeral procession, with John in white (clergyman), Ringo in black (undertaker), George in denim jeans (grave-digger), and Paul with his eyes closed, bare feet and a cigarette, also known as a "coffin nail", in his hand (clearly, the deceased).

And on and on it goes…

The first time I learnt of this theory was while I was visiting some of my American relatives in New York, a few weeks after the original article by Tim Harper was published. The rumour was starting to gain some traction, and the media were looking for people who might be "in the know". Suddenly, I received a phone call at my relatives' place, from a certain WABC radio station. I have no idea how they got my number. Perhaps they had rung my flat in London, and Louisa had passed on my contact number to them.

At first, I thought it had to be some kind of joke. And a pretty grim sort of joke too. Paul dead? A fake Paul impersonating him for the past two years? It was just daft. And yet the radio journalist on the line seemed deadly serious.

"Look, wait a second," I said to him at one point, becoming exasperated with the man's insistence. "I don't care what you hear if you play their songs backwards. I can assure you that the Paul I know now is the same Paul I have always known."

"How can you be so sure?" he challenged me.

How can I be sure? I thought to myself. For a moment, he had me stumped. I mean, the Paul whose hair I'd styled just a few weeks before looked like the old Paul, and he sounded like the old Paul. But it was true that a close lookalike might have been able to fool me. Then, suddenly, I had an idea.

"I'll tell you why I'm sure," I said. "A person's hair, the specific way it's patterned on the scalp, is as particular to him or her as a fingerprint. Everyone's is different. I cut Paul's hair before and after that supposed accident, and I'd have noticed if anything was different. There's simply no way an impostor could have fooled me."

The radio journalist, however, was not convinced. He had such a long list of "Paul is dead" clues that, in the end, I even began to doubt myself.

When I got back to England shortly afterwards, Derek's press office was being flooded with phone calls from all over the world, demanding proof that Paul McCartney was alive. At Apple, this bizarre media storm was the cause of both amusement and frustration. Derek had initially issued a statement, to the effect that it was "a load of old rubbish". But the phone calls wouldn't stop. So he eventually sent a reporter from *Life Magazine* up to Scotland, where Paul had been spending some quiet time with his new wife Linda Eastman and their children. The resulting article, "Paul Is Still with Us", did manage to stem the tide, but the rumour didn't die down completely.

It was something of a relief when my favourite client eventually returned from his northern retreat and called for me to go round to St John's Wood. I could at last put my mind at rest.

As we were setting up the "salon" in the upstairs bedroom, we got to chatting as usual. But at one point I went quiet as I ran my fingers through his hair, paying close attention to how it fell across his forehead.

"What are you up to, Leslie?" he asked, noticing my furtive mood.

"Oh, just checking to see if you are dead or alive," I said.

Paul broke into peals of laughter. He'd obviously had it up to his ears with the insistent rumours of his demise.

"So, what's the verdict?" he asked

"I am delighted to confirm that you are the one and only Paul McCartney."

"Well, thank you, Leslie," he chuckled. "I am very relieved to hear it. Now perhaps we should tell the rest of the world…"

I did tell everyone who brought up the topic. In fact, it still does crop up from time to time, to my continuous astonishment. Fred LaBour eventually admitted that he fabricated many of the "clues" in his original article, and that the piece was meant as a joke. But I suppose that the conspiracy theorists will never be fully satisfied. After all, they say, Fred LaBour could have been threatened into recanting. As for the Beatles' hairdresser, why shouldn't he have been brought into the plot, along with Jane Asher and all the rest of them? *Of course he'd go along with it*, they'd say. *He had everything to gain by claiming that he was still cutting the real Paul McCartney's hair! And they repaid him handsomely for his silence by opening up his very own salon in the basement of Apple Tailoring…*

Believe what you wish. But first record yourself saying "number nine" several times, and play the recording backwards. Doesn't it sound a little like "Turn me on, dead man"?

12

How Fame Nearly Got Me Killed

I think it must have been at Dave Clarke's party. His huge residence in Mayfair was full of hip people in bell bottoms and flowery shirts, shaking to the rhythms and flashing lights that pumped out of his jukebox, or examining the strands of his shaggy white carpet with tripped-out amazement. Unlike Paul's unassuming home, Dave's penthouse really did look like a proper pop-star's pad. I'd been there many times before, since he'd become a regular client of mine by 1968, and I'd often ring his doorbell just for a friendly chat. But this was the first time he'd invited me along to one of his famous showbiz parties.

At one point, I walked outside onto the balcony and perched myself on the edge, looking down over Curzon Street in Mayfair. Suddenly, I heard a deep velvety woman's voice.

"Fancy a joint?" she said.

I looked up, and my eyes fell on a striking black woman I immediately recognized. It was Nina Simone.

"Don't mind if I do," I said, taking the rolled-up ciggie between my fingers.

I guess that's when it struck me: I wasn't that kid from Burnt Oak any more. I wasn't even just a hairdresser who worked at the trendiest of salons. I was a guest of Dave Clarke. I was making small talk with Nina Simone. Over in the corner was Paul McCartney, who'd come to the party with Jane.

Richie Havens, soon to be the Woodstock Festival's opening act, had been chatting with me a bit earlier. The luxurious penthouse was absolutely packed with famous faces. And so I finally accepted that I'd become one of them. I too was a celebrity of sorts.

Before then, I'd resisted the idea. I'd seen my name in the papers, of course. And, increasingly, the most fashionable people in town not only wore, but spoke of the "Cavendish cut", recommending me to their friends and colleagues as a trustworthy private hairdresser to the stars. But I'd continued to feel like an outsider, unable really to believe that I belonged to that scene. Up on that balcony, though, looking out over the city, it dawned on me how much things had changed in only a couple of years, since Suzanna Leigh had been too embarrassed to introduce me to her famous friends. Now, here I was, with my own celebrity crowd. A celebrity myself! Not a pop star, certainly, but just about as celebrated as a hairdresser could possibly become.

Fame, however, comes with a price.

*　　*　　*

Even before leaving Vidal Sassoon and opening my own salon, I'd learnt that sky-rocketing to the heights of success can be a risky business. As I've mentioned on several occasions, my boss Roger resented my work with Paul McCartney from the very beginning. As time went on and I became known throughout the country as the Beatles' hairdresser, his envy only got worse.

Roger never said anything to me. He never once mentioned Jane Asher or Paul McCartney, or any of the others. But I could see the bitterness simmering inside him. I felt its heat every time he made a show of correcting my haircuts in full view of the whole salon. Then, when he fired me after the Magical Mystery Tour, his triumph was cut short as Vidal forced him to take me back. After that humiliating blow, he could hardly bear to look me in the eye.

What made him finally explode was that article in the *Evening Standard*. Until then, he'd been the only hairdresser, aside from Vidal Sassoon himself, who had been featured in newspapers and fashion magazines. Roger Thompson had been the up-and-coming styling star, the revered artist, the "hair architect". But now Leslie Cavendish, his recent junior, that upstart barely out of his teens, was being interviewed by none other than Ray Connolly, the famous pop-music journalist. That was simply too much for Roger. He just couldn't stand for it.

One afternoon, at the Grosvenor House salon, I'd been cutting Chris Stamp's hair on the top floor, after hours. Male customers still weren't allowed to mix with the normal clientele at Vidal Sassoon's, but my little side operation on the top floor continued to grow unabated. After the Who's co-manager had gone, I came down the stairs and was surprised to find Roger waiting for me, a dark look in his eye. Every time we'd crossed paths in the past year, the tension between us had been palpable. But this time, it was about to come out in the open once and for all. The salon was empty except for the two reception girls at the entrance. We were on our own.

"That's it, Leslie!" he shouted at me. "This is not a men's hairdresser's! From now on, you are not to be cutting men's hair on these premises!"

"What's your problem, Roger?" I asked, getting riled up myself.

"You're charging outrageous prices for men's haircuts," he continued. "Where's all that money going to, eh?"

"Into Vidal's till!" I shouted back, outraged. "Where do you think, you... you..."

Now, I'm not a violent type. Even before I was reading *Siddhartha*, listening to Joan Baez and smoking hash, I'd always been a peaceful sort of chap. When I was a kid, I did love to watch the boxing matches on Sundays with my father, grandfather and Uncle "Pinky" at the Shoreditch Town Hall. Uncle Pinky was involved, together with his brother-in-law Archie Kasler and Bernie Grossmith, in organizing the matches, and his wife, my Aunt Sophia, would prepare a hot stew for all the boxers in their house in Shoreditch, like a good Jewish momma. In that house on Hanbury Street, right over the place where Jack the Ripper committed his second murder, I met many of the day's biggest boxers, including world champions such as Terry Downes and John Conteh. Once, in a gym, I even tried my hand at the sport, thinking that I knew all the moves. But after I took my first punch in the face, I decided it wasn't for me. The only occasion I remember getting into a real fight was that time in my school days, when I ended up with a black eye and both Lawrence and me got caned by the headmaster. I suppose I learnt my lesson well, because I never again resorted to physical violence.

This time, though, Roger's unfair accusations rammed into me like a power punch to the stomach, and I found myself striking back. I couldn't help myself. In fact, I wasn't even conscious of doing anything at all. My left hand seemed to form into a fist of its own accord, flying through the air until it whacked Roger right in the eye socket, a cross-punch hard enough to throw him back onto the floor. Perhaps all those times at the ring with my Uncle Pinky had taught me something after all.

Roger was shocked, for sure. But so was I. What had I done? How could I have punched my own boss? And not just any boss, but Roger Thompson, Vidal Sassoon's right-hand man, his most celebrated stylist? However he'd treated me in these past months, I admired the socks off this man, and was immensely grateful for everything he'd taught me. I would never have become a stylist, let alone Paul McCartney's, if it hadn't been for his patient lessons. He was a hairdressing guru in his own right. And now I'd smacked him one right in the face.

Roger lay on the ground, stunned and moaning. One of the reception girls helped him to crawl up onto a couch, while I apologized clumsily for my inexplicable action. I could see that his eye was beginning to swell. Meanwhile, the other receptionist had phoned Roger's brother-in-law, the manager of the Bond Street salon.

"Joshua's on his way," she announced breathlessly.

That was bad news for me. Joshua was not only built like a middleweight boxer, but he had actually practised boxing for a time. What was I to do? Run away? Face Joshua? Try to appease Roger? In the event, I just stood there, frozen, watching as the receptionists tended to my boss's swollen eye and mentally reviewing the boxing techniques my grandfather would get so excited about.

Finally, Joshua burst into the salon, his well-toned body bulging under his smart suit.

"Look, Joshua…" I stammered, stepping back. "I don't know what to say… Roger had a go at me… He's been needling me for ages… I just lost my temper in the end, and I hit him… It's over."

As he advanced towards me with a grim look on his face, I braced myself for the worst. The reception girls stared at us in horror. He pulled his arm back, and then it came straight at me… as a handshake. Grabbing my hand in his thick fist, he looked me in the eye and said:

"Thank you, Leslie. If it hadn't been you, it would have been me!"

Though amazed, I could see why Joshua might have wanted to throw a punch at his brother-in-law. I had first-hand knowledge that Roger, who was married to his sister Shirley, wasn't the most faithful of husbands. During my training as a junior, on model nights, my mentor would sometimes ask me to ring up his wife and explain that he'd be working late that evening – even though he'd already finished his haircuts. Joshua and I never spoke of this matter, but I think we shared an understanding.

As for Roger and me, the little skirmish mercifully ended the tension that had built up between us. I think that, from the next morning, he resigned himself to the new state of affairs. I was no longer his junior at Vidal's: I'd become a successful stylist in my own right and, in any case, I wasn't going to let myself be pushed around by him just because he was my manager.

In 1969, Roger Thompson was promoted to the new role of International Creative Director at Vidal Sassoon's and moved to New York to head its Madison Avenue salon. By then I was fronting my own Apple studio on the King's Road, but before he left, I visited him at Grosvenor House and thanked him for teaching me to be a hairdresser. We shook hands, and I wished him the best of luck. As far as I'm concerned, Roger remained the top haircutting artist Vidal ever produced. His haircuts and styles have never been forgotten.

* * *

Another hazardous side effect of fame came my way in mid-1968. I received a phone call at my Apple Tailoring salon from the posh-sounding secretary of a certain Mr Stigwood, who "requested my private services" at his home in Stanmore, an affluent suburb in North London. The whole thing sounded to me like a royal summons. Who was this Stigwood character? Some sort of crusty aristocrat? A wealthy businessman? The most powerful mobster in town?

At Apple, Derek Taylor couldn't believe my ignorance.

"He's the coming man in pop business, my friend," the press officer told me, with a glass of whisky in one hand and a phone in the other. "He's managing Eric Clapton, the Bee Gees... He's the one who's bringing *Hair* to Shaftesbury Theatre."

Wow. *Hair*! As far as I was concerned, that tribal love-rock musical was the most astounding show to hit the stage ever. Though I hadn't seen it yet, I already knew the soundtrack by heart, a compendium of our whole hippy scene: love, nudity, sex, drugs, music, flowers, pacifism, spirituality, rebellion, mind-expansion, racial equality, environmentalism and, of course, long, flowing, wildly growing hair. From what I'd heard, at the end of the final act, right after the famous 'Age of Aquarius' climax, the audience was invited on stage to participate in a Be-In with the cast, everyone joining in a communal sing-and-dance rendition of 'Let the Sunshine in". What a trip! In fact, *Hair* seemed so in tune with what the Beatles were doing that I'd even dared to bring my imported copy of the album into Paul McCartney's house, and played it for him after one of his haircutting sessions. Unfortunately, he hadn't seemed very impressed...

"Sounds like a good client to have," I said to Derek.

"Not bad at all." Derek raised his glass in my direction. "Here's to cutting both the Beatles' and the Bee Gees' hair."

On the day of my appointment, I drove up, past Burnt Oak, to Robert Stigwood's leafy suburb. As I reached the tall gates of his residence, which dwarfed my Mini, I began to feel a little intimidated. *This isn't a house*, I thought, *it's a palace!* I'd never visited such a ritzy home. There was a collection of go-karts near the entrance, which Robert and his friends evidently used to race around the grounds. A young, uniformed butler greeted me at the door.

"Good morning," I said, feeling very much out of place. "I've come here to cut Mr Stigwood's hair and… This *is* the Stigwood home, isn't it?…"

"Oh yes," the butler said. "Mr Stigwood can't *wait* to meet you. He's just upstairs, in the main bedroom."

With that, he turned on his heel sharply and strode away across the marble floor. By then, I'd been exposed to plenty of camp behaviour, both at work and in my social circles. That butler registered at the very top of the camp-o-meter. In fact, as I walked towards the grand stairway, between tall columns that rose up to a lofty ceiling, I noticed that all of the male personnel that glided from one room to another seemed equally feminine in their movements.

By the time I made it to the first floor, my heart was beating hard in my chest, and it wasn't just the exertion. What was I getting myself into? Another of the boyish servants noticed my hesitation and waved his arm encouragingly at the ornate, semi-open door of the master bedroom. I tapped a couple of times on the door before entering.

"Do come in," a voice called from somewhere inside.

I stepped into the lavishly decorated bedroom, which was dominated by a huge four-poster bed. A bare-chested Robert Stigwood lay inside its pink satin sheets, looking for all the world like a member of the Roman Triumvirate. As I came closer, the impresario slithered out of the bed and stood before me, wearing only his silk pyjama trousers and an unmistakable "come hither" look.

I froze. This was not right. Though I didn't wish to upset my wealthy and influential client, I certainly wasn't going to encourage the fantasies he seemed to have prepared for our private session.

"Mr Stigwood," I said, trying to sound as professional as possible. "Please call me back when you're dressed."

I turned around and retraced my steps out of the room, feeling a huge sense of relief as soon as I was back in the hallway. I waited nervously for a few minutes, clutching my portable hairdressing kit for support, while the servants eyed me with curiosity.

Eventually, Stigwood called me back in. This time, I found him not in the bedroom but in his enormous en-suite bathroom. He greeted me fully clothed, and in a much more businesslike manner – as if our first meeting had never taken place. This suited me just fine. Clearly, he'd got the message, and the rest of our session proceeded quite normally. In fact, it was something of a quick one, as Stigwood didn't have that much hair.

The powerful manager didn't seem offended by my lack of interest. Though he never called me back to his residence, I did begin to work for the Bee Gees soon after, first on fashion shoots, then at the BBC studios, where *Top of the Pops* was recorded, and eventually also in their private homes. These sessions were much more enjoyable than the hair-raising experience with their manager. I was a big fan of their music, and would melt into the ground every time Barry Gibb pulled out his twelve-string guitar and played me a tune. The only hazard I had to face was trying to handle Robin Gibb's coiffure. His high forehead and thin hair texture were a real stylist's nightmare.

* * *

I've read somewhere that pop and film stars tend to live shorter lives than would be expected, by about seven years on average. I can certainly confirm that many of the people I associated with during my Swinging London days met with untimely deaths. Much of it undoubtedly had to do with the hedonistic lifestyle they indulged in. Jayne Mansfield died in a late-night road accident three years after I was stuck in that lift with her and Diana Dors. Brian Jones was found dead in his swimming pool only a few months after his last shopping expedition to Apple Tailoring. Keith Moon, Jimi Hendrix and Brian Epstein all overdosed on drugs. And many others left us long before their normal life expectancies, including Neil Aspinall, Mal Evans and Derek Taylor.

John Lennon, however, was a victim of fame itself. Shy by nature, he was particularly loath to the grabbing and groping of his adoring teenage fans, and often worried about being literally "torn apart" someday. In the end, he wasn't too far off the mark. Mark David Chapman, a troubled youth who initially idolized Lennon, became increasingly enraged with the singer after converting to Christianity. His anger was fuelled by the "more popular than Jesus" quip, by the lyrics of the song "God" and by the perceived "phoniness" of Lennon's appeals to peace and love when he lived like a millionaire. Finally, on

8th December 1980, Chapman waited for Lennon outside his apartment building, asked him to autograph his latest album, *Double Fantasy*, and then returned a few hours later to gun him down with five shots from a .38 special revolver.

Lennon's assassination was perhaps the most shocking celebrity death of my generation. But it wasn't the first time the Beatles had inspired a deranged mind to commit murder. A decade earlier, the lyrics from their *White Album* had been twisted into the sick justification for one of the grisliest serial killings in the history of America. And I, Leslie Cavendish should have been there.

This bizarre tale began in the summer of 1969, when I received a phone call, out of the blue, from the United States.

"Hi," the voice began. "Is this Leslie Cavendish?"

From the accent, I could tell the young man was from the West Coast.

"Yes, how can I help you?"

"I hear you're the hairdresser to the Beatles."

"I have that honour, yes."

"Well, it's great to meet you, Leslie. My name's Jay Sebring, and I'm a stylist like yourself here in California. Maybe you heard of me?"

"Of course," I lied. Like me, Jay was famous, but not *that* famous. "Good to talk to you, Jay."

"Yeah, well, thing is, here in the States I'm in a similar position to yours. I'm cutting Sinatra's hair, Sammy Davis Junior's, Jim Morrison's – you know, from the Doors?"

"Yeah, sure," I said, feeling instantly connected to this distant colleague.

"Lots of film stars, too: Steve McQueen, Warren Beatty, Kirk Douglas..."

"Not a bad line-up," I said, with growing curiosity. "And what can I do for you, Jay?"

"Oh, yeah: down to business. Listen, I got some backers here who want me to open a bunch of new salons, top-notch design, high-end clients… and, well… I'd love for you to work with me. With both our reputations together, we'd be quite a team, huh?"

"Um… yeah, could be," I said, not wanting to commit myself too much.

"Oh, we'd have to talk it all over, of course. Get to know each other. In fact, here's what I was thinking, Leslie. A few of us are going over to LA, to hang out at Sharon Tate's place. You know, the actress? Polanski's wife? She's a real good friend of mine."

"Yeah, I know Sharon," I said. "She was a client of Vidal Sassoon's when she was living in London."

"Cool, man, that's like total synchronicity. We're all going over to her house in a couple of weeks, so why don't you join us? A little work, a little fun, you know the scene…"

It was tempting to say the least. By mid-1969, the world of the Beatles was quickly beginning to unravel. Despite selling millions of singles and LPs, the complete lack of financial control at Apple Records was pushing the company towards bankruptcy. When Allen Klein, the manager of the Rolling Stones, was asked to re-establish some order at the start of the year, he discovered that the spending spree wasn't limited to the £600 per month Derek's office splurged on liquor, but included roast beef and caviar in the office kitchen, a mountain of bills from London's top restaurants, unjustified transatlantic plane tickets and extended phone calls to Canberra, Kathmandu and Acapulco. Not to mention the thousands of pounds being lost from thieves walking off with

TVs, electric typewriters, adding machines, cases of wine, boxes of records and even the lead on the roof...

Klein immediately set up a strict accounting system, reduced the number of Apple artists being promoted and fired anyone he decided wasn't strictly necessary, including Ron Kass, Alistair Taylor and Neil Aspinall. Apple Electronics, among other branches of the corporation, was also shut down, after "Magic Alex" failed to produce any revolutionary technologies whatsoever, or even a properly functioning studio downstairs. Inevitably, these changes caused plenty of friction, most notably between the Beatles themselves. In fact, Paul McCartney had refused to take on the American manager, favouring his new girlfriend's father and brother, Lee and John Eastman. Outvoted three to one by his bandmates, Paul was becoming increasingly alienated from the others, and I had a feeling that things might soon be coming to a head. John Lennon had just released 'Give Peace a Chance'. As the first solo single by one of the band's members, it sounded more like a declaration of war – or at least of independence.

As for my hairdressing business, things were also becoming harder for me. At the salon, my relationship with John Crittle had continued to deteriorate since Apple pulled out of our enterprise, and we were now facing a lot more competition from other boutiques and fashionable hairdressers. In addition, the cutbacks at Apple had affected my income, with fewer styling gigs for staff and not as many artists being promoted by the record company. So it certainly seemed like a good time to move on professionally. Jay Sebring's proposal offered me a fresh start across the Atlantic, plenty of new clients and a salon that wouldn't be stuck at the bottom of someone else's shop. Two years after Vidal had invited me to work at his studio in New York, here was a second chance to make it big in America.

Nevertheless, the idea of meeting the Californian stylist in two weeks' time, at Sharon Tate's party, didn't attract me, for some reason. Maybe it was my sixth sense. Maybe it was my talent for being at the right place at the right time – or, in this case, not being in the wrong place at the wrong time. Whatever it was, I decided that I wasn't going to be rushed into such a momentous change. The Beatles were back in their studio; I was hoping the situation at the salon might improve and, more generally, I needed to consider if I was ready to move away from London.

"Wow, Jay," I said. "That all sounds great, and yes, I am definitely interested. But listen, I'm very busy at the moment with the Beatles. Do you think we could speak again in about a month's time?"

"Sure Leslie, that's cool," Sebring said. "Just call me when you're ready."

After I hung up, I did some research and found confirmation that Jay Sebring really was the hippest hairdresser in the States. A few years later, he would become one of the inspirations for the character George Roundy in the film *Shampoo*, played by his ex-client Warren Beatty. At a time when a typical man's haircut and style cost $2 in the US, he was charging $50. His company, Sebring International, was now franchising salons and introducing hair products in his name. It certainly did sound like a perfect career move.

Two weeks later, however, I was in for a shock. Walking down the King's Road, I glanced at a newspaper on display, and a headline instantly grabbed my attention: SLAUGHTER IN LOS ANGELES: MOVIE-STAR WIFE OF ROMAN POLANSKI MURDERED. *Polanski's wife? Wasn't she the very Sharon Tate my future business partner had mentioned?* I picked up the paper and read the article with growing horror. The story described the gruesome killings in excruciating detail: mangled bodies, signs of torture and a single word scrawled on the front door in Tate's blood: PIG. Among the victims were two friends of the actress, her unborn child (she was eight months pregnant) and a prominent hairdresser called Jay Sebring. I looked at the date of the murders: 9th August. My blood ran cold. Had I taken up Jay's offer, I would have been staying at Sharon Tate's house during the very party that became a massacre. It took me weeks to recover from the fright.

However, the awful story would still take a further twist, both sinister and darkly ironic. A few months later, in December 1969, the culprits of the Tate massacre were finally apprehended, suspected of a whole slew of additional murders in which similar bloody messages had been left on walls. The odd thing, though, was that this group of psychopaths were not, as had first been assumed, drug dealers or low-life criminals. On the contrary. The "Manson Family" were a merry band of long-haired, pot-smoking hippies who had lived together in a Haight-Ashbury commune during the Summer of Love. Afterwards, they'd taken their own "Magical Mystery Tour", from San Francisco to Los Angeles, on an old school bus refurbished with colourful rugs and pillows instead of seats. Charles Manson, a guitar-playing musician and the group's guru, was obsessed with the Beatles and had hoped to publish music just like theirs, to "programme the young love" and spark off a revolution.

Except that Manson's revolution, which he prophesied as imminent, had to do with a "coming race war between blacks and whites". Believing himself to be the reincarnation of Jesus Christ, he had ordered the serial killings as a ploy to kick-start this conflict, which he called "Helter Skelter", just like the title of the Beatles' song. In fact, when Manson first listened to the *White Album*, he became convinced that the Beatles had channelled his own spirit (i.e., the truth) and crafted the entire record as a coded version of his demented prophecies. 'Sexy Sadie' referred to Susan Atkins, one of Tate's killers, who had worked as a topless dancer and was known as "Sadie Mae Glutz" within the group. The "Blackbird" who was waiting "for this moment to arise" confirmed the black man's imminent rebellion. The "Piggies" in the song (and later in the bloody scrawls) were the white people who would get "a damned good whacking". The two songs about "revolution" foretold the coming struggle, and 'Happiness is a Warm Gun' – well, that one was an outright incitement of violence. In short, Manson thought that the Beatles had encouraged him and his believers to go ahead with their madness.

I followed the subsequent Manson Family trials with the mesmerized horror that impels you to look at a road accident. I had survived, but my American twin was dead. And in any case, the Manson Family had killed off a part of me. They had inflicted a hundred stab wounds into the hippy dream of a new age of peace and love. It wasn't just my impression. No one could get their head around it. How could this be? How could these chilled-out hippies, with their colourful dresses and flowers in their hair, perpetrate such atrocious crimes? And how could the Beatles' lyrics have inspired their bloody rampage? Did it mean that our generation was just as mixed up as any other? That the Age of Aquarius was much farther off than we'd anticipated? That it was all a lie?

To make things worse, on 6th December 1969, the very week that the Manson Family members were arrested, the notorious Altamont Speedway Free Festival was held in California. Six months after the legendary Woodstock Festival, it featured many of the same bands, including Santana, Jefferson Airplane and Crosby, Stills and Nash. But for some reason, it ended disastrously. As for other similar events, the San Francisco Hells Angels – including my "buddies" Frisco Pete and Sweet William – had been hired to provide security. Apparently, on this occasion, the Angels had been paid in crates of beer, which they consumed during the festival itself. Violent fights broke out near the front of the stage, including an incident in which one of the Hells Angels punched out Marty Balin, one of Jefferson Airplane's lead singers. As a result, the Grateful Dead, despite having organized the festival, cancelled their appearance and left the venue. Finally, when the Rolling Stones came on, the situation escalated, and a drugged-out audience member, Meredith Hunter, jumped on stage and pulled out a gun. One of the Angels ran up to him and knifed the intruder to death, right in front of Mick Jagger and 300,000 fans. Elsewhere at the site, another three people died from accidents, and many were injured. The entire show was an extended nightmare: the bad trip to end all trips. The warmth, colour and fruits of the Summer of Love had been replaced by a cold wind that ushered in this Winter of Death.

So ended the 1960s, with Richard Nixon in the White House, Timothy Leary in jail and all of our idealistic hopes and fantasies shattered. But there was still one more nail to be hammered into the rainbow-streaked coffin of the counter-culture. On the tenth of April 1970, coinciding with the launch of Paul McCartney's first solo album, my long-time client announced that he was leaving the Beatles – an ironic development for the band, considering he'd always been the most committed member.

I won't here go into all the causes, versions and theories of the breakup. Frankly, I think that too much fuss has been made over the whole thing over the years. A whole slew of reasons can be compiled to explain the mounting friction that arose between the four Beatles, but I think the truth is much simpler. In my humble opinion, John, Paul, George and Ringo were four immensely talented people who increasingly didn't want to be defined by the initial project which had launched them into worldwide fame. Since they stopped touring, each of them had begun to explore his own interests, and tried pulling the rest of the band onto his boat. But inevitably, the boats drifted too far from each other. Or maybe their Yellow Submarine had become too small and stifling for the four of them. In any case, I think the breakup of the band was just a part of the natural order of things. Like the hair on their heads, it grew according to its own shape and texture. You could shape it, brush or even cut it, but you couldn't stop it from growing. The four musicians had been trying to bury the Beatles since their impersonation of Sgt. Pepper's marching band – and, finally, they'd managed to do it. Having witnessed a lot of the backstage tensions, I suppose it was about time.

I say all of this now, with the wisdom of age. In the spring of 1970, though, I was as gutted as everyone else. More so because their split signified the end of an era for me, professionally and personally. I still had my salon, of course, and I could continue to work with Paul and maybe some of the others as private clients. But never again would I be the "Beatles' hairdresser". At least we all had a consolation prize, in the form of a final release by the band as a whole. The title of the album held a parting message for us all: *Let It Be*.

13

When We Get Older, Losing Our Hair

Louisa and I broke up around the same time that the Beatles did. Looking back on it now, I can say that our romance was as melodramatic and heart-wrenching as any of the Italian operas I've started to appreciate in my later years. I promise that I'm not making anything up – not even the names.

The Stylist of Chelsea

ACT I

Mr Rabaiotti's imposing corporate offices.

Leslie and Louisa, hippy dreamers of Swinging London, have both discovered true love at last. For the first time, the working-class boy, who was driven to hairdressing simply to be surrounded by glamorous women, has decided to marry and settle down with a family.

Leslie visits Louisa's father, a Catholic businessman, at his offices in central London, to inform him of his intentions. Mr Rabaiotti, who had sympathized with Mussolini's Fascist regime, is not happy with the idea of a Jew marrying his daughter. Moreover, he has his own plans to wed Louisa to Rocco, the son of his equally wealthy business partner.

"What will you do with the trust fund my daughter will inherit when she turns twenty-one?" he sneers at Leslie at one point.

"That's for her to decide!" sings the idealistic youth. "I'm not interested in that."

The old man laughs bitterly.

"Don't make the same mistake I made," he warns mysteriously.

Leslie leaves, shaken by the meeting. He is still committed to marry Louisa, but runs off towards dark thunderclouds.

ACT II
Leslie and Louisa's flat in Chelsea.

Louisa has discovered the delights of cocaine and heroin, which help relieve the tedium of her pampered life. Her Irish mother was an alcoholic, and now she too begins to slide down the road towards addiction. As Leslie arrives at the flat, Louisa tries to conceal her drugs, but he confronts her once again over her destructive habits. In the heat of the argument, he decides to call off their marriage plans, though it breaks his heart.

ACT III
A Catholic convent in Hertfordshire.

Louisa has spent the last few months secluded in a convent in the countryside, trying to overcome her addictions. She is now clean, but depressed, and all she will say to the nuns that care for her is "please get Leslie". Mr Rabaiotti has no option but to call that despised Jewish boy and beg for his help.

Leslie arrives at the convent on a midsummer night. The nuns assure him that Louisa is now free of the evil drugs, and she pleads with him, "Let us marry, now!" But Leslie tells her it is impossible. By then he has found a new girlfriend, Jocelyn, who is crazy about him. Mr Rabaiotti's call interrupted Leslie while he was preparing Jocelyn's twenty-first birthday party, and he must now go back to her. However, Leslie discovers that his feelings for Louisa are stronger than he'd supposed. In fact, he begins to suspect that Jocelyn was only his way of forgetting about his true love. Finally, in a moment of weakness, he agrees to marry Louisa.

ACT IV
Julie's Restaurant, Notting Hill.

Just before her twenty-first birthday party, Leslie announces to Jocelyn that he has something important to tell her. The poor girl is convinced that the wedding proposal she has long awaited is finally about to arrive, just in time for her birthday. Instead, Leslie confesses to her that Louisa has returned to his life, and that he has decided to marry his old flame. Jocelyn weeps bitter and desperate tears as the ruined birthday party begins, with both of their friends and family in attendance.

ACT V
A beach on the French Riviera.

Louisa and Leslie seem happy together, once again, and plan their upcoming wedding. As they stroll by a swanky outdoor cocktail bar, however, Leslie is torn by a terrible thought.

He cannot take his beloved to the bar and have a drink or smoke a cigarette, or even order wine at a restaurant, without tempting her to fall once again into the pit of addiction. In fact, if he marries her, he will spend his whole life as a nursemaid for a recovering drug addict. Louisa notices his sadness and asks him for the reason, leading to his final, tragic decision. He will break up with Louisa once again, and give up on love completely.

I suppose that, in a real opera, it would have ended worse. Louisa or her father would probably have killed Leslie in a fit of rage with a nearby beach-umbrella pole, and she would have drowned herself in the Mediterranean, by tying her foot to the cocktail bar's decorative anchor. But it was bad enough as it was. My true love hated me, Jocelyn and her entire family had good reason to curse Leslie Cavendish for ever, and I'd given up hope of ever finding my one true love.... On top of all that, the Beatles had broken up.

Having always been an irrepressible optimist, I'd never understood why someone would take their own life. Suicide just didn't fit with my way of thinking. Normally, whatever the matter was, I could just go to my club and sweat it off in a good game of tennis. But for a few terrible moments in 1970, I did flirt with that operatic temptation. I was haunted nightly by a dream in which I struggled to climb out of a narrow, dark, slippery and absurdly tall tennis-ball can, trying to reach the tiny dot of sky at the top. Then, when I awoke, I'd find myself confronted with that dreadful question: is my life worth living?

Luckily, I still had my dog Ernie around the house. He couldn't answer any existential quandaries for me, of course, but he did urgently need to go walkies in the morning. Outside, in the fresh air, things didn't seem quite as bad. And eventually, I did climb out of that bloody tennis-ball can.

* * *

I closed my salon in 1972.

I still took on a few freelance hairdressing jobs, but they didn't amount to much of an income, so I sold my Mini and my flat in Chelsea, moved to a house in cheaper Fulham and hugged Ernie a lot. The brilliant thing about dogs is that they couldn't care less about status, wealth and all those other silly things we humans get so hung up on. So while I was trying to adjust to my new, diminished existence, he was the best companion I could have possibly had.

Around that time, I'd sometimes bum lifts from Barry Gibb's chauffeur, Billy, who had become a friend of mine thanks to my work with the Bee Gees. When I signed on for unemployment benefits, Billy used to drive me to the unemployment office. This was convenient, but for the fact that his car was an enormous Rolls-Royce. I could hardly turn up to collect my benefits in a Roller, of course, so he would park just around the corner. I suppose that image sums up what my life became after the Beatles' breakup. I was stuck at a ridiculous halfway point between poverty and glitz.

Apart from the Bee Gees and a few other loyal clients, I was still Paul's preferred hairdresser, and felt privileged to visit the ex-Beatle during that period, when he was rarely seen outside his house on Cavendish Avenue. He had adopted a thick beard and shaggy hairstyle, and became generally unkempt. On the many times I dealt with his increasingly unruly hair, I found him relatively serene. Thoughtful, yes, and undoubtedly sad, but not in a desperate state as the rumours tended to suggest. Like myself, Paul was an eternal optimist, and I'm certain that his new family helped him keep his balance – including his trusty sheepdog Martha.

His wife Linda was also collaborating with him on a new project, Wings, together with the Moody Blues' guitarist Denny Laine. In March 1973, the band held a charity concert at London's newly opened Hard Rock Cafe, for the launch of their album *Red Rose Speedway*. When my client invited me to this event, I was finally able to see Paul McCartney on stage, for the first time since that early Pigalle Club concert. I was delighted to find that he was back in top form, and didn't doubt for a second that Wings would be a success – which it eventually was.

Shortly afterwards, however, Paul and Linda moved to their new home in Peasmarsh, in East Sussex. Though Paul kept the house in St John's Wood, the couple didn't visit London that often, so I finally lost touch with the McCartneys, as Ernie did with Martha.

I picked up one last memento from that period. I'd been over to cut Linda's hair, while Heather, her daughter, was half watching me at work and half concentrating on drawing a picture with her crayons. Before I left, Linda asked me if I wouldn't mind cutting little Heather's hair too. Once I'd finished the job for my young client, under her mother's close supervision, Heather ran back to the table.

"Would you like to see my picture now?"

"Yes, please," I answered.

Heather was about to hand it over when she seemed to have second thoughts. The little girl pulled the sheet back onto the table, scrawled something right over her drawing, and then handed it to me proudly. What she'd written was: "This is a princess. Love to Leslie. Heather McCartney". The drawing, which shows many heads of longer- and shorter-length hair embroidered on the dress of the princess, is one of my most treasured possessions.

* * *

After I closed down my salon, I couldn't bear the idea of going back to hairdressing full-time. What was I going to do? Join Vidal Sassoon again? In my profession, working for the Beatles was like scaling Mount Everest. Anything else would seem like a barren hillock in comparison. So the idea of joining even the fanciest salon just didn't excite me any more. Instead, my parents helped me set up a men's fashion boutique near their footwear shop in East Street Market. I'd learnt a lot about the business from John Crittle, and it was also a way of staying in familiar territory, right where my grandfather had planted his horse-drawn shoe stall so many years before. Plus, with my parents' help, I'd be able to juggle the running of the boutique with my unpredictable private hairdressing work.

During the Sixties, business had been booming at my family's shoe shop in Elephant and Castle. Alex Shoes, named after my grandfather, was only a few streets away from Aylesbury Estate, one of the largest public-housing projects in Europe, so my family supplied work boots, school shoes and slippers for many of its ten thousand residents. My business-savvy grandfather had chosen his premises right next to the market's toilets, which meant that people would always be queuing up outside his window display. This provided the shop with a never-ending stream, you might say, of customers. Also, East Street was one of only two London markets with a royal charter to open on Sundays, long before high-street shops and shopping centres were able to do so. And to top it off, my grandfather had managed to secure the exclusive rights to sell Dr Martens boots in South London, just as they were becoming fashionable.

At Leslie Cavendish's Boutique, I began to sell smart two-tone suits, Crombie overcoats and DM boots to the trendy working-class mods who'd zip into East Street Market on their curvy Italian scooters. So I suppose that, in a way, from the 1970s onwards, I managed to keep myself at the cutting edge of fashion. Still, there's no doubt my clientele was a far cry from the foppy King's Road celebrities I'd become used to dealing with.

*　*　*

How did I adapt to my fall from the heights of fame and success? Not too badly, all in all. I did miss my wild Beatles adventures, undoubtedly. Every time I heard their music, or any of the new songs John, Paul, George and Ringo began to publish in their separate solo careers, I'd get nostalgic for that Sixties dream that receded, year by year, into history. 'Yesterday', in particular, took on a whole new meaning for me. But in the end, I just got on with it, like my beloved Queens Park Rangers, who'd dropped back down to the Second Division after their brief moment of glory around the Summer of Love. Ob-la-di, Ob-la-da, life really does go on – and it was time for me to grow up with the rest of my generation. I suppose I'd had enough lucky breaks during that magical decade to last me a lifetime. In any case, I'd always been something of an outsider to the world of pop stardom, and felt as comfortable down the pub in South London as in

Dave Clark's glitzy Mayfair parties. I decided I could still be cool in a streetwise, rough-and-tumble sort of way, which was the direction youth culture was moving in anyway. *Fair's fair, see? Sorted. No troubles, mate.*

Still, I did have my wistful moments. A particularly poignant one arrived together with a frail-looking elderly man whose face in my window display seemed strangely familiar. It was a cold winter morning in 1975 when I noticed this distinguished gentleman stooping over his cane outside my shop and looking inside, his silver hair neatly combed back under a trilby hat. The more I gazed on the man's thick lips and wise, wrinkled face, the more I got the feeling that I'd met him before. Why else would he be peering into my shop with such curiosity, anyway? Perhaps he was a forgotten family friend, or even one of my grandfather's old clients. So I stepped outside the door.

"Hello, sir," I said. "What brings you down here?"

"Oh." He smiled up at me. He was rather short in stature, and his pronounced stoop made him seem even smaller. But he had a lively spark in his eye. "Well, I haven't been down this street in a long time, but I was born very close to here. Just past your shop, in fact. And it brings back many memories..."

So he wasn't an old acquaintance. His warm and friendly voice wasn't particularly familiar to me either. The accent was distinctly mid-Atlantic, so I assumed that if the gentleman was originally English, he must have lived in the United States for a good part of his life. But still, there was something about his smile, and the way his eyebrows moved under his hat, that instinctively made me want to chuckle. And it convinced me that somehow, somewhere, I'd come across this man before. Just as I was about to ask him, though, he did an odd thing. He put his finger to his lips, said "Shhh" and gave me a wink.

A moment later, without any further explanation, he was off, hobbling down the street.

As I watched him walk away, slowly and with evident difficulty, I noticed his distinctive waddling gait. At first I put it down to his age, and then, suddenly, it struck me. I knew where I had seen that gait before. Even though he wasn't twirling his walking stick around as he used to in his movies, there was no mistaking it. That wizened figure was none other than Charlie Chaplin.

The legendary actor had come to London for his knighting by Queen Elizabeth, which took place a few days later, on the fourth of March 1975. As a kid, I'd probably been more of a Marx Brothers fan, but I'd loved *The Great Dictator*, long before I knew I'd get into the haircutting business like the Jewish barber he played in the movie. Now, years later, I found myself identifying with the man himself. Like me, Chaplin had risen from humble beginnings to the heights of success, and then, with the arrival of talking movies and advancing age, his star too had faded. In fact, his last great film was the melancholy *Limelight*, an autobiographical tale about a washed-up comedian, much like himself. That image of Chaplin looking into my shop window, recalling his childhood, seemed perfectly to mirror my nostalgia of that period, towards my own more recent glory days. The great man's warm sense of humour also struck me as the right kind of attitude in facing the ups and downs of life: a wink and a smile.

* * *

I didn't completely lose touch with the celebrity world. For the next decade or so I'd still go out socially to some of the trendiest nightclubs in London, including one of the most exclusive members-only venues in the world, Tramps. Through an ex-client of mine, I'd become friends with the owner, Johnny Gold, and he provided me with a lifetime membership to this oak-and-chandelier den of iniquity for the stars. In the meantime, I remained in contact with several people from the Swinging London scene, including Ray Connolly, Pattie Boyd and Chris O'Dell, who by then had moved on from the Beatles to touring with the Rolling Stones and Bob Dylan.

Funnily enough, these friendships allowed me to frequent one of the Beatles right into the 1980s: Ringo Starr. Pattie Boyd used to give great dinner parties, and on many occasions Ringo would also be there with his new wife, the film actress Barbara Bach. These evenings together were always great fun and reminded me of the old scene. It was then that I got to know the warm and funny side of Ringo, which had been stifled in those tense recording sessions I'd witnessed at Abbey Road. This new side to his personality made me reflect that the breakup of the band was probably something of a release for the drummer. He no longer had anything to prove to the others, and could simply get on with his music and film careers, as well as his family life.

It was at Tramps that I met my first wife, Ellie Smith, a six-foot tall American model who kept getting deported from the UK for doing photo shoots without a work permit. She was fun and beautiful, and after I'd rescued her at the airport for the tenth time, we decided it would be easier if we just got married. Ever the innocent romantic, I actually convinced myself it was love, and got excited once more with the idea of having a family.

"If we get married," I told Ellie, "I want to have kids."

"Whatever you want, Leslie," she said, and gave me a kiss.

We had a huge wedding in a Mayfair club, with over a hundred guests, and then a few months later I discovered she was secretly on the pill.

"You're too immature to have children," was her explanation.

Those six words burst my romantic fantasy in an instant. It hadn't been love at all. Ellie had found her work permit, and the streetwise Leslie Cavendish had been played for a fool. From then on, our relationship became one great big drawn-out argument, right down to the last bitter details of our divorce papers.

"I could have told you six months ago," my mother concluded when I broke the news to her.

By the time I turned forty, and the customers at my shop had gone from Mods to Punks and New Romantics, I'd practically given up on the idea of raising a family. My days just seemed to plough on ahead through the age of Thatcher and Reagan, in which the cute little Yellow Submarines of our youth seemed to have been bombed out of existence. "There is no such thing as society," Maggie had told us. "There are individual men and women, and there are families." Quite a far cry from the utopian Be-Ins of the hippy scene, which my generation had expected would usher in a new age of sharing.

At the same time, I was beginning to lose a lot of the people around me. My father had passed away from heart failure shortly after John Lennon was shot, and my grandparents had also left us by then. Even Ernie was gone. It was just my mum, me and her two sisters running the family's shoe shops in East Street Market, and the growth of shopping centres was taking a further toll on our business. We managed to make a good living, but it was only a question of time before we'd have to close down.

Outside of work, I concentrated on my two passions: music and sports. I was still devoted to Queens Park Rangers, of course, and in the Eighties my beloved team had returned to the First Division under the management of Terry Venables. In the meantime, I'd developed a love for that all-time English game, cricket, and continued to play tennis at the Hurlingham Club, of which I'd become a member.

It was on my way to a tennis tournament, in fact, at the exclusive Queen's Club, that I met a woman who would completely transform my life. Charlotte Stridh was staying with my friend Dympna, a TV agent who lived three houses away from me in Normand Mews, right around the corner from the club. Stopping by Dympna's house, I was so taken by this beautiful twenty-five-year-old from the southern Swedish village of Helsingborg that I never actually made it to the match. We hit it off straight away, got married in 1989 and, before I knew it, I found myself the father of two wonderful boys, Aidan and Oliver. Moreover, once the last of my family's shops had been sold off at the end of the Nineties, Charlotte and I decided to move to the small town of Alhaurín el Grande, near the southern Spanish coast, and I became a house-dad full-time. The new, responsible Leslie Cavendish even gave up smoking, the last of my unhealthy hippy habits. Amazing, but even my freewheeling old friend Chris O'Dell, after abusing every illegal substance in the books, had become a drugs counsellor in Tucson, Arizona.

For a few years, Charlotte ran a *cafetería* near Malaga with her Swedish friends, while I took the boys to school. As in my kibbutz days, I was living the Mediterranean dream again, cooking our home-grown vegetables, picking oranges from the orchard and pressing oil from our own olives. A new millennium was dawning, and though it may not have been the Age of Aquarius, it certainly felt like Charlotte and I were setting up our own little international utopia. What could possibly go wrong?

Well, it turned out the Mediterranean dream wasn't for me. Once the initial excitement wore off, my chilled-out life in the tiny rural town of Alhaurín, with all of those hours to myself, began to make me restless. Eventually, I tired of the back-breaking work in the orchard and the hours of driving around in my 4x4. I never quite managed to fit into the native culture, either, or that of the British expats in the area – many of whom turned out to be unbearably bigoted and closed-minded. Even Queens Park Rangers, whose games I followed on satellite TV, let me down, with a string of poor results and a slide into financial chaos and corruption scandals. As a result, the fifty-five-year-old Leslie Cavendish gradually became a grumpy, nagging bore. It wasn't so much that Charlotte couldn't stand me. I couldn't stand myself. I guess I was too much of a Londoner in the end. I missed the buzz. I missed the noise. I missed the helter-skelter.

So began my second divorce. Fortunately, this time around things were a lot more civil. Charlotte and I still loved and appreciated each other: we'd simply grown apart. I will always be tremendously grateful to her for the privilege of bringing up my children – who are more important to me than any pop star I ever met. I don't regret any of the decisions I made with her. As in the case of the Beatles' breakup, I think it was just part of the natural way of things. Nevertheless, like any divorce, whether personal or professional, it hurt – like all the tragic love songs said it would.

* * *

By the time Charlotte and I separated, I was nearing my sixtieth birthday, and supposed that my days of romance were over. I was feeling a bit sorry for myself, and also rather embarrassed, frankly, at this new failure in my life. I fretted about how to break the news to my mother, who would probably be disappointed by her wayward son, or maybe tell me that she knew it would happen all along. I still occasionally listened to the old music though, on a 1964 Wurlitzer jukebox I'd acquired, and I don't know about you, but every time I play 'Here Comes the Sun', it rekindles that part of me that still hopes for a third, a fourth or a sixteenth chance. Amazingly enough, it was Betty Boots who came to the rescue.

My mother was still living in Burnt Oak, retired, but still going strong in her eighties, swimming at a local pool early in the mornings and then hanging out at the bingo parlour with her East Street friends. On a recent visit to London, I'd asked her for the keys to the garage so I could dig out my old barber-shop chair from the King's Road salon. Beatles memorabilia seemed to have sky-rocketed in price around the turn of the century, with items the Beatles handled, including guitar picks and microphones, selling at Sotheby's for tens of thousands of pounds. I was sure my beautiful crushed-velvet chair from Apple's very own hairdressing studio, which had seated George Harrison, Keith Moon, Dave Clark and so many others, would be worth a fortune by now.

"Oh, that moth-eaten thing," my mother scoffed. "I chucked it out ages ago..."

"No you didn't, Mum," I said, thinking she *had* to be joking.

"Yes, I did, Les. It was rubbish, and it was in the way. The dustman took it."

Speechless, I stormed off to the garage to check for myself. That enormous beast of a chair had always been there, in the corner. It weighed a ton, and one of its wheels was broken, so moving it was no easy feat. I simply refused to believe my mother could have got rid of it. But when I opened up the garage, my wonderful antique was nowhere to be seen. It had vanished into thin air, as if my Apple-backed salon had never existed in the first place – as if I'd never met any of the Beatles all those years ago and my precious memories were nothing but an old man's wishful fabrications.

But then I pulled myself together. That barber-shop chair had *definitely* existed. It had sat right there in the corner, gathering dust, for years.

"Mum!" I shouted back to her. "Do you realize what you've done? Beatles stuff is being sold for hundreds of thousands of pounds! You've thrown away an absolute fortune!"

"Well, it's gone now, Les," she pointed out matter-of-factly. "What do you want for dinner?"

I thought I could never forgive her for that. But I was wrong. Shortly after I broke up with Charlotte, my mother made up for the loss of that priceless historical relic – a hundredfold.

Back in my childhood, there was a cute little girl who lived across the road from us in Burnt Oak. I remember Susan as bright and friendly, but since she was eight years younger than me, I only ever saw her as my cousin Lynn's best friend. When Lynn got her precious signed album and lock of hair from Paul McCartney, these gifts from "Cousin Leslie" must have made quite an impression on the twelve-year-old Susan, who had already screamed her way through one of the Beatles' early concerts at the Finsbury Park Astoria Theatre in 1964. Forty years later, little Susan had become a successful businesswoman who sold knitwear to the major UK high-street retailers, and she also happened to have a home in Marbella.

My mother, unaware that I'd separated from Charlotte, suggested to Susan that she ring me up when she next travelled to Spain. We met for a coffee and, within minutes, Sue and I fell into a comfortable, playful banter that was bizarrely familiar, as if we'd always known each other – which, in a way, of course, we had. We shared a Jewish upbringing in the same neighbourhood, the experience of the Sixties and Seventies, our work in the world of fashion and a love of going out on the town. Plus, it turned out Sue was an even bigger fan of the Beatles than me! I suppose we can't say it was love at first sight, but it was no less fresh and exciting. We've been together now for eleven wonderful years.

Thanks to this relationship, I've also finally discovered what my mother had been telling her best friends about her son throughout my whole life. Incredibly, considering how little she seemed to have been impressed by my celebrity connections when I'd told her about them, Betty Boots had been bragging about "My Les who cuts the Beatles' hair, you know", behind my back, for years. On the other hand, Sue had got the impression that I was some kind of hopeless playboy. Rather embarrassing, but I suppose I can see how someone could have got that, um... *completely erroneous* impression.

My old friend Lawrence, who was living between London and the French Riviera after retiring from hairdressing, just couldn't believe it. After all that chasing after movie stars, models and celebrities, Leslie Cavendish had found his soulmate across the street in good old Burnt Oak. Paul McCartney had told me as much a hundred times, but had I listened? *Get back to where you once belonged!*

* * *

Speaking of Paul McCartney, in 2012 I received an invitation to the British Film Institute, on London's South Bank, for a special screening of a BBC Arena documentary titled *The Beatles' Magical Mystery Tour Revisited*. I was particularly excited with the idea of viewing previously unseen footage from the movie, including the fish-and-chips scene in which I featured prominently. Paul had also been invited, of course, and it was announced to the press that he would be in attendance.

I went with my son Aidan, who looked forward to meeting his dad's old client and friend. Naturally, I was also thrilled at the idea, but I found myself, as in the old days, hiding my enthusiasm. Just in case.

Didn't want to be too disappointed, you see.

"Dad," Aidan asked me as we headed towards the BFI. "Do you think he'll recognize you after all these years?"

"Don't be silly," I answered. "Of course he will."

Or not, I secretly worried. Four decades is a long time. I'd watched Paul McCartney age through the press, but he would have no idea what I looked like these days. Wrinkles aside, I had put on some weight since we'd last met; my face was rounder, and my hairstyle had become more formal. Also, I could imagine someone like the ex-Beatle must have met a lot of people in the intervening years. Even if he did recognize me, though, would he still meet me? Would he still greet me? Now that we were both well past sixty-four?

When we arrived at the cinema, I was pleased to bump into a number of people I hadn't seen for ages, such as Pattie Boyd and some of the few remaining cast members from the Magical Mystery Tour coach. I also noticed that Liam Gallagher from

Oasis was there, among other more recent celebrities. Aidan and I kept looking around for Paul, but couldn't see him anywhere.

Finally, after we sat down, and just as the film was about to start, my old client walked down the central aisle with Giles Martin, George Martin's son, who was by then an established record producer in his own right and had remixed the soundtrack for the new *Magical Mystery Tour* DVD. Paul and Giles found their seats, the lights went out and the screen flickered into life.

Watching that bizarre piece of cinematic art was like a time-travel journey to the Sixties – not just the real Sixties I'd experienced day by day at Vidal Sassoon's, Abbey Road, the Apple Corps and the swinging Chelsea scene, but the technicolor fantasy my generation had invented: the coming utopia of flower children, the global spiritual awakening, the peaceful revolution that would have policemen dancing arm in arm.

Fifty years on, I reflected that perhaps we hadn't got it completely wrong. We'd certainly been naive in believing that those four pop musicians, in their cheap wizards' costumes, could change the world from one day to the next with a wave of their wands, a few catchy tunes, some good-quality marijuana and the help of their many long-haired friends. And yet, many of the counter-culture's idealistic dreams had indeed been coming true, though perhaps they were taking a little longer than originally anticipated. America had moved on from racial segregation to electing Barack Obama, gay people were now celebrating legal weddings and women had more freedoms and opportunities than ever before. Despite 9-11 and its aftermath, the world really was a more peaceful place on the whole, and the threat of an all-out nuclear conflict seemed now a distant Cold War memory. Many other far-out quirks of the counter-culture

– environmentalism, meditation, sexual freedom – had all gone mainstream in the intervening decades. The Internet allowed any talented musician, film-maker or artist to achieve worldwide fame with a single viral video, making Apple Records' mission come true in a way none of us could have imagined back then. Even drug use had been wholly or partially decriminalized in some countries, a move that was also being seriously considered by the UK government. The twenty-first century was certainly no Age of Aquarius, with its economic inequality, terrorism, collapsing ecosystems and a thousand and one other challenges. Nevertheless, I got the impression that, over the past fifty years, we'd come a little closer to our spaced-out utopia. And these whimsical wizards on the BFI's screen had played their part, as the spokesmen for our generation.

Aside from those headier reflections, I laughed of course, and cried, and repeatedly flipped out at the extended two-hour flashback, together with all my companions from that ridiculous Magical Mystery Tour. As for my son Aidan, who was then about the same age as the shaggy-haired stylist on screen, I think he was simply stunned to see this new side to the "boring old dad" he'd always known.

When we made our way out of the auditorium, I saw Paul again, engrossed in a conversation with a group of people I didn't recognize.

Should I go up and say hi? I wondered nervously. *What if he fails to remember me?* My old habit of not wanting to seem like an annoying groupie kicked in automatically. *Best not to bother him*, I thought.

At that moment, though, we caught each other's eye.

Paul suddenly raised his eyebrows at me, in that familiar manner of his, and his face lit up with joyful surprise.

"Is it... Leslie?"

"Yes!" I replied, hugely relieved.

In a moment I will never forget, Paul put his arm around me as we walked out of the theatre. I told him how much I had enjoyed the documentary and we exchanged impressions, amazed that nearly half a century had elapsed since those scenes had been filmed.

"Congratulations on your recent marriage," I said at one point.

"Thank you, Leslie, and how are things with you?"

"I'm good, thanks." I said. "I've been divorced twice, but I'm now in a happy relationship, and I have two lovely boys. This is my eldest, Aidan."

I remembered to leave out the bit about QPR returning to the Premier League. Then, as we were about to go, I pointed my finger at his head.

"Paul, you see, I was right all along..."

"What do you mean?" he asked.

"When we first met, you played me that song of yours. *When I get older, losing my hair...* But I told you we never would lose our hair. And we haven't!"

We both burst into laughter, pulling on the hair from our scalps – as if we were lounging around in his music room, back at 7 Cavendish Avenue – as if no time had passed at all.

As if everything in the past fifty years

       had been nothing but a momentary hallucination,

         inspired by a puff

           of magical

             smoke

              o o o o

Acknowledgements

I'd like to thank Jane Asher (for making this happen), Lawrence Falk (Boy Scout), Vidal Sassoon (the Conductor), Chris O'Dell (blondes have more fun), Neil McNaughton (my Magnet), Susan Kaye (for being there for me), Eduardo Jáuregui (the Pump), Aidan and Oliver Cavendish (for politely putting up with my bedtime stories), Ernie Sutton and Terry Bloxham (from *British Beatles Fan Club* magazine), my many friends and family who made this book (and my life) possible; and, of course, the Fab Four themselves – Paul, John, George and Ringo: without your hair, there wouldn't have been such a magical story to tell.

Neil McNaughton would like to thank his writing coach Hud Saunders for his experience and wisdom, and *The Times*' Ed Potton for reading the manuscript and offering encouragement.

Eduardo Jáuregui would like to thank Leslie and Neil for their time and patience, and Emanuela Lombardo for her support and comments.

The three of us would like to thank Lorenzo Rulfo, Pierdomenico Baccalario, Antonia Reed, Alessandro Gallenzi, Andrea Cavallini ("Dr Bestia") and everyone at Book on a Tree and Alma Books for believing in this project, and for all their continued support and ideas.

Finally, we're all grateful to the creators of the following valuable sources of Beatles and Sixties lore, which we've used to jog Leslie's memory and fill in the gaps:

WEBSITES

The Beatles Bible (www.beatlesbible.com)
The Internet Beatles Album (www.beatlesagain.com)
The Beatles Interview Database (www.beatlesinterviews.org)
The *Jewish Chronicle* Archive (www.thejc.com/archive)
Spotify
IMDb
Wikipedia

BOOKS

Bugliosi, Vincent, and Gentry, Curt, *Helter Skelter: The True Story of the Manson Murders*, (New York: W.W. Norton, 1974).

Davies, Hunter, *The Beatles* (New York: W.W. Norton, 2004).

DiLello, Richard, *The Longest Cocktail Party* (Chicago: Playboy Press, 1973).

Gould, Jonathan, *Can't Buy Me Love: The Beatles, Britain and America* (New York: Three Rivers Press, 2008).

Loker, Bradford E., *History with the Beatles* (New York: Dog Ear Publishing, 2009)

Miles, Barry, *Paul McCartney: Many Years from Now* (London: Harvill Secker, 1997)

Norman, Philip, *Shout! The Beatles in their Generation* (New York: Touchstone, 2011)

O'Dell, Chris, *Miss O'Dell: Hard Days and Long Nights with The Beatles, The Stones, Bob Dylan and Eric Clapton* (New York: Touchstone, 2010)

Selvin, Joel, *Altamont: The Rolling Stones, the Hells Angels, and the Inside Story of Rock's Darkest Day* (New York: Dey Street Books, 2016)

Schaffner, Nicholas, *The Beatles Forever: How They Changed Our Culture* (New York: Fine Communications, 1997)

Spitz, Bob, *The Beatles: A Biography* (New York: Back Bay Books, 2006)

Thompson, Hunter S., *Hell's Angels: The Strange and Terrible Saga of the Outlaw Motorcycle Gangs* (New York: Random House, 1966)

Wolfe, Tom, *The Electric Kool-Aid Acid Test* (New York: Farrar, Straus and Giroux, 1968)

ARTICLES

Boucher, Caroline, 'John Lennon Is Likely to Go Bald', *Disc and Music Echo*, 26th April 1969.

Carpenter, Julie, 'The Father Who Darcey Bussell Rejected', *The Daily Express*, 26th April 2012.

Cohen, Allen, 'The Gathering of the Tribes', *The San Francisco Oracle*, vol. 1, 5, 1967.

Connolly, Ray, 'Don't Call Leslie a Barber, He Believes in Hair', *The Evening Standard*, 17th August 1968

Hickey, William, 'Ernie Hopes for a Hit – We Think', *The Daily Express*, 1968.

Lacey, Hester, 'Elvis and Me? Now There's a Story', *The Independent*, 7th February 1999

MUSIC

The Beatles, *Please Please Me*, Parlophone, 1963

The Beatles, *With the Beatles*, Parlophone, 1963

The Beatles, *A Hard Day's Night*, Parlophone, 1964

The Beatles, *Beatles for Sale*, Parlophone, 1964

The Beatles, *Help!*, Parlophone, 1965

The Beatles, *Rubber Soul*, Parlophone, 1965

The Beatles, *Revolver*, Parlophone, 1966

The Beatles, *Penny Lane/Strawberry Fields Forever* (double single), Parlophone, 1967

The Beatles, *Sgt. Pepper's Lonely Hearts Club Band*, Parlophone, 1967

The Beatles, *Magical Mystery Tour*, Parlophone, 1967

The Beatles, *The Beatles* ("*White Album*"), Apple, 1968

The Beatles, *Yellow Submarine*, Apple, 1969

The Beatles, *Abbey Road*, Apple, 1969

The Beatles, *The Ballad of John and Yoko* (single), Apple, 1969

The Beatles, *Let It Be*, Apple, 1970

The Grateful Dead, *Anthem of the Sun*, Rhino Entertainment, 1968

Harrison, George, *All Things Must Pass*, Apple, 1970

MacDermot, G., Ragni G. and Rado, J., (1968) *Hair: An American Tribal Love-Rock Musical*, RCA Victor, 1968

FILMS

Lester, Richard, *A Hard Day's Night*, United Artists, 1964

Harrison, George, Lennon, John, McCartney, Paul and Starr, Ringo, *Magical Mystery Tour*, Apple Corps/BBC, 1967